AFTER HIROSHIMA

AMERICA SINCE 1945

Albert C. Ganley

Thomas T. Lyons

Gilbert T. Sewall

Independent School Press

Wellesley Hills   Massachusetts

To
Our Students

0-88334-121-2

79808182
12345678

£8.50
USA

val

we believed in monolithic
communism. But in
essence it wasn't that

① got us going — misconception —
simplistic Commie

fear of commies

② supporting govs to
propagate an own self interest.
Chile —
Dominican Rep.

ALBERT C. GANLEY, a graduate of Williams and Cornell, has taught American history at Williams, Manhasset (N.Y.) High School, La Jolla (Calif.) Country Day School, and in the Newton program. A former John Hay Fellow at Harvard, he is at present a member and former chairman of the Phillips Exeter Academy history department. He is author of *The Progressive Movement.*

THOMAS T. LYONS, a graduate of Harvard College and Graduate School of Education, taught American history at Dartmouth and Mt. Hermon School. Earlier a fellow at Wesleyan and Stanford, he is currently chairman of the history department at Phillips Academy, Andover. He is author of *Presidential Power in the New Deal, The Supreme Court and Individual Rights in Contemporary Society, Reconstruction and the Race Problem, Black Leadership in American History,* and other books.

GILBERT T. SEWALL, a graduate of Berkeley, Brown and Columbia, is a former instructor of history at Phillips Academy, Andover. He is now an associate editor at *Newsweek.*

THE I.S.P. AMERICAN HISTORY SERIES
William O. Kellogg, *Editor*
St. Paul's School, Concord, New Hampshire.

PREFACE

After Hiroshima: America Since 1945 represents the efforts of three secondary school history teachers to provide their students with a specialized narrative about the United States in the decades following World War II. Rather than a detailed, all-inclusive account of the years from 1945 to 1979, we have written eight narrowly focused, self-contained essays, divided equally between foreign relations and domestic events. In foreign affairs the narrative stresses the development of American efforts to secure United States interests in a dangerous world of nuclear weapons, ideological conflict, national tensions and power struggles. The first four chapters describe the evolution of post 1945 American policies in Europe, East Asia, Latin America, the Middle East, Africa and Southeast Asia. At home the last four chapters focus on economic growth and the social consequences, the Supreme Court's initiatives to secure individual liberty and promote equality, the long struggle of Black Americans to gain equal rights, and Presidential power and politics.

There is no attempt to get into historiographical debate. We have not adopted any historical school of interpretation such as revisionist or post-revisionist, or busied ourselves or the readers with a particular theory of history. Neither heroes nor villains appear in this book, although history may eventually furnish some. Our limited time perspective, the elusiveness of objectivity in one's own age, and the fragmentary documentary record available at this time preclude such judgments.

The chapters represent eight narratives. rich in historical detail, concrete events, and influential personalities. We have made a conscious effort to define terms explicitly and to write in a vocabulary that is clear to secondary school students. We have avoided vague generalizations and personal biases.

This book is not simplistic. The student will learn not only the meaning, but also the application of concepts such as national security, gross national product, and affirmative action. Statistics are used to document statements and to provoke reader analysis. The authors believe that the book fills a void left by textbooks, specialized monographs and journalistic essays. *After Hiroshima: America Since 1945* joins *The Expansion of the Federal Union, 1801-1848* to become the second of six volumes to be published comprising the Independent School Press American History Series.

Contents

List of Illustrations

List of Maps

Chapter One

The Cold War In Europe

"I believe that it must be the policy of the United States to support free peoples who are resisting attempted subjugation by armed minorities or by outside pressures."
—Harry S. Truman, 1947

"For us to think that what the central struggle is about is just Berlin would be a great mistake. They're fighting for New York and Paris when they struggle over Berlin. Therefore, I think we would have to make it cold — and mean it — that we would fight.
—John F. Kennedy, 1959

ORIGINS OF THE COLD WAR

A New Leader and Signs of Trouble The seventy-seven year old Secretary of War lingered behind as cabinet members walked silently from the somber meeting. He had an urgent message for the man who had started the day as Vice-President but had just met the cabinet as President of the United States. When the room was empty of all other officials, Henry L. Stimson calmly told the tense President that he wanted an appointment to inform him in detail about an immense project to develop an explosive of incredible power — a super weapon to win the war quickly. Thus, within minutes of the swearing-in ceremony on April 12, 1945 President Harry S. Truman learned for the first time the specific purpose of the Manhattan Project, the secret code name for the effort to construct an atomic bomb. Later that evening Stimson recorded in his diary: "The new President on the whole made a pleasant impression, but it was very clear

1

that he knew very little of the task into which he was stepping and he showed some minor vacillation on minor matters . . . as if he might be lacking in force."

Stimson's reservations were understandable, for in his ten years in the Senate Truman had little opportunity or inclination to become knowledgeable in foreign affairs. His effective work as Chairman of a Senate Committee to investigate defense expenditures had earned Roosevelt's respect and made Truman acceptable as FDR's running mate in 1944. Never an insider in the administration, Vice President Truman had not participated directly in any serious discussion of postwar planning. Charles "Chip" Bohlen, Roosevelt's interpreter at Big Three Conferences, described Truman as ". . . an obscure vice-president, who got to see Roosevelt less than I did and who knew less than I did about United States foreign relations." Truman did not attend the Yalta Conference in February 1945 at which the Big Three (Roosevelt, Churchill, Stalin) agreed that the peoples of Europe liberated from Nazi and Fascist domination could "create democratic institutions of their own choice." Truman knew little detail of the agreement on territorial adjustments whereby Poland would gain German territory east of the Oder and Neisse Rivers (map, p. 6) in exchange for territory east of the Curzon line ceded to the Soviet Union. No one apparently had told the Vice President about a secret protocol whereby Stalin in return for certain concessions in East Asia had agreed to enter the war against Japan within three months after the defeat of Germany.

The transfer of power to Truman came at a crucial moment. The war against Germany was entering its final weeks, and a United Nations Conference was scheduled to convene in San Francisco on April 25th to draft the charter for the new international organization. Truman conveyed his own concerns about the awesome task ahead when on his first full day in office he told a group of reporters:

> Boys, if you ever pray, pray for me now. I don't know whether you fellows ever had a load of hay fall on you, but when they told me yesterday what had happened, I felt like the moon, the stars, and all the planets had fallen on me. I've got the most terribly responsible job a man ever had.

It soon became clear to Truman that FDR and his advisers had assumed: first, that the Soviet Union would cooperate in the establishment of a postwar world based on justice and democracy as stated in the Atlantic Charter; second, that a strong international association of free nations was essential for the maintenance of peace, and would make power politics unnecessary to maintain a balance of power; third, that the greatest threat to world peace would be a strong, united Germany; fourth, that the United States within two years of the end of the war in Europe would be able to withdraw all its military forces. But, on that first afternoon as President of the United States, Truman received a State Department report with the ominous statement: "Since the Yalta Conference the Soviet government has taken a firm and uncompromising position on nearly every major question that has arisen in our relations."

Trouble in Eastern Europe Sharp differences over which Polish leaders to include in the Warsaw government had erupted at a March meeting of the British and American Ambassadors in Moscow with V.M. Molotov, the Soviet Foreign Minister. Having liberated Poland from the Nazis at great cost, the Russians had no intention of broadening the Polish government in any way that might enable anti-Soviet Poles to take control. But the American Ambassador to Russia, W. Averell Harriman, insisted on implementing the exact language of the Yalta Declaration committing the Big Three ". . . to form interim governmental authorities broadly representative of all democratic elements in the population and pledged to the earliest possible establishment through free elections of governments responsible to the will of the people. . . ."

The extent of the rift over Poland soon became painfully clear. As a gesture honoring the late President Roosevelt, Stalin consented to send Molotov to the San Francisco Conference. The Soviet Foreign Minister stopped in Washington for talks on April 22, just ten days after Truman became President. Preliminary conversations with his advisers convinced the new President that "It was now obvious. . . that our agreements with the Soviet Union had so far been a one-way street and that this could not continue." The discussions with Molotov, called "Old Ironpants" by Americans who had experienced his rigid and imperturbable manner, went badly. A heated exchange over Poland provoked the Soviet Foreign Minister to exclaim: "I have never been talked to like that in my life." Truman shot back: "Carry out your agreements and you won't get talked to like that." Afterwards the President, always proud of his tough decisiveness, bragged to an aide, "I gave it to him straight one-two to the jaw."

Stalin's chilling message that followed left no doubts about the seriousness of the Polish issue. "You apparently, do not agree," said the Soviet dictator, "that the Soviet Union has a right to make efforts that there should exist in Poland a government friendly toward the Soviet Union, and that the Soviet government cannot agree to existence in Poland of a government hostile to it."

American leaders found themselves trapped between the democratic ideals of the Atlantic Charter and the realities of Russian military presence in Eastern Europe. In view of a public opinion suspicious of Soviet intentions and hostile to Soviet ideology, Truman could hardly abandon, without a word of protest, Poland or any of the liberated nations to puppet governments controlled by the Kremlin. In the United States the administration in power must pursue a foreign policy attuned to domestic political realities or be swept from office. Yet, without resorting to the unacceptable method of military force or the threat to use it, Washington had little chance of persuading the Russians to accept a free, democratic Europe.

Another dilemma faced the United States as a result of the rapid destruction of Nazi resistance by Allied forces on the western front and Russians advancing from the East. Having bridged the Rhine in March 1945 and encircled the industrial Ruhr valley, General Dwight D. Eisenhower, Commander of the Allied forces in Europe, decided to strike through central Germany to the remaining industrial centers rather than drive along the coastal plain of northern Germany to Berlin. Truman left to the judgment of Eisenhower and the Joint Chiefs of Staff (JCS) the decisions about the use of Allied forces, and military rather than political goals dominated Eisenhower's analysis of the situation. In order to win the war as quickly as possible, destruction of the enemy's military forces seemed much more important than the capture of the enemy's bombed-out capital city. To the dismay of Churchill and Americans who attached great psychological importance to beating the Russians to Berlin and Prague, capital of Czechoslovakia, Eisenhower ordered the American Ninth Army to concentrate on cutting the German forces in half.

The Hopkins Mission Washington also had to deal with another problem because many Americans were reluctant to spend American dollars in Europe for nonmilitary purposes. Responding to this public mood, Truman, on the day the war ended in Europe, May 8, 1945 (V-E Day), approved an order embargoing all lend-lease shipments to Europe. Subordinates promptly ordered ships en route to Europe to return to United States ports without unloading their cargoes. A storm of protest at home and abroad engulfed the President. In excusing his failure to notify Russia and America's other allies, Truman claimed that he had not read the cancellation document. Urgently needing American supplies, Stalin took Truman's action as a deliberate affront. Truman's subsequent modification of the embargo failed to improve feelings or curb suspicions.

In an effort to arrest the deterioration in relations with the Soviet Union, Truman sent to Moscow an ailing Harry Hopkins, one of Roosevelt's key advisers. Hopkins found Stalin deeply resentful of both the Allied stand on Poland and the abrupt curtailment of lend-lease. Dismissing American complaints about Soviet domination of Poland as unnecessary and unrealistic, the Soviet dictator pointed to the way in which the Western Allies had organized the new governments of Italy and Belgium without even consulting him. He also reminded Hopkins that the Soviets had made it clear at Yalta that "Poland is not only a question of honor but of life and death for the Soviet Union." Twice in the twentieth century German armies had crossed Poland to invade Russia which lacked a natural boundary in the West.

Potsdam Conference   Although the odds against reversing a process in Eastern Europe so far advanced were overwhelming, Truman made the effort at a summit meeting in Potsdam, Germany in July 1945. But Stalin countered every American argument. Facing for the first time not only a new American President but also a new British Prime Minister, Clement Atlee, the Soviet leader demanded British and American recognition of the new "People's Democracies" in Rumania, Poland, Yugoslavia, Albania, and Hungary. Although he promised "free elections" in Poland, Stalin persisted in his demand that the western border of Poland be extended to include western Silesia and the cities of Breslau and Stettin. As he doodled heads of wolves with a red pencil, Stalin also insisted on huge reparations from Germany (he mentioned $20 billion) regardless of economic costs to the zones administered by the Allies.

Anticipating a tough stance by the Soviets, Truman had arranged that the Potsdam Conference would coincide with the scheduled test of the atomic bomb. Evidence suggests that the President and his closest advisers had begun to think of the bomb, not only as a military weapon against Japan but as a powerful diplomatic tool for securing a satisfactory settlement of postwar problems. Not until July 24, 1945, eight days after the successful test of the secret bomb in New Mexico, did an elated Truman "casually mention" to Stalin that the United States "had a weapon of unusual destructive force." Nonchalantly blowing cigarette smoke towards the ceiling, the Red dictator, probably well briefed about the American nuclear project through Soviet espionage, grunted disinterestedly. Unable to resolve any of the issues with the Soviets, a frustrated Truman left the conference convinced, as he later wrote in his *Memoirs*, that ". . . the Russians were not in earnest about peace"

POSTWAR DIVISION OF GERMANY

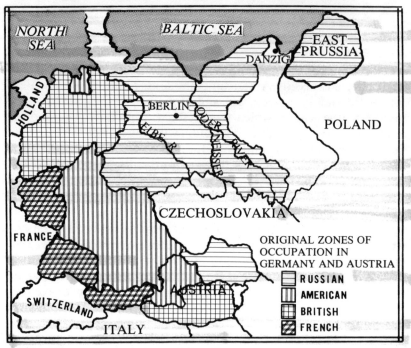

DIVIDED BERLIN

and ". . . were planning world conquest. . . ." The President concluded that "Force is the only thing the Russians understand."

The Disintegration of the Grand Alliance   The wartime marriage of convenience lacked the deep faith and mutual admiration necessary to sustain an enduring close relationship. Sharp disagreements over basic principles had so poisoned the association that only deep changes in attitudes could prevent a disastrous quarrel. Such different values and aspirations divided the United States and the Soviet Union that only exceptional patience and willingness to compromise could maintain good will and cooperation.

Badly mangled by the war, the Soviet Union had suffered fifteen million dead, nine percent of its pre-war population, and had sustained heavy losses in its European industrial plant and agricultural resources. Russian national interest demanded guaranteed military security against any repetition of invasion from Western Europe. Centuries old dreams — control of the Turkish Straits, the outlet for the Black Sea, and the union of all Slavs under Russian leadership — likewise remained prime objectives of the Kremlin. In addition, the rebuilding of a war-torn country demanded immediate attention, and prompted the Soviets as early as January 1945 to ask the United Stations for a six billion dollar loan for postwar reconstruction. In pursuing these national interests, Stalin and his associates intended to act according to Marxist-Leninist principles while keeping the leadership of the Communist world in Moscow. Communists believed that elimination of economic classes and establishment of a society of social equals were more important than expansion of the liberty of the individual. The good of the society, according to Communists, took precedence over individual freedom to acquire property, to have free speech, and to vote for one's own candidate.

By contrast, the United States had lost 400,000 dead, or less than .03 percent of its population, and its great industrial and agricultural productivity was undamaged by the war. American leaders saw the national interest best served by a restoration of a free Europe as it existed before Hitler, with Fascism eradicated, democracy installed, and no one power dominant. Some hard-learned lessons of the past seemed obvious. The error of appeasing the aggressor who threatened to use force must be avoided whatever the cost. World trade, upon which American prosperity and security depended, must be restored by rebuilding disrupted capitalist economies of Europe and Asia. Contrary to Communists, Americans valued human liberty above economic security and equality. Individual freedom to acquire and use property had first priority, even if it led to inequality of living conditions. Communist denial of the existence of God and of the right to private property, Stalin's bloody purges of rivals, and his 1939 non-aggression pact with Hitler demonstrated to Americans the wickedness of the Soviet system.

But Americans looked at the Soviet Union through a lens blurred by two images — one, an aggressive nation state suppressing human freedom while expanding its power — the other, an international Communist conspiracy, with headquarters in Moscow, spreading revolutionary doctrine throughout the world. Predictably, confusion about the appropriate response to these threats divided Americans. A few assumed that Russian concern for security against attack justified Soviet expansion into Eastern Europe. Viewing America's atomic monopoly as inciting the Soviet Union to a "defensive aggressiveness," holders of this position opposed any use of the bomb as a bargaining weapon. Some even believed it would be wise to offer Russia full partnership in atomic development since scientists had warned that only a short time would elapse before the Russians built a bomb of their own. Strongly opposed to any deal whatsoever with the Communists, a small minority even toyed with the idea of preventive war while the United States still held the atomic monopoly. But, in general, Americans desired peace without making any concessions to the Russians. Suspicious of schemes for international control of atomic energy without foolproof safeguards and worried about Soviet expansion, most Americans wanted their government to maintain a firm anti-Communist stance.

In this inauspicious climate regular meetings of the Foreign Ministers of the big powers bogged down. The American monopoly of the atomic bomb failed to give James F. Byrnes, the new Secretary of State, the leverage in negotiations so confidently expected. Publicly stating that the bomb would frighten only the "weak-willed," Stalin manifested little interest in an American plan for international control of atomic energy. Failure of Byrnes to obtain acceptable agreements at the Moscow meeting of Foreign Ministers in December 1945 increased the pressures on Truman "to get tough with Russia." A disappointed President concluded that: "Unless Russia is faced with an iron fist and strong language another war is in the making. Only one language do they understand — how many divisions have you?" On this low note the President said to Byrnes: ". . . I'm tired of babying the Soviets."

The Iranian Crisis, 1946 As the split in Europe widened, a new trouble spot — Iran — enlivened the first meeting of the United Nations General Assembly and Security Council in London in January 1946. The Soviet Union had failed to withdraw its 30,000 troops from Iran after the war as promised. According to Iran, these Soviet forces, originally sent to protect Lend-Lease supply lines, were aiding a Communist inspired separatist movement in the province of Azerbaijan. The Iranian government, backed by the United States and Great Britain, lodged a complaint against the "interference of the Soviet Union. . . in the internal affairs of Iran." Functioning as a world forum, the United Nations so publicized Soviet misconduct toward Iran that the U.S.S.R. evacuated all Red Army troops by May. The lesson seemed clear — take a strong stand, marshall world opinion, and the Russians will back down.

The Iron Curtain   But in Germany the problem defied such a simple solution. The first winter after the war revealed disastrous consequences of the division of Germany into four zones. Suffering from a food shortage in their zones, the British and Americans had to import food, an expense that an insolvent Britain could hardly afford. Interested only in reparations from the western zone, the Russians refused to export any surplus food produced in their zone. To make matters even worse, the western zones would lose machinery and tools necessary to develop self-sufficiency if they allowed the Soviets to obtain reparations demanded.

Winston Churchill, visiting the United States in early March 1946 as a private citizen, described a disturbing scene in a speech made in Fulton, Missouri. The famous wartime leader warned:

> From Stettin in the Baltic to Trieste in the Adriatic an iron curtain has descended across the Continent. . . . The Communist parties, which were very small in all these eastern states of Europe, have been raised to preeminence and power far beyond their numbers and are seeking everywhere to obtain totalitarian control. . . .

The phrase "iron curtain" immediately crept into the vocabulary of the West, amidst growing public disillusionment with the effort to negotiate with Russia. A Gallup Poll in March revealed that sixty percent felt that the United States was being "too soft" in its policy toward Russia. A majority of Americans also believed that the Soviet Union was engaged in hostilities as threatening as armed conflict. Although no fighting had taken place, a deadly Cold War had shattered dreams of a world without international tensions.

Bizonia   In the early spring of 1946 Moscow's flat rejection of Byrnes's proposed twenty-five year Big Four Treaty to keep Germany disarmed, a remarkable departure from traditional American policy of non-entangling alliances, brought into sharp focus the deep disagreement over Germany. The American Commander in Germany, General Lucius D. Clay, halted delivery of reparations from the German zone in May. Byrnes, meanwhile, called for the elimination of all economic barriers between zones. When the Russians showed no inclination to move towards economic integration, Washington began discussions with London that culminated in an agreement in December to combine their zones for economic administration.

Demobilization   Despite the danger signals emanating from Europe, the American public continued to demand a return to the conveniences and bounty of peacetime. A "bring the boys home" refrain reached a crescendo during 1946 that no candidate for national office could ignore. That the Russians continued to keep over five million men under arms mattered less to most Americans than the prompt return of their men to private life once World War II ended. By the end of 1946 the American military force in Europe was reduced from over three million men to just under four hundred thousand. Truman even felt compelled to promise that the American Army would be cut to just over one million men by July 1, 1947.

Bipartisanship   But no serious domestic challenge to the administration's foreign policy developed. When Henry A. Wallace, Truman's predecessor as Vice President and now a holdover from Roosevelt's cabinet as Secretary of Commerce, attacked the "get tough with Russia" approach, the President fired him. Truman also carefully emulated FDR's tactic of blunting partisanship by involving key Republicans, notably Senator Arthur H. Vandenberg (R., Mich.) and foreign affairs expert John Foster Dulles, in the formulation and execution of policy. Such practical political expedients helped to stop politics "at the water's edge" on several occasions and avoided the tragic error made by President Wilson in failing to consult opposition leaders about the Treaty of Versailles. Labeled "bipartisan" by the press, this non-partisan policy attracted wide approval.

But some prominent Republicans, notably Senator Robert A. Taft of Ohio, refused to endorse the concept of a bipartisan foreign policy, especially since they disagreed with its premise that foreign policy was above politics. Claiming the responsibility of the party out of power to alert the public to policy decisions that might jeopardize the nation's interests, Taft insisted on retaining his freedom to criticize administration policy when he disagreed with it. He warned that the limitation of dissent in foreign policy could promote tyranny at home and abroad.

The accumulating frustrations of many Americans with Soviet

behavior and with such peacetime problems of reconversion as inflation, shortages, and labor disputes invited partisan exploitation. In the 1946 mid-term elections, Republicans, gleefully proclaiming "To err is Truman" and campaigning on the slogan "Had enough? Vote Republican," won a big victory with a gain of thirteen seats in the Senate and fifty-six in the House. For the first time since 1930 the G.O.P. controlled both Houses of Congress.

DEVELOPMENT OF CONTAINMENT POLICY

The Truman Doctrine, 1947   Soon after the end of the war the Soviets began to exert heavy pressure on the Turks to place the Dardanelles and Bosporous under joint Turkish-Russian defense. Late in 1946 Edwin G. Wilson, American Ambassador to Turkey, reported that "Turkey will not be able to maintain indefinitely a defensive posture against the Soviet Union."

Simultaneously a serious situation developed in Greece. British efforts to establish political stability and to promote economic recovery were undermined by intense hostility between conservative royalists in power and Communist-dominated groups who waged guerrilla war from bases in the northern hills. Finding it increasingly difficult to maintain a garrison of 40,000 men in Greece, the British sounded out American officials about furnishing help to the Greek government.

In February 1947 the American Ambassador to Greece, Lincoln MacVeagh, alerted the State Department to rumors that Britain was considering withdrawal of its forces because of its own precarious financial condition. Shortly thereafter, Mark Ethridge, the American representative on a United Nations Commission of Investigation in Greece, advanced the concept, subsequently called the "domino theory," when he asked: "(1) If Greece goes through our default, have we released forces in Azerbaijan and Turkey? (2) If that force is released, where does it stop?" When the British government officially notified the United States that it would have to pull out of Greece by April 1, 1946, a committee of experts under the leadership of General George C. Marshall, the new Secretary of State, recommended immediate aid to Greece and Turkey to prevent the entire region from falling under Soviet control.

Effective action by the Truman administration required the support of an unfriendly, Republican controlled Congress. True to campaign promises, the Republicans proposed both deep cuts in the budget to bring it into balance and more conservative fiscal policies so that taxes could be cut twenty percent. Sharp disagreements with the President over these domestic programs threatened to affect foreign policies.

Banking on the appeal of non-partisanship in foreign policy, Truman invited a group of Congressional leaders of both parties to the White House for a briefing on the Greek crisis. After hearing Under Secretary of State Dean Acheson's convincing description of the threat, Vandenberg exclaimed: "Mr. President, if you say that to Congress and the country, I will support you and, I believe that most of its members will do the same." The Michigan Senator understood full well the American people's intolerance of ambiguity. Before making sacrifices, they needed to see themselves arrayed against a wicked enemy.

Two weeks later on March 12, 1947, Truman addressed Congress in a speech described as "the opening gun in a campaign to bring people up to the realization that the war isn't over by any means." Taking Vandenberg's advice, the President painted a scene designed, according to one aide, "to scare hell out of the country." Carefully refraining from direct charges against the Soviet Union, Truman said: "Greece must have assistance if it is to become a self-supporting and self-respecting democracy. . . . As in the case of Greece, if Turkey is to have the assistance it needs, the United States must supply it. . . ." Then describing a much bigger, world-wide struggle, he warned: "We shall not realize our objectives, however, unless we are willing to help free peoples to maintain their free institutions and their national integrity against aggressive movements that seek to impose upon them totalitarian regimes. . . ." Employing the "domino theory" as his basic premise, the President concluded: "If Greece should fall under the control of an armed minority, the effect upon its neighbor Turkey would be immediate and serious. Confusion and disorder might well spread throughout the entire Middle East."

Truman asked Congress to appropriate $400 million through June 1948 to assist Greece and Turkey in their hour of need. His proposal, soon labeled the Truman Doctrine, assumed that Communism, always seeking to expand, fed on despair and discord, and that economic and military aid could enable a regime, resisting Communist penetration, to satisfy the needs and desires of its people.

Not all Americans agreed. Some critics denounced Truman for by-passing the United Nations, while others protested that the President's request was imperialistic and would inevitably involve the United States in a war. A few disliked the idea of bolstering corrupt and undemocratic regimes in Greece and Turkey. And some thought that ". . . there was a little too much flamboyant anti-communism in the speech."

But Truman had another ace to play. To further dramatize the case against the Communist danger, the President issued, later in March, a loyalty order to root out of government jobs all security risks. Public opinion swung behind the President, and within two months, Congress, by large margins, appropriated funds to aid Greece and Turkey.

The Truman Doctrine marked both a beginning and an end in American foreign policy. While abandoning the nation's historic policy of non-involvement in Europe's internal affairs, the Doctrine initiated an unprecedented commitment of American resources to aid other nations to resist Communism. Having taken this first plunge, the United States would find it difficult to resist requests for similar ventures.

The Marshall Plan   During the debate over the Truman Doctrine, an economic crisis in Western Europe worried American leaders. Economic activity was slowed by inflation, acute shortages of food, fuel, and raw materials, as well as by strikes. French opposition to increased German industrialization and to centralized administration of German economic enterprise frustrated British and American efforts to restore normal economic activity. Without German production of industrial goods for export, the economic recovery of Europe faced long delays. A State Department group under George F. Kennan worked all spring to develop a program satisfactory to the United States while requiring vigorous efforts by the Europeans themselves. Such a design, it was hoped, would avoid a storm of protest against an "American give-away."

At Harvard's Commencement on June 5, 1947, the tall, graying Secretary of State, George C. Marshall, in soft, almost inaudible tones, outlined in general terms what Europe and the United States might do together to save the former from economic collapse. He explained that:

> The truth of the matter is that Europe's requirements for the next three or four years of foreign food and other essential products — principally from America — are so much greater than her present ability to pay that she must have substantial help or face economic, social and political deterioration of a very grave character. . . .
>
> Our policy is directed not against any country or doctrine but against hunger, poverty, desperation and chaos. . . . The initiative, I think must come from Europe. . . .

If further division of Europe occurred, Marshall contended, the Russians would have to bear the responsibility, for he offered the

Kremlin the opportunity to become an integral part of the European economic community. Almost immediately a favorable press identified the new American proposal as the Marshall Plan.

Within two weeks the British and French foreign ministers met with Molotov to discuss how Europeans might cooperate in a recovery plan. Although the Soviet Foreign Minister urged the British and French to reject it as interference in their internal affairs, the latter invited twenty-two European nations, including the Communist bloc, to a July meeting. When Czechoslovakia accepted, Moscow pressured her to withdraw. But by September sixteen European nations had set up a Committee for European Economic Cooperation (CEEC) that requested $590 million in aid from the United States for the next six months.

After consultation with leaders of both parties, Truman called Congress into special session and asked for that amount of emergency foreign aid through March 1948 to help Europeans survive the coming winter. Although the *New York Daily Mirror* called economic aid to Europe "the greatest fool's gamble ever proposed with a straight face to an intelligent nation," the American press generally portrayed a disturbing picture of the Communist threat and supported the Marshall Plan.

On September 27, 1947, the very day when the CEEC sent to Washington its report on the Marshall Plan, representatives of Communist parties meeting in Poland founded the Cominform (Communist Information Bureau) "to meet the aggressive and frankly expansionist course to which American imperialism had committed itself since the end of World War II." Ironically, these Soviet words and actions helped to push an Interim Foreign Aid Bill through Congress by the end of the year.

The Mr. X Article   In the midst of the debate over the Marshall Plan an article in *Foreign Affairs* directed wide attention to the assumptions on which American policy was now based. Published in July over the signature "Mr. X," George Kennan's essay gave birth to the concept of "Containment" as the cardinal principle of American foreign policy. Kennan argued that:

> . . . . it will be clearly seen that the Soviet pressure against the free institutions of the western world is something that can be contained by the alert and vigilant application of counter-force at a series of constantly shifting geographical and political points, corresponding to the shifts and maneuvers of Soviet policy. . . .

Although Kennan later protested that he did not mean an inflexible policy of military resistance either to Soviet expansion or to seizure of power by national communist parties, his widely praised essay was so interpreted by many American political and military leaders.

The Debate Over Foreign Aid   Despite the economic implications of containment, Truman was eager to maintain the balanced budget deemed vital in the fight against inflation. Accordingly he set an arbitrary ceiling for fiscal 1948-1949 on arms expenditures well below that advocated by the Defense Department. Yet at the same time he asked Congress for $17 billion in foreign aid over four years, including $6.8 billion to cover the first fifteen months (to June 30, 1949) of the European Recovery Program (ERP). Each proposal was unpopular in certain quarters, but the foreign aid program attracted the sharpest attack.

U.S. Foreign Grants and Credits To Western Europe **July 1945 - Jan. 1, 1956 (in millions of dollars)**	
Country	**Amount of U.S. Aid**
Austria	1,019
Belgium & Lux.	726
Denmark	284
Finland	86
France	5,477
Germany	3,907
Iceland	34
Ireland	146
Italy	2,795
Netherlands	1,051
Norway	309
Portugal	67
Spain	195
Sweden	108
United King.	6,920
Yugoslavia	860
Total	23,984

Source: *Statistical Abstract*

A strange array of opponents condemned the $17 billion request. On the Left, Henry Wallace and pro-Soviet sympathizers denounced the Marshall Plan and ERP as a blatant scheme to extend America's economic domination over Europe. On the Right, Senator Taft criticized ERP as "a global W.P.A. .... pouring money down a rat-hole." Economy-minded Congressmen pointed out that already in the first two years of peace the United States had funneled about $11 billion into the reconstruction of Europe. Could the nation afford, they asked, to give much more aid without causing bankruptcy, higher taxes, and inflation?

The size of the request astonished even the administration's strongest supporters. Sam Rayburn, House minority leader, said: "It will bust the country," but Truman soon won him over. Diverse economic groups such as important farm and labor organizations and the National Association of Manufacturers lined up in support of the Marshall Plan. The shock of a Communist minority seizing control of the democratic government in Czechoslovakia in February 1948 helped to sway both Houses of Congress in March 1948 into approving by large majorities an authorization of $5.3 billion for the first twelve months.

Although a minority led by Taft, attempted each year to cut the ERP grant, Congress between April 3, 1948 and June 30, 1952 appropriated $13 billion in foreign aid, none of it of a military nature prior to June 1950. By helping the West Europeans, Americans also helped themselves. The dramatic European recovery process stimulated the American economy and benefited worker, farmer, and investor. The Marshall Plan appeared to be a master stroke.

The Berlin Crisis of 1948-1949 The Cold War's division of Europe into East and West caused greatest tension in Germany and Austria where families, as well as nation and capital city, were cut in two. Berlin, over one hundred miles inside the Russian zone of Germany, and Vienna, forty-five miles inside the Russian zone of Austria, presented difficult military and economic problems for the western powers. With strong military forces close at hand, the Russians could easily sever access and take over either city or both at any time. Since Berlin served as a gap in the iron curtain through which East Germans could see the attractions of a free society and escape into it, the temptation to the Kremlin to close that breach was great.

Late in March 1948 the Soviets withdrew their representative from the Allied Control Council in Berlin, and began to delay train and truck convoys to West Berlin at border points with allegations that they did not conform to agreed upon regulations. At the same time the Communists procrastinated in establishing a uniform German currency, desired by the United States to curb inflation caused by currency printed in the Russian zone. General Lucius Clay, Commander of American forces in Europe, described the atmosphere as "exceedingly grave." When the Soviets demanded more direct control of American military train service through the Soviet zone into Berlin, Clay ordered soldier guards on the trains "to prevent Soviet military from entering U.S. passenger trains but not to shoot unless fired upon." A concerned Marshall warned: "If we mean. . . to hold Europe against communism, we must not budge."

Throughout the spring, tension over Berlin mounted. On June 1 the three western powers announced plans to convene a constituent assembly, elected by Germans, before September 1, 1948 to draft a federal democratic constitution for Germany. A Russian warning that the policy of the West was ". . . pregnant with such consequences as can suit only all kinds of instigators of a new war" was ignored. On June 18 Clay informed the Russians of the introduction of a new currency for the western zones of occupation, excluding Berlin, to take effect in two days.

Denouncing the "illegal new western currency," the Soviets suspended all interzonal passenger traffic and incoming traffic on all roads, including pedestrian entry into the Russian zone. Interdiction of land traffic into Berlin left western officials with a difficult decision that would test their firmness and patience. In a letter to his daughter, Truman said: "We are faced with exactly the same situation with which Britain and France were faced in 1938-39 with Hitler." American officials emphasized that they were in Berlin by right and intended to stay. There would be no "Munich appeasement."

As the crisis worsened, the administration hit upon an ingenious solution — go by air until the land routes were reopened. Clay quickly organized air lifts to ferry necessary supplies into Berlin. After sending a sharp warning to Moscow by dispatching to Britain and Germany two squadrons of B-29 bombers, the only aircraft capable of delivering an atomic bomb, Truman confided in his diary: "I do not pass the buck, nor do I alibi out of any decision I make." If the Russians played tough, America could more than match them.

A Gallup Poll in July indicated that eighty percent of those interviewed agreed that the United States and its allies should stay in Berlin even if it meant war. Facing a difficult uphill political campaign for re-election, the President had correctly gauged public opinion. The Russian blockade of Berlin made it very difficult for Republicans to wage an all-out attack on the containment policy without appearing disloyal.

For 321 days a great battle of wills continued as the Russians blockaded Berlin via land while the United States airlifted on an around-the-clock schedule the supplies necessary for sustaining life in the German capital. American and British planes made over 270,000 flights and carried nearly 2.5 million tons of cargo. In Truman's words, "Berlin had become a symbol of America's — and the West's — dedication to the cause of freedom."

Complicating the Kremlin's task in the Berlin crisis was the appearance of internal dissension in the Communist camp   — the defiance of Marshall Tito, Communist leader of Yugoslavia. Tito's refusal to sacrifice his nation's independence to the interests of the Soviet Union caused a break between the two nations in June 1948 at the beginning of the Berlin showdown. Although this crack in the monolithic image that the Soviets wished to present to the outside world opened infinite possibilities for exploitation by the West, few western leaders understood that a nation with a communist government could act independently or as a neutral in the East-West struggle. This lack of perception would plague American policy-making for two decades.

Clearly losing the propaganda war and failing to dislodge the West from Berlin, the Kremlin opened secret negotiations that resulted in the lifting of the blockade in May 1949. Steadfast determination had produced success for the United States without a "hot war." Again the lesson seemed clear — firm resistance would foil aggressors.

THE DEFENSE OF WESTERN EUROPE

The Brussels Pact, 1948   The fragmented defense system of the West, in which each nation maintained a force for its own protection, with a total of no more than fifteen divisions, faced a powerful Russian juggernaut of an estimated 125 divisions when the Berlin crisis erupted in 1948. America's unwillingness, in deference to world opinion, to use its atomic weapons even to force Russia to lift the blockade, nullified the West's best potential counterforce. No evidence exists that the American government ever considered using the atomic bomb in the early years of the Cold War, the issue never even appearing on the agenda of the National Security Council. In the eyes of western policy makers, therefore, the build-up of their conventional military strength was crucial.

Early in 1948 Britain, France, and the Benelux nations took preliminary steps toward a united defense in Western Europe by signing the Brussels Pact, a fifty-year treaty pledging unprecedented economic and military cooperation for their collective defense. Truman responded: "I am sure that the determination of the free countries of Europe to protect themselves will be matched by an equal determination on our part to help them do so."

The Vandenberg Resolution   Conditions favored the administration. Any faith in the effectiveness of the United Nations in promoting peace and justice had been seriously weakened by the Soviet Union's frequent use of the veto to paralyze the Security Council. Consolidation of Communist power in Czechoslovakia and the ominous rumblings in Berlin prompted scare headlines in the American press that nourished strong anti-Soviet feelings. Truman's request in March 1948 for $3 billion in addition to the $11 billion military budget already proposed for the next fiscal year, and the campaign by the Air Force for a seventy group air force, rather than the planned fifty, spotlighted the need for American strength in a hostile world. A Gallup Poll in the spring of 1948, showing sixty-five percent of the American people in favor of a western alliance, indicated public readiness for action by Washington.

In this setting Vandenberg introduced a resolution in the Senate in May 1948 advising the President, in accordance with Article 51 of the Charter of the United Nations, to seek the "Association of the United States by constitutional process with such regional and other collective arrangements as are based on continuous and effective self-help and mutual aid, and as affect its national security." By including the phrase "by constitutional process," a reference to the power of Congress to declare war, Vandenberg blunted the opposition of foes of an alliance requiring the nation to fight in support of an ally. On June 11, 1948, the eve of the Berlin blockade, the Senate after only eight hours of debate approved the Vandenberg Resolution, sixty-four to six. But further action on a collective security treaty was delayed until after the 1948 election.

Generally considered the underdog in the presidential race, Truman faced three tough challenges: first, from Republican Governor Thomas E. Dewey of New York; second from Henry Wallace, candidate of a new Progressive Party; third, from a group of Southerners angry over Truman's Civil Rights proposals, who organized a Dixiecrat Party with Senator Strom Thurmond of South Carolina as standard bearer. A vigorous "whistle stop" campaign enabled Truman to upset Dewey by carrying twenty-eight states with 303 electoral votes.

The North Atlantic Treaty   With his new mandate and a Democratic Congress, Truman pledged in his inaugural address ". . . to strengthen freedom-loving nations against the dangers of aggression" by negotiating ". . . a joint agreement designed to strengthen the security of the North Atlantic area." To give teeth to this pact he offered "military advice and equipment to free nations which will cooperate with us in the maintenance of peace and security." Negotiating the precise language of a North Atlantic Treaty became the task of Truman's new Secretary of State, Dean Acheson, who replaced the ill Marshall. Acheson, long convinced that it was futile to negotiate with the Soviets, believed in making the West so unified, strong, and prosperous that Moscow would have no choice but to cease its aggressive actions. The treaty was ready for the twelve participating nations early in April 1949. The powers pledged that they ". . . by means of continuous and effective self-help and mutual aid, will maintain and develop their individual and collective capacity to resist armed attack." In addition, they agreed "that an armed attack against one or more of them in Europe or North America shall be considered an attack against them all. . . ."

Although public opinion polls throughout the spring of 1949 indicated strong public support for ratification of the North Atlantic Pact, critics rushed to the attack. Henry Wallace asked, "Supposing the Soviets had military bases on the Mexican border? The Canadian border? On Cuba? Could a treaty which put guns in our faces be called a pact of peace?" And in ten days of Senate debate in July, diehard opponents of the treaty focused on the military obligations of the United States as well as the treaty's possible dangerous impact on the Soviet Union. Taft deplored the American tendency ". . . to assume that we are a kind of demigod and Santa Claus to solve the problems of the world. . . ." He defended his intention to vote against the treaty on the ground that ". . . the pact carries with it an obligation to assist in arming at our expense, the nations of western Europe, because with that obligation. . . it will promote war in the world rather than peace. . . ."

The Ohio Senator attracted few adherents in either party, as Senators tended to be more impressed by the polls, and by such arguments as that of Senator Tom Connally (D., Tex.) who said: "The Atlantic Pact is but the logical extension of the principle of the Monroe Doctrine." After voting down an amendment barring arms aid, the Senate ratified the treaty by 82 to 13, eleven of the negative votes being Republican. On July 25, 1949 Truman signed the North Atlantic Treaty, the first military pact between the United States and a European nation since the 1778 alliance with France was ended in 1800.

Proponents of the pact proclaimed that the United States and its allies now had "the shield" to make it less likely that America would ever have to use "its sword" — the atomic bomb. But, as usual, an indifferent public took little notice. A national poll taken two years later showed only one-third of the people able to give a reasonably correct description of NATO or its purposes.

Although the North Atlantic Treaty had no termination date, it contained a provision for review at the end of ten years and an option permitting a signatory to withdraw after twenty years. Three non-Atlantic nations were admitted later, Greece and Turkey in 1952 and West Germany in 1954. Despite repeated Communist efforts to sow division and weaken NATO, it has remained the keystone of United States policy in Europe. (map, pp. 22-23)

A Deterrent Force in Europe   Ratification of the North Atlantic Treaty was only the first step in creating a conventional deterrent force to discourage direct or indirect aggression in Europe. But when Washington turned to the next step — the building of a strong European military force equipped with non-nuclear weapons — it became clear that a large infusion of American military aid was necessary. Truman's request in mid-1949 for $1.45 billion in military aid to strengthen NATO nations encountered stiff opposition in Congress. For fiscal 1949-1950 Congress had exceeded the President's budget request for defense by appropriating $15.9 billion, the largest defense budget ever in peacetime and by providing for seventy combat air groups, fifteen more than Truman requested. But giving the President money for arming other nations was a different matter, and opponents fought for a new measure with less money and with limits on the President's authority.

Once again events outside the United States aided the administration. In the midst of the debate Truman dropped a bombshell with the cryptic announcement: "We have evidence that within recent weeks an atomic explosion occurred in the U.S.S.R." The House responded by accepting the Senate version of military assistance. In October 1949 the President signed into law the Mutual Defense Assistance Act authorizing $1.13 billion in aid to NATO nations. The latter soon agreed upon a strategic concept based on a "balanced force" to which each power would contribute its share "in the light of its geographic position, economic capability, and population." As America's share, Truman assigned two American divisions in Europe to NATO — hostages, in effect, to prove the nation's good will.

NSC No. 68   The Soviet Union's development of an atomic bomb prompted Truman late in 1949 to order the National Security Council (NSC), created two years earlier to advise the President, to devise a plan for guaranteeing the security of the United States.

UNITED STATES COLLECTIVE DEFENSE ARRANGEMENTS

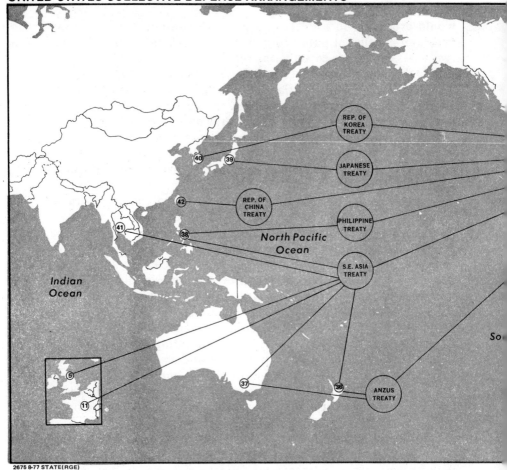

2675 8-77 STATE(RGE)

NORTH ATLANTIC TREATY (15 NATIONS)

A treaty signed April 4, 1949, by which "the Parties agree that an armed attack against one or more of them in Europe or North America shall be considered an attack against them all; and . . . each of them . . . will assist the . . . attacked by taking forthwith, individually and in concert with the other Parties, such action as it deems necessary, including the use of armed force . . ."

1	UNITED	9	LUXEMBOURG
	STATES	10	PORTUGAL
2	CANADA	11	FRANCE
3	ICELAND	12	ITALY
4	NORWAY	13	GREECE
5	UNITED	14	TURKEY
	KINGDOM	15	FEDERAL
6	NETHERLANDS		REPUBLIC
7	DENMARK		OF
8	BELGIUM		GERMANY

ANZUS (Australia — New Zealand—United States) TREATY (3 NATIONS)

A treaty signed September 1, 1951, whereby each of the parties "recognizes that an armed attack in the Pacific Area on any of the Parties would be dangerous to its own peace and safety and declares that it would act to meet the common danger in accordance with its constitutional processes."

1   UNITED STATES
36   NEW ZEALAND
37   AUSTRALIA

PHILIPPINE TREATY (BILATERAL)

A treaty signed August 30, 1951, by which the parties recognize "that an armed attack in the Pacific Area on either of the Parties would be dangerous to its own peace and safety" and each party agrees that it will act "to meet the common dangers in accordance with its constitutional processes."

1   UNITED STATES
38   PHILIPPINES

SOUTHEAST ASIA TREATY (7 NATIONS)

A treaty signed September 8, 1954, whereby each party "recognizes that aggression by means of armed attack in the treaty area against any of the Parties . . . would endanger its own peace and safety" and each will "in that event act to meet the common danger in accordance with its constitutional processes."

1   UNITED STATES
5   UNITED KINGDOM
11   FRANCE
36   NEW ZEALAND
37   AUSTRALIA
38   PHILIPPINES
41   THAILAND

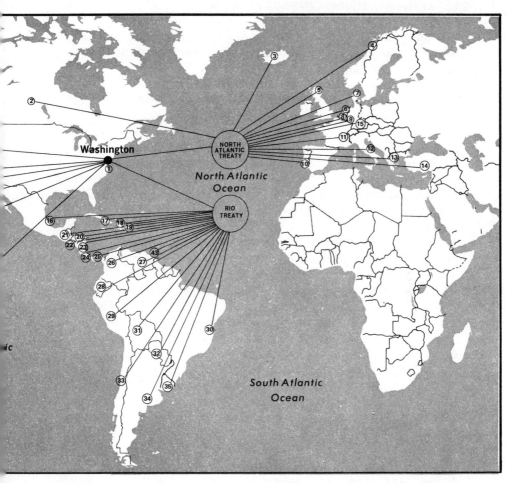

North Atlantic
Ocean

South Atlantic
Ocean

REPUBLIC OF CHINA TREATY (BILATERAL)

A treaty signed December 2, 1954, whereby each of the parties "recognizes that an armed attack in the West Pacific Area directed against the territories of either of the Parties would be dangerous to its own peace and safety . . ." and that each "would act to meet the common danger in accordance with its constitutional processes." The territory of the Republic of China is defined as "Taiwan (Formosa) and the Pescadores."

1 UNITED STATES
42 REPUBLIC OF CHINA (FORMOSA)

JAPANESE TREATY (BILATERAL)

A treaty signed January 19, 1960, whereby each party "recognizes that an armed attack against either Party in the territories under the administration of Japan would be dangerous to its own peace and safety and declares that it would act to meet the common danger in accordance with its constitutional provisions and processes." The treaty replaced the security treaty signed September 8, 1951.

1 UNITED STATES
39 JAPAN

REPUBLIC OF KOREA TREATY (BILATERAL)

A treaty signed October 1, 1953, whereby each party "recognizes that an armed attack on either of the Parties . . . would be dangerous to its own peace and safety" and that each Party "would act to meet the common danger in accordance with its constitutional processes."

1 UNITED STATES
40 REPUBLIC OF KOREA

RIO TREATY (22 NATIONS)

A treaty signed September 2, 1947, which provides that an armed attack against any American State "shall be considered as an attack against all the American States and . . . each one . . . undertakes to assist in meeting the attack . . ."

1 UNITED STATES	**26 COLOMBIA**
16 MEXICO	**27 VENEZUELA**
17 CUBA	**28 ECUADOR**
18 HAITI	**29 PERU**
19 DOMINICAN REPUBLIC	**30 BRAZIL**
20 HONDURAS	**31 BOLIVIA**
21 GUATEMALA	**32 PARAGUAY**
22 EL SALVADOR	**33 CHILE**
23 NICARAGUA	**34 ARGENTINA**
24 COSTA RICA	**35 URUGUAY**
25 PANAMA	**43 TRINIDAD AND TOBAGO**

Assuming that American goals could not be achieved by negotiating with Russia, NSC Paper No. 68 in April 1950 recommended a "bold and massive program of rebuilding the West's defensive potential to surpass that of the Soviet world, and of meeting each fresh challenge promptly and unequivocally." This comprehensive statement of strategy, emphasizing that "security must henceforth become the dominant element in the national budget" would long influence American policies. For two decades the nation would confront each Communist threat, real or suspected, with the counter-threat of military force.

Nuclear Superiority   The loss of nuclear monopoly re-kindled the debate whether to initiate, early in 1950, a crash program to build a super weapon — a hydrogen bomb — to regain nuclear superiority. Every scientist on the Advisory Committee to the Atomic Energy Commission counseled that such a project "might weaken rather than strengthen the position of the United States" by encouraging an unlimited race in the development of nuclear weapons of mass destruction. Holders of this view pointed out that every Congressional increase in spending for arms merely resulted in a Soviet response to match or exceed it. This cycle offered no pleasant ending — bankruptcy or annihilation.

Proponents of the hydrogen bomb weighed in with strong counter arguments. The Pentagon told Truman that the Russians, unless deterred by greater American destructive power, might employ their nuclear capability to achieve their objectives. Acheson, hawkish as usual, warned that ". . . we are in a situation where we could lose without firing a shot." The American people, eighty-one percent of whom believed, according to a 1950 Gallup Poll, that Russia was trying to become the ruling power of the world, demanded a "military posture" second to no one.

In a Congressional election year political considerations loomed large in the debate over national security policy. With Senator Vandenberg silenced by illness, new Republican voices betrayed restiveness with bipartisanship. The Communist triumph in China, the outbreak of war in Korea in June, and the shock of the trials of Americans accused of spying for the Soviet Union furnished the G.O.P. the issues of Democratic mismanagement and negligence. Small wonder then that Truman gave a green light to the project that resulted in November 1952 in the detonation of the first hydrogen bomb. As the nation applauded, an awed President wrote to his daughter: "So powerful was the explosion that an entire island was blown away and a large crater left in the coral."

Effort to Rearm Germany   Finding a way for Germany to

share in the cost of the defense of Europe remained a primary objective of the administration, but France continued to block this step. Truman tried to reassure France that America was committed to Europe's defense by offering to send more troops to supplement the two American divisions already there. To spur France to raise twenty divisions by 1953 Washington offered military aid of $2.4 billion, including $500 million for Indo-China. Prolonged negotiations to get French approval of German rearmament produced at the end of 1950 a tentative agreement for gradual integration of German combat teams into a European army and in the appointment of General Eisenhower as Supreme Commander of NATO forces. But the French had no enthusiasm for a rearmed Germany, and they continued to frustrate American efforts to bring it about.

The Great Debate   Meanwhile, a great debate erupted as Republican leaders, bolstered by impressive gains in the 1950 elections, criticized not only the further abandonment of traditional non-involvement in Europe but also the "unconstitutional extension of Presidential power in military and economic aid programs." Seventy-six year old ex-President Hoover denounced the sending of "another man or another dollar" to nations of Western Europe until they themselves had "organized and equipped combat divisions of such large numbers as would erect a sure dam against the red flood." Basing his faith in a "Fortress America," Hoover urged overwhelming American air and sea power "to preserve for the world this Western Hemisphere Gibraltar of civilization." Taft, hopeful of winning the Republican presidential nomination in 1952, seized the chance to argue that it was ill-conceived to fight Communism "on the vast land areas of the continent of Europe or on the continent of Asia, where we are at the greatest possible disadvantage. . . ."

In defense of the administration's position, Acheson observed that the threat to Western Europe was "singularly like that which Islam had posed centuries before, with its combination of ideological zeal and fighting power." He also upheld Truman's constitutional right to deploy American troops as he thought necessary for national security. To administration officials the Hoover-Taft position appeared dangerously akin to the foolish isolationism of the 1920's and 1930's.

The public backed the administration. A Gallup Poll taken in the midst of the "great debate" indicated that almost half of the people were even "willing to risk their lives to keep the Russians from taking over Western Europe." And despite efforts by Republican spokesmen to direct attention to Asia, Americans believed that it was more important for the United States to stop Russia in Europe.

In April 1952 the Senate in a sense of the Senate resolution approved the dispatch of the four divisions to Europe, while implying no more without congressional approval. Thereby the Truman-Acheson grand design of collective security in Europe was completed except for the establishment of a European Defense Community that included a re-armed West German Republic. Truman's decision not to seek another term left that task to a new President.

A New Look Republicans entered the 1952 primary campaign confident of victory after five straight losses. Following a bitter primary fight with conservative and isolationist groups backing Taft, the sixty-two year old General Eisenhower, a war hero yet a man of peace and a warm father figure popularly called "Ike," captured the nomination. The party's foreign policy plank, carefully fashioned by John Foster Dulles, attempted to distinguish "Republican principles" from Democratic policies. It deplored "the negative, futile and immoral policy of 'Containment' which abandons countless human beings to a despotism and godless terrorism. . ." and proclaimed that "The policies we espouse will revive the contagious, liberating influences which are inherent in freedom."

While echoing the conventional view that Russia sought "the economic containment and gradual strangulation of America," Eisenhower took a hard line against the Soviets. In a campaign speech to the American Legion, he hinted at the replacement of containment by liberation when he declared that ". . . until the enslaved nations of the world have in the fullness of freedom the right to choose their own path, that then, and then only, can we say that there is a possible way of living peacefully and permanently with Communism in the world."

With Vice Presidential candidate Richard M. Nixon leading the way, Republicans exploited national frustration over the failure of America's nuclear and economic dominance to produce victories over Communism. Nixon denounced "the Dean Acheson College for Cowardly Containment of Communism," while party stalwarts charged Democrats with "Communism, Corruption, and Korea." They blasted Truman's "soft" reaction to Communist aggression as willingness "to live with it, presumably forever." Accusations against the loyalty of Alger Hiss and State Department officials in recent Democratic administrations trumpeted incessantly by Senator Joseph McCarthy (R., Wisc.) drowned out voices of moderation.

The election outcome was never in doubt, especially after Eisenhower's dramatic announcement that he would go to Korea, if elected, in an effort to end the war. Following a precedent first set in

1828 with Andrew Jackson, the American people gave their popular war hero a landslide win over Governor Adlai E. Stevenson of Illinois.

Eisenhower assigned responsibility for an aggressive foreign policy to his Secretary of State, John Foster Dulles. A sixty-four year old lawyer and life-time student of foreign affairs, Dulles had strong convictions about right and wrong and a tendency to moralize. His analysis of Truman's programs, expressed in countless articles and speeches, called for a "new look" in foreign policy. Political reality required that he pursue relentlessly total victory over America's enemies. Negotiation and accommodation would not do. Senator McCarthy gave his blessing to the "new look" by ridiculing containment as "a big word which grew out of the Groton vocabulary of the Hiss-Acheson gang."

An opportunity to apply the Dulles liberation concept appeared in June 1953 when rioting broke out in East Berlin against Soviet labor policies and quickly spread to other East German cities. But beyond claiming that these convulsions behind the Iron Curtain were at least the indirect result of the administration's pronouncements, Washington made no move. Critics quickly pointed out that the heralded new look bore an amazing resemblance to the old.

Continuity of Truman policy also characterized the new administration's effort to secure a European Defense Community Treaty. Although Dulles pressured the French by implying that their failure to ratify EDC". . . would compel an agonizing reappraisal of basic United States policy," the French Assembly in August 1954 rejected the treaty. But France did join Britain and the United States in an agreement to end the military occupation of Germany. Eventually, in May 1955 West Germany was admitted to full membership in NATO. Shortly thereafter the Soviet Union reacted by forming the Warsaw Pact, a mutual security treaty with its East European allies. Two armed camps divided Europe.

Soviet announcement, in mid-summer 1953, of the explosion of a hydrogen bomb revived interest in an international agreement on atomic energy before a nuclear holocaust occurred. In a speech to the United Nations in December, Eisenhower attempted to break the deadlock by proposing "atoms for peace." Inviting the two governments to "begin now and continue to make joint contributions from their stockpile of normal uranium and fissionable materials to an International Atomic Energy Agency," Eisenhower challenged the Soviet Union to show its peaceful intentions. No favorable response came from the Kremlin.

Massive Retaliation   In an article in *Life Magazine* before the

1952 convention met, Dulles had suggested a new strategy for dealing with the Communist military threat. He proposed that the free world "develop the will and organize the means to retaliate instantly against open aggression by Red Armies, so that if it occurred anywhere, we could and would strike back where it hurts by means of our own choosing." Early in 1954 Dulles again advanced this idea in a speech suggesting that the modern way for a nation to "get maximum protection at bearable cost" was "to place more reliance on deterrent power and less on local defensive power." Such a policy, Dulles repeated, would ". . . depend primarily upon a great capacity to retaliate, instantly, by means and at places of our choosing."

As viewed by administration officials, this "New Look" assumed that only a surprise nuclear attack could knock out the United States, and that the Korean War had taught an unpleasant lesson against fighting brush fire wars with conventional weapons on other continents. Mere brandishing a nuclear deterrent, according to this view, would convince an enemy not to risk annihilation. Equipped with atomic weapons, the United States Strategic Air Command (SAC) would be more efficient and less costly than an army to match the 175 Soviet divisions in Europe. In defense of the "New Look," Eisenhower explained in his *Memoirs* that: "I refused to turn the United States into an armed camp. . . . I saw no sense in wasting manpower in costly small wars that could not achieve decisive results under the political and military circumstances then existing."

Labeled "massive retaliation" by critics and ridiculed as designed primarily to produce "a bigger bang for the buck," the "New Look" generated an uproar at home and abroad. Some charged that domestic political considerations, namely a balanced budget to appease conservative Republicans, was the motivating force. Opposition came from the Navy and Army who saw the Air Force winning the lion's share of resources, and from Congressmen worried about economic consequences of a projected cut of $4 billion in the 1954-55 budget. Paradoxically the administration drew fire from those who feared it might start a nuclear war as well as from those who believed that it was bluffing because it would never use such weapons. Both Eisenhower and Dulles found it necessary to reassure the world of America's peaceful intentions and to acknowledge that no radical change in American policy had occurred. "Massive retaliation" soon joined "liberation" in the limbo populated by campaign hyperbole of the past.

PEACEFUL COEXISTENCE?

Soviet Overtures   Stalin's death in March 1953, a few weeks after Eisenhower's inauguration, encouraged hopes of reversing the course of the Cold War. New leaders in the Kremlin began to soften Soviet language toward the West. Georgi Malenkov, the new Soviet Premier, suggested "peaceful coexistence" and "competition between the capitalist and socialist systems." Dulles remained skeptical. He interpreted this new Soviet line as the result of internal weakness and outside pressures, so he advised Eisenhower ". . . to keep up those pressures right now."

The Decline of McCarthyism   In truth, the Eisenhower administration was the prisoner of public opinion molded by years of anti-communist rhetoric by American leaders and the press. To accede to specific Soviet proposals, however promising, would challenge the McCarthy interpretation that previous deals with and sell-outs to the Communists had cost the nation so much. As long as McCarthy's following appeared numerous and strong, the individual who crossed him risked humiliation and defeat at the polls. Few public officials were so brave.

Television, now available to the masses, rescued the administration. In the spring of 1954 millions of Americans watched the hearings conducted by McCarthy's Special Senate Committee investigating charges of Communism in the United States Army. What they saw was so disturbing that McCarthy's influence waned rapidly, and by the end of the year his Senate colleagues dared to censure him for contempt of a Senate Subcommittee

Geneva Conference, 1955   With McCarthy muffled, it was possible to consider a relaxation of tension with the Communist bloc. When the Soviet Union announced its intention early in 1955 to sign a peace treaty with Austria, it appeared that the post-Stalin generation of Soviet leaders really wanted a thaw in the Cold War. Although Dulles feared that a summit conference, proposed by the Soviets, might "be nothing but a spectacle and promote a false euphoria," a skeptical Eisenhower was encouraged by others to agree to meet with the heads of state of Britain, France, and the Soviet Union at Geneva, Switzerland in July 1955.

On the fourth day of the conference Eisenhower, looking directly at the Soviet delegation, declared that "The United States will never take part in an aggressive war." Then the President made a dramatic "open skies" proposal that would allow each side unrestricted aerial surveillance of the other's territory to inspect for surprise military moves. By such an exchange of military blueprints another Pearl Harbor could be avoided. But Nikita Khrushchev, the new Soviet leader, dismissed the idea as "nothing more than a bald espionage plot against the U.S.S.R."

The generally cordial atmosphere, however, and agreement on measures to increase friendship between peoples of the West and the Soviet Union raised hopes that "the spirit of Geneva" promised a reduction in the intensity of the Cold War. Whereas seventy-three percent in a March 1955 Gallup Poll had believed that there would be a war in their lifetime, after Geneva less than half thought so. Yet the hard truth was that changes in style and personality did not mean settlement of divisive issues. Dulles cautioned that no development at Geneva "justifies the free world relaxing its vigilance or substantially altering its programs for collective security. . . . We must assume that the Soviet leaders consider their recent change of policy to be an application of the class of maneuver known as 'Zig-zag'."

Such reservations did not obscure the reality of a relaxation of international tension that endured through Eisenhower's recovery from a heart attack in 1955 and through most of his successful campaign for re-election in 1956. Not even two serious crises in October 1956 — one in the Middle East (p. 97), the other in Hungary — escalated the Cold War. Hungarian "freedom fighters" elicited many admiring words from Americans, but no liberating weapons. Washington had no intentions of risking war to aid the oppressed peoples of Europe.

Nuclear Arms Race   The post-Geneva calm was shaken by an astonishing Soviet feat in October 1957 — the launching of Sputnik into orbit 560 miles above the earth. Any lingering doubts about the ability of the Soviets to deploy an intercontinental ballistic missile (ICBM) vanished. Alarm spread that Russia might be ahead in the Cold War and might be tempted to use its ICBM superiority to destroy a vulnerable United States. Such fears increased after the Gaither Report, prepared by a special government appointed committee of private citizens, testified in November 1957 to the ability of the Soviet Union within two years to launch one hundred ICBM's with megaton nuclear warheads against the United States. Washington rushed to equip NATO bases with short range missiles capable of hitting Soviet targets. Many saw civilization teetering on a "delicate balance of terror."

A confident Nikita Khrushchev, having gained the premiership after a bitter internal struggle, now moved to exploit the leverage of the Soviet Union's new nuclear capability. But throughout the spring of 1958, Eisenhower, wary of Russian efforts to dismantle NATO and to stop nuclear testing after their own successful tests, parried the Kremlin's overtures for another summit meeting.

Berlin Crisis, 1958-1959 Then in November 1958 Khrushchev initiated a new crisis. Turning over the administration of East Berlin to Moscow's East German satellite, the German Democratic Republic, the Soviet Premier set a six month deadline for withdrawal of all troops from Berlin and the transfer of authority over the West's access to Berlin to East Germany. In December Moscow warned that after it turned over control to East Germany "any attempt to force a way into Berlin" would lead to a "military conflict" involving "the most modern means of annihilation. ..." By rattling his nuclear sabre, Khrushchev hoped to pry loose from NATO the more vulnerable nations. But fortunately Khrushchev was not Stalin. Confining his aggressiveness to threatening language, the new Red leader allowed Allied convoys to move through the Russian zone to West Berlin. Only desperate East Germans, attempting to flee to freedom encountered gunfire.

Nor was Eisenhower a Neville Chamberlain, intimidated by threats. Standing fast by American rights in the German capital, as had Truman a decade earlier, the President held the Russian government "directly responsible for the discharge of its obligations undertaken with respect to Berlin under existing agreements."

Confronted by such American firmness, Khrushchev, in Eisenhower's words, "executed a remarkable diplomatic retreat." By March 1959 the Red leader was calling for a new summit conference and downgrading the six months "ultimatum" to a negotiable deadline. By May the Big Four foreign ministers were meeting in Geneva trying to resolve the deadlock over Berlin and over nuclear testing. By August Khrushchev and Eisenhower were agreeing to exchange visits. By September Khrushchev was in Washington saying that "we and all peoples should live in peace and friendship. ..." And by the end of his tour of America, from Disneyland to an Iowa farm and a Pittsburg steel mill, the Soviet leader was convincing many Americans that peaceful coexistence was here to stay. A surprising twenty percent in a Gallup Poll even believed that he was "sincere in wanting to work out an effective disarmament plan."

The U-2 Incident, 1960 Eisenhower never returned the visit. In early May 1960 the Soviets shot down a U-2, an American photo-reconnaissance plane, some thirteen hundred miles inside the U.S.S.R. Khrushchev waited until the State Department attempted to disguise the ill-fated U-2 flight as a weather-gathering mission that had wandered off course due to mechanical failure. He then paraded the captured pilot and displayed fragments of the U-2 as evidence of American espionage and dishonesty. At a news conference Eisenhower admitted to the U-2 flights, initiated in 1956, as a "distasteful but vital necessity" to obtain accurate intelligence in the absence of agreements on disarmament and cessation of nuclear testing. Although the President stopped further flights, he refused Khrushchev's demand that those responsible for U-2 missions be punished. The summit conference in Paris was scuttled on its first day, and Eisenhower's subsequent trip to Moscow was postponed indefinitely. On this sour note, progress toward relaxation of East-West tension ended as the nation entered the 1960 election campaign.

The Berlin Crisis of 1961   In his campaign for the Presidency John F. Kennedy took a hard anti-Communist line and criticized the Eisenhower administration for allowing a missile gap to develop. Assuming that the Communists prepared for peace only if America prepared for war, Kennedy stressed the need to "strengthen our conventional forces" and then ". . . move ahead full time on our missile production." In this fashion the United States would possess what Kennedy called a "flexible response." Missing from his campaign speeches was a commitment to negotiate with the Soviets to strengthen peaceful coexistence. Although Kennedy's tough talk may have garnered votes, it failed to faze Soviet leaders. Evidence suggests that Khrushchev regarded the youthful American President as inexperienced and likely to back down if pushed to the brink.

At the very outset of his term Kennedy faced a new Soviet engineered crisis over Berlin, where the United States, according to a campaign statement, had "a commitment that we have to meet if we're going to protect the security of Western Europe." Early in January Khrushchev issued a six months ultimatum requiring the end of allied occupation of West Berlin and recognition of it as a demilitarized city. If the West did not agree, then the Soviet Union would sign its own peace treaty with East Germany thereby terminating the legal agreement for the western presence in Berlin.

With the firm Berlin stands of Truman and Eisenhower as precedents, Kennedy could ill afford any sign of indecision. In his State of the Union Message on January 30, 1961 he warned that the country faced ". . . . an hour of national peril. . .", and that ". . . the tide of events has been running out and time has not been our friend." But the new President's willingness, early in his term, to accept a humiliating defeat in the abortive Bay of Pigs venture (p. 70) rather than risk war apparently encouraged the Kremlin to believe that Kennedy's boldness was confined to words.

Exhilarated by the achievement in April 1961 that sent a Soviet cosmonaut on the first manned space flight, a confident Khrushchev proposed a meeting with Kennedy. But the Soviet leader had mis-judged his opponent. The President, suspecting that the Russians were testing the American will to resist and his own toughness, refused to abandon West Berlin. Before leaving for the Vienna meeting with Khrushchev he asked Congress for a massive arms build-up and increased defense expenditures of almost $3 billion. Kennedy warned that: "The Free World's security can be endangered not only by a nuclear attack, but also by being slowly nibbled away at the periphery, regardless of our strategic power. . . . ".

At the two day Vienna meeting in June, the Soviet Premier, eager to halt the embarrassing flow of four thousand refugees each week from East Germany into West Berlin and freedom, held fast to his deadline. Kennedy painted a somber picture in his report on the talks in Vienna. Claiming that ". . . the adversaries of freedom plan to consolidate their territory. . .", he found the nation facing ". . . a contest of will and purpose as well as force and violence — a battle for minds and souls as well as lives and territory. And in that context, we cannot stand aside." Vienna had settled nothing.

Khrushchev kept up the pressure with a July announcement of a one-third increase in Soviet military spending and a suspension of the partial demobilization of the Red Army. In this deadly game of nuclear poker, each round of increases led to another round with no end in sight. Presidential adviser Arthur M. Schlesinger, Jr. deplored the tendency to define the issue as: "Are you chicken or not?" Failure to retaliate in kind should not be construed, according to Schlesinger, as being "soft, idealistic, mushy. . . ."

Yet Kennedy knew that there could be no negotiations under the threat of an ultimatum. He told the nation on July 25 that: "We cannot and will not permit the Communists to drive us out of Berlin, either gradually or by force. . ." After announcing that he was asking Congress for $3.25 billion more for defense, he said that he was calling up certain reserve and National Guard units. After reviewing the steps being taken for civil defense, the President assured the nation that: "In the coming months, I hope to let every citizen know what steps he can take without delay to protect his family in case of attack." Despite such alarmist talk, Kennedy claimed that ". . . we are willing to consider any arrangement or treaty in Germany consistent with the maintenance of peace and freedom, and with the legitimate security interests of all nations."

Throughout the summer of 1961 tension over Berlin mounted as 30,000 refugees fled to West Berlin in July alone. On August 13, East German troops began to install roadblocks and barbed wire barricades along the line dividing East and West Berlin. Four days

later the Communists began construction of a concrete wall along
the line. Eventually the wall wound its way through over one
hundred miles of Berlin streets and alleys. Resisting pressure from
the "hawks," who as usual advocated retaliating with bombs,
Kennedy avoided war while insisting on American rights in Berlin.
He ordered 1500 combat troops to move from West Germany to
Berlin, and he sent Vice-President Lyndon B. Johnson to reassure
the German people of America's commitment.

By the end of August the administration's firm stand had persuaded the Russians to begin negotiations. Again it appeared that
holding fast to an established position against threats was the wisest
approach in dealing with the Soviets. Although the talks on Berlin
dragged on sporadically for a decade, a compromise agreement
upholding Western rights was reached in 1973. But long before this
satisfactory conclusion of the crisis in Europe, developments in
other parts of the world had heated up the Cold War.

Chapter Two

Conflict in East Asia

The unfortunate but inescapable fact is that the ominous result of the civil war in China was beyond the control of the government of the United States."
Dean Acheson, 1949

"This strategy would involve us in the wrong war, at the wrong time, and with the wrong enemy."
General Omar Bradley, 1951

THE UNITED STATES AND THE CHINESE CIVIL WAR

The Failure to Achieve Wartime Unity in China A few hours before Harry Truman swore the oath as President of the United States on April 12, 1945, a C-54 of the Air Transport Command landed in Washington, D.C. Aboard was a career officer in the State Department, John S. Service, whose activities in China soon embroiled the Truman administration in sharp controversy. Eleven days earlier Service had held official conversations in Yenan, China, with Communist leaders at the residence of Mao-Tse-Tung (Mow Zuh-dung), leader of the Chinese Communist Party. Now, although Service did not know it, he had been recalled to Washington at the insistence of American Ambassador to China, Patrick J. Hurley.

Eight months earlier President Roosevelt had sent Hurley to China as his personal envoy to try to settle the twenty year internal conflict between the governing Nationalist Party, the Kuomintang (Gwaw Minh-dang) under the leadership of fifty-seven year old Chiang Kai-shek (Jyang Ki-sheck), and the Communists. Americans viewed these two Chinese rivals as more interested in fighting each other than in promoting the welfare of the Chinese people. Even after the first Japanese attack on Manchuria in 1931, the two Chi-

35

nese parties had carefully husbanded their resources for use against each other. Renewed Japanese attacks on China in 1937-1938 deprived the Nationalists of a chance for victory over Mao and forced them to retreat hundreds of miles inland to Chungking on the upper Yangtze River. (map p. 41)

The entry of the United States into the war against Japan in December 1941 failed to unite the Chinese Nationalists and Communists in a cooperative military effort. Assuming that the United States would eventually defeat Japan, both Chinese parties believed that postwar control of China would fall to the one in the strongest position to take over. But American officials were eager to bring maximum pressure against Japan. They urged Chiang to refrain from attacking Chinese Communists, to settle differences with them, and to carry out reforms to expedite the war effort against Japan.

The idea of deserting the leader of the legitimate government of China, even though incompetent, was unthinkable for the Roosevelt administration. Americans, traditionally sympathetic toward and protective of China through the Open Door Policy, had readily accepted Roosevelt's elevation of China to the rank of great power and equal partner in the war, despite the open skepticism of Churchill and Stalin. American journalists and radio commentators had long found it fashionable to extol the greatness of Chiang Kai-shek and the beauty and charm of Madam Chiang, educated at Wellesley College, and along with her husband a convert to Christianity. *Time* magazine, published by Henry Luce, son of an American missionary in China, had set the pattern for an idealized image of the Generalissimo and his wife by naming them "Man and Wife of the Year" for 1937. An American public, hungry for heroes, embraced Chiang as a valiant fighter for western ideals and an enlightened leader deserving all possible aid. Madam Chiang rose to a top spot on annual most admired women lists. China's internal disunity and weakness were conveniently blamed on the long war with the ruthless Japanese.

This widely held romanticized view of the situation in China inevitably influenced government policy. In the midst of the 1944 election campaign, Roosevelt saw little choice but to cater to the Generalissimo's wishes by appointing General Albert Wedemeyer as Commander in the China-India-Burma theatre, replacing General "Vinegar Joe" Stilwell, whose blunt criticism of China's war effort had incurred Chiang's displeasure. Unwilling to manipulate American aid to coerce Chiang to reform his government, FDR found it less risky politically to send Hurley to try to persuade the Generalissimo to cooperate with the Communists in fighting the Japanese.

Hurley had served as Secretary of War in Hoover's cabinet and as a factfinder on several wartime missions for the President, who regularly tried to muffle G.O.P. criticism of foreign policy by involving prominent Republicans in its planning and execution.

First impressions convinced Hurley that Communist strength was greatly exaggerated by American foreign service officers in China and that the Nationalists had little to fear. The primitive living conditions and Spartan simplicity of Mao's accommodations contrasted strikingly with Chiang's headquarters with its cordon of brisk guards and fleets of long black American limousines. Hurley assumed that only minor differences divided the two parties and that a coalition government could be arranged. After all, Molotov and Stalin had described the Chinese Communists as "radish communists" (red on the outside only) who "had no relation whatever to Communism." Hurley's own first hand observations of private enterprise in Yenan led him to accept a widely-held theory that the Chinese Communists were not real Communists in the Russian mold. American observers in Yenan also contributed to this view by consistently reporting the absence of Soviet advisers, arms, and supplies in Chinese Communist areas as evidence that Mao and his followers were "agrarian reformers" and not Soviet puppets.

That American officials became confused about Chinese Communism was not surprising. Communists were supposed to be urban industrial workers, a propertyless, oppressed class seeking under Russian direction to overthrow capitalist exploiters who owned the factories and controlled the government. Chinese peasants hardly fit that stereotype. Many Americans thought that Mao's goals would be reached as soon as the large property holdings of the landlords were broken up and redistributed among the peasants. Guided by this simplistic analysis of Chinese Communism, Hurley believed that his skill as a negotiator could bring the two sides together to concentrate on fighting Japan.

The fact that Stalin continued diplomatic relations with the Nationalist government, and formed no open ties with the Chinese Communists, nurtured Hurley's suspicions that the latter's weakness would eventually force them to make concessions. The Ambassador returned to Washington in February 1945 to urge vigorous support of the Nationalists as a loyal ally while denying aid to the Chinese Reds.

Although agreeing with Hurley that the Chinese Communists were not true Communists of the Soviet variety, some veteran professional foreign service officers in China questioned the wisdom of full support of Chiang. Disenchanted with the Generalissimo and the KMT because of flagrant corruption, incompetence, and blind resistance to reforms, these "China hands" had become pessimistic about Chiang's capacity to suppress growing Communist strength by force and to nullify Communist appeal to the Chinese masses. General Stilwell put it succinctly with his observation that Chiang was "a man trying to fight an idea with force. He doesn't understand the idea and he doesn't know how to use force." After Hurley had arrived back in Washington several foreign service officers, including John Service signed a message to the State Department proposing that:

> . . . the President inform the Generalissimo in definite terms that we supply and cooperate with the Communists and other suitable groups who can assist the war against Japan. . . and that we are taking direct steps to accomplish this end. . . . we can point out the advantage of having the Communists helped by us rather than seeking Russian aid or intervention.

When he saw the wire, Hurley, suspecting a move to undermine his position, exploded: "I know who drafted that telegram: Service! Service! I'll get that S.O.B. if it's the last thing I do." Hurley had Service and the other signers recalled to the United States, and Washington rejected the advice of the State Department's career men.

Although Stalin had agreed at Yalta "to conclude with the National Government of China a pact of friendship and alliance," Truman in his early weeks in office became concerned about Russia's intentions in China. The President instructed Harry Hopkins on his special mission to Moscow in late May to promote a formal agreement between Chiang and Stalin to forestall new troubles in Asia. Hopkins did obtain from the Soviet dictator a pledge to "do everything he can to promote unification under the leadership of Chiang Kai-shek." In Washington hopes now revived for a coalition government dominated by the Nationalists.

A long summer of negotiations between Chungking and Moscow produced on August 14, 1945, the day of the Japanese surrender, a Treaty of Friendship and Alliance. But real agreement between the KMT and the Chinese Reds failed to materialize. As the war ended the immediate task of disarming the Japanese generated friction between the two Chinese parties. The Generalissimo, reassured by the treaty with Russia as well as by the steady flow of aid from the United States, would not over-rule his Generals and KMT officials who opposed any sharing of power with the Communists. Chinese Red leaders, disappointed by Russia's treaty with Chiang, hoped that direct involvement of the Soviet Union in disarming the

Japanese in Manchuria would improve their own position.

The Failure of The Hurley Mission   Although the July 1945 Potsdam agreements called for Chiang to disarm more than one million Japanese troops in China, he was not prepared to forestall similar action by Mao. Claiming equal rights to liberate enemy held territory, Communist General Chu Teh (Choo Deh) ordered his armies to disarm the Japanese in northern China provinces where there were no Nationalist troops. Hurley tried to resolve this new crisis by bringing Mao and Chiang together in Chungking for talks early in September, but the two adversaries could not reach an agreement.

Bolstered by the extension of emergency Lend-Lease aid for six months, Chiang began to transport with American assistance some of his troops to key spots in northern and eastern China. "Descending like a swarm of locusts," Nationalist troops and civilian officials alienated local populations by confiscating gold, houses, cars, and women. But Communist forces blocked Nationalist movement into the most northeastern provinces. In Manchuria, Soviet armies rapidly disarmed the Japanese, established control over the provinces and began to dismantle factories and industrial equipment for shipment back to the Soviet Union. Despite Stalin's pledge at Potsdam, the Russians allowed the Chinese Communists to take possession of Japanese arms while refusing to allow Nationalist troops to land at Darien, southern Manchuria's major port.

Washington faced a tough decision. General Wedemeyer, Army Secretary Patterson, and Navy Secretary Forrestal favored all-out military aid to Chiang. Truman and his closest advisers, however, believed that to guarantee a Nationalist victory would require American intervention on a scale matching the military effort against Nazi Germany. Given the mood of the American people, who wanted the return of their servicemen now that World War II had ended, such a step was unthinkable. United States Marines and Air Force personnel, therefore, were instructed to assist only in the transfer of Nationalist forces to North China.

Emotionally and physically exhausted, Hurley returned to Washington late in September 1945 as fighting broke out in North China. Stung by press and Congressional criticism of his diplomacy and incensed by the recent appointment of his old adversary, John Service, to the Far Eastern Commission under General MacArthur, Hurley concluded that the Chinese Affairs Division of the State Department was trying to thwart his efforts to carry out, as he put it, "Roosevelt's Asian policy based on the Atlantic Charter." A scathing condemnation of Hurley's "blank check" support of Chiang by

Congressman Hugh DeLacy (D. Wash.) so infuriated Hurley that, without first informing the President, he gave the press his blistering letter of resignation charging that "a considerable section of our State Department is endeavoring to support Communism generally as well as in China."

Hurley's tirade against a Democratic State Department whipped into action Congressional Republicans impatient with Truman's China policies and eager to find a winning issue. Senator Styles Bridges (R., N.H.), who had repeatedly condemned the administration's "softness" towards Communism and its tolerance of disloyal career men in the State Department, urged Hurley to "shoot the works" by disclosing the secret Yalta agreement. Even Taft joined the chorus praising Hurley's support of Chiang and criticizing Truman's "bankrupt" China policies.

Bipartisanship had never been the rule in American Asian policy. Republican leaders, proud of their party's institution of the Open Door Policy early in the century, protested that they had not been consulted when basic decisions about China had been made at Big Three Conferences. Having had no voice in making policy that, in their eyes, left Nationalist China in jeopardy, many Republicans clamored for a greater American effort to save China from Communism. Although a Senate investigation in December dismissed Hurley's charges as unfounded, they poisoned the dialogue. Ultimately politicians and journalists, hostile to the Democrats, embellished the accusations of betrayal in China and flooded the media with allegations of wrong doing in high places.

The Marshall Mission and Civil War in China Moving quickly to counter the uproar instigated by Hurley, an angry President asked retired General George C. Marshall to succeed the Ambassador. Truman feared that civil war in China would enable the Russians to extend their control because of the weakness of the Nationalist Government. Hurley's failure to bring the two sides together did not mean that the idea was unsound. Therefore, to nudge the Generalissimo toward democratic reforms and unity, Truman authorized Marshall to announce ". . . that a China disunited and torn by civil strife could not be considered realistically as a proper place for American assistance. . . ." But the United States had no real alternative other than to continue to back the Nationalists.

A superhuman task confronted Marshall. A confident Chiang counted on American aid, which amounted to over $700 million in Lend-Lease alone after V-J Day, to assure ultimate victory. He viewed any coalition with the Communists as not only undesirable

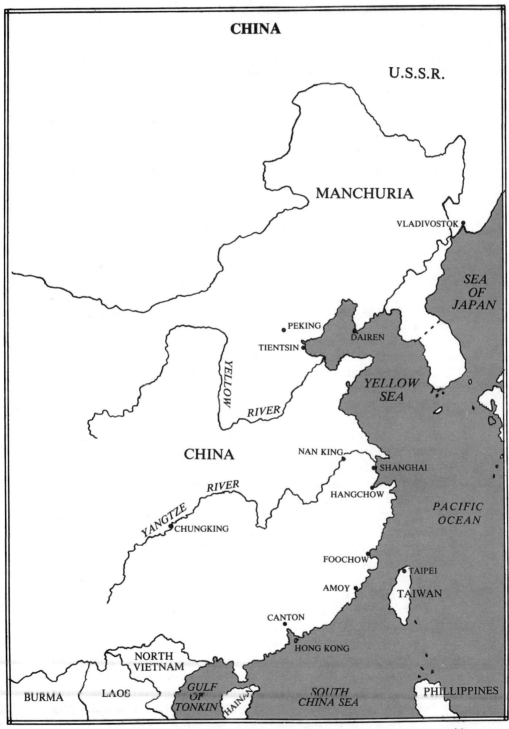

CHINA

U.S.S.R.

MANCHURIA

VLADIVOSTOK

SEA
OF
JAPAN

PEKING

DAIREN

TIENTSIN

YELLOW

RIVER

YELLOW
SEA

CHINA

NAN KING

SHANGHAI

RIVER

HANGCHOW

YANGTZE

CHUNGKING

PACIFIC
OCEAN

FOOCHOW

TAIPEI

AMOY

TAIWAN

CANTON

HONG KONG

NORTH
VIETNAM

BURMA

LAOS

GULF
OF
TONKIN

HAINAN

SOUTH
CHINA SEA

PHILLIPPINES

but as unnecessary. According to the metaphor used by conservatives in the KMT, the small Communist strongholds could be
removed as easily as a surgeon cuts out an inflamed appendix. The
other side, the Communists, outnumbered two and a half to one,
without American aid and confined to the northern provinces,
favored American mediation to establish a coalition government in
which they would occupy a legitimate place. Playing for time to gain
position, Red leaders visualized a broadening of their base in the
North and expanding their appeal. They counted on Nationalist
blunders and resistance to reforms to shrink Chiang's support until
the overwhelming majority of Chinese people turned to the Communists to take over control of China. The construction of such different plots in the minds of the principal actors foreshadowed
frustration for any director attempting to blend the two into one
scenario.

Marshall's prestige and skill did produce a cease-fire in North
China and Manchuria on January 25, 1946 and adoption of procedures for negotiations. But meetings in Chungking to work out
details of a coalition government stalled when Chiang refused to
participate in joint truce teams to supervise a cease-fire in Manchuria. A disappointed Marshall explained to Truman that Chiang was
". . . in an extremely difficult position struggling with the ultra conservative and determined wing of each group [the army and KMT],
many if not most of whom will lose position and income, all or in
part by the changes proposed. . . ." The precarious truce collapsed
soon after Marshall's return to Washington in mid-March for consultations. When the Russians finally began to withdraw from Manchuria in early April 1946, Chiang ignored military advice of
American officers, including Wedemeyer, and sent troops into Manchuria to destroy the Red Chinese forces.

Upon his return to China in April, Marshall blamed both sides
for the fighting. He chided Nationalist General Yu Ta-wei (Yoo Da-
way): "I do not know who the Generalissimo's advisers are but
whoever they may be, they are very poor ones. Instead of constructive action they got the government into trouble." In a message to
Truman, Marshall criticized the Communists for violating the
cease-fire agreement by resisting the government's efforts to establish sovereignty in Manchuria.

Neither side was happy with American mediation efforts. Chinese Communist spokesmen condemned United States policy that
professed to be neutral and committed to peace, but continued to
furnish extensive military and economic aid to the Nationalists. Red
leaders refused to accept Chiang's terms that threatened the very

existence of their own party. On the other side, the Generalissimo saw no reason to make concessions to an enemy seeking to destroy him. Convinced that extension of territorial control spelled military success, Chiang marched on. Unable to defeat Communist forces who avoided battle, KMT officials complained that Marshall's policies held them back from total victory. Caught in the middle, General Marshall labored to prevent the full scale conflict that appeared imminent.

Growing polarization in the United States paralleled this division in China. An influential group, the so-called "China Lobby," funded by wealthy Chinese and American businessmen, was hard at work in America propagandizing the cause of the Nationalists. On May 15, 1946, sixty-five prominent Americans, including Representatives Walter Judd (R., Minn.), a former medical missionary in China, and Clare Booth Luce (R., Conn.), wife of the publisher of *Time* and *Life*, condemned the Yalta agreement for pledging "to deliver the promised concessions in Manchuria and Mongolia to Soviet Russia whether the Chinese government agreed or not." This charge that the United States had sold out China at Yalta attracted Roosevelt haters and those convinced that Asia was more important than Europe to America.

Arrayed against the China lobby were die-hard opponents of more aid to the "decadent" KMT. They found a new argument in a June 1946 United Press story charging that ". . . there was solid evidence that a clique of officials in the Kuomintang, the Generalissimo's party, under the inspiration of German Nazi advisers, were opposed to peace with the Communists under any conditions." Subsequent news articles supported the contention that the obstacle to unification of China was a Nazi influenced group in the KMT, notably Generals Ho Ying-chin and Tu Yu-ming (Doo Yoo-ming), and the so-called CC clique headed by Minister of Organization Chen Li-fu (Chun Lee-foo), whom Marshall identified as "the man most opposed to my efforts," and his brother Chen Kuo-fu (Chun Gwaw-foo). On June 30 the United States officially protested the Chinese government's removal of four hundred persons from a list of "dangerous and objectionable Nazis to be shipped to Germany." Apparently these Germans had bribed KMT officials with sums ranging from $15,000 to $75,000 in order to remain in China. Understandably many Americans felt bewildered as they tried to identify the "good guys" in China.

As government forces, meanwhile, advanced in sharp fighting in Shantung province, the Chinese Communist attitude toward the United States turned bitter. Red propagandists accused the Nationalists of using Marshall's mediation as a cover for expanded military operations. Not even Marshall was spared the invective of Communist radio broadcasts, and newspaper stories accusing him of deliberately promoting civil war in China in behalf of "imperialist circles" in America. Mao himself ridiculed the "so-called mediation as a smokescreen for strengthening Chiang Kai-shek in every way. . . ."

Marshall's warning of impending financial collapse failed to deter the Nationalists from military expenditures consuming about seventy percent of their budget and promoting ruinous inflation. Discouraged by the continued irresponsibility of Chiang's government, Truman, at Marshall's request, imposed in August a temporary embargo on further shipment of military supplies to China as a means of forcing reforms. Administration leaders thought that the Nationalists could not win a military victory and that their only hope of retaining power was to make a political settlement with Mao.

The American public, absorbed in debate over continuation of wartime wage and price controls and disturbed by an epidemic of strikes, paid little heed to disturbing events in China. Newspaper accounts tended to be buried in the middle pages as Soviet actions in Europe and the Middle East dominated the news. The *New York Times* relegated to page nine the June 25th warning by Mao that continuation of American aid to the Nationalists would plunge China into civil war.

In an effort to mollify some of his critics, Chiang in October summoned a National Assembly to meet on November 12, 1946. Communist General Chou En-lai (Zhou Un-lie) denounced this call as a violation of previous agreements and as "nation-splitting." The National Assembly convened without any Communist delegates and drafted a constitution to take effect after elections in December, 1947. Satisfied with this window dressing, Chiang steadfastly resisted serious reforms on the grounds that they would only feed the fire of rebellion.

Late in 1946 Marshall sadly advised Truman to terminate American participation in the mediation effort and to withdraw the 10,000 marines still in China. Blaming both sides for the civil war, a disenchanted Marshall left China for the last time early in January 1947 and flew back to Washington to replace James Byrnes as Secretary of State

The Wedemeyer Mission and The Debate Over U.S. Policy in China   Each Nationalist reverse in the early weeks of 1947 built up pressures in the new Republican-controlled Congress to resume aid to Chiang. In House hearings on Truman's proposal to aid Greece and Turkey, Judd asked why the administration did not show the same concern for the Chinese resisting Communism. Secretaries Patterson and Forrestal, supported by the Joint Chiefs of Staff, argued for the removal of the embargo on munitions as necessary to prevent a Communist triumph. Signs of a major debacle for Nationalist forces in Manchuria amidst new reports of student strikes for peace in many Nationalist cities, persuaded Marshall to lift the ten month old embargo in May.

Washington, however, had no desire to become more deeply involved in China. Marshall later admitted that ". . . the thing that concerned me was that the Chinese [Nationalists] have long been intent on the United States going to war with the Soviet Union with the expectation that the United States would drag the Chinese government out of its difficulties." Truman also feared that partisan debate over China might jeopardize the European Recovery Program. It was decided, therefore, to send General Albert C. Wedemeyer to China on a fact-finding mission. The President saw in Wedemeyer, highly regarded by the Generalissimo, an opportunity to quiet discordant notes arising from Republican ranks in Congress and from the pro-Nationalist press. Wedemeyer was instructed to tell Chinese officials that the United States "can consider assistance in a program of rehabilitation only if the Chinese Government presents satisfactory evidence of effective measures looking toward Chinese recovery. . . ."

A grim picture confronted the American general, who reported soon after his arrival in China that the Nationalists "do not understand why they should die or make any sacrifices. They have lost confidence in their leaders, political and military, and they foresee complete collapse. Those in positions of responsibility are therefore corruptly striving to obtain as much as they can before the collapse."

A month's investigation confirmed Wedemeyer's first estimates. Uncontrolled inflation had driven the price index in Shanghai from 92 in January 1946 to 686 a year later and to 2993 in June 1947. Conditions were so bad that Wedemeyer warned Nationalist leaders that ". . . the Central Government cannot defeat the Chinese Communists by the employment of force, but can win the loyal, enthusiastic and realistic support of the masses of the people by improving the political and economic situation immediately."

Despite these misgivings, Wedemeyer in his September report to Truman argued that criticism of the Nationalist Government "should be tempered by a recognition of handicaps imposed on China by eight years of war, the burden of her opposition to Communism, and her sacrifices for the Allied cause." The General recommended "moral, advisory, and material support to China and that Manchuria be placed under a Five-Power Guardianship or under a United Nations Trusteeship." In an explicit criticism of recent American policy in China, he declared that ". . . it may be said that the American mediation effort has been to the advantage of the Chinese Communists and conversely to the disadvantage of the Nationalist Government."

Wedemeyer's report did not sit well with the administration. Marshall contended that the proposals for Manchuria might offend the Nationalists and perhaps encourage the Soviet Union to urge a similar trusteeship for Greece, thereby jeopardizing the Truman Doctrine. The Secretary of State advised Truman that: "It seems to be mandatory that we treat Wedemeyer's report strictly top secret. . . ." Wedemeyer was left, as he later complained, "to twiddle my thumbs" while his report was buried in "foggy bottom," the critics' team for the Department of State.

But the China Lobby did not observe a respectful silence. Judd and Bridges charged that Wedemeyer's report was suppressed because it favored Chiang. They implied that the Truman administration was abandoning China to the Communists at a time when additional aid, modest in comparison to the billions allotted to Europe, could save China. Judd revealed that the Generalissimo had asked him "why the U.S. took a different view of Communism in the East than in the West. . . . was it a racial matter, that the United States cared for white people but not for yellow?" William R. Johnson, a former American missionary in China, joined the attack on the administration in an essay titled "The United States Sells China Down The Amur." Sensing a winning issue, New York Governor Thomas E. Dewey, a leading candidate for the Republican presidential nomination in 1948, began to speak out for more aid to Chiang. A wave of public sentiment in favor of assistance to the Nationalists inundated Washington.

"Three Cheers" For The Nationalists   In February 1948 President Truman, bending to Republican pressure, asked Congress for $570 million in economic aid for fifteen months to assist "in retarding the current economic deterioration and thus give the Chinese government a further opportunity to initiate the measures necessary to the establishment of more stable economic conditions." Testifying in support of this request, Marshall claimed that in order to reduce the Communists to a negligible force in China the United States "would have to be prepared virtually to take over the Chinese Government and administer its economic, military, and governmental affairs." Such a step, the Secretary argued, "would inevitably play into the hands of the Russians. . . ." Marshall made it clear that the administration had no intention of falling into the abyss of a land war in China.

In March a National Security Council report supported the administration's position with the conclusion that any economic and military assistance program in China "should be regarded as subordinate to the efforts to stabilize conditions in areas of more strategic importance." Although Wedemeyer still contended that limited military aid could be effective, a majority of Congressmen would support only a token gesture. Behind the closed doors of Executive Session on the China Aid Bill, Senator Vandenberg candidly admitted: "I think it is perfectly obvious that this is essentially three cheers for the Nationalist government in hope that it can get somewhere in the face of Communist opposition." Congress at length passed a bill that appropriated only $338 million for economic support to China for one year and, as a sop to Judd and his allies, a meager $125 million for military supplies. Lest anyone misunderstand America's intent, Vandenberg cautioned that the act "should not be interpreted to include the use of any of the armed forces of the United States for combat duties in China."

William C. Bullitt, a former Ambassador to Russia, sent to China by *Life* magazine for an on-the-spot study in the spring of 1948, undercut the administration by telling KMT leaders that Marshall blocked more aid for China. In addition, Bullitt suggested that "if the Chinese can only manage to hold on until after the coming Presidential elections they can count on the fuller measure of assistance which they require because Mr. Truman will not be elected. . . ." But Truman did not waver in his China policy. In fact, implementation of military aid to China under the 1948 Act proceeded so slowly that by the end of September only about $3 million of military supplies had been sent.

Throughout the summer and early fall, Ambassador Stuart's communications from China matched the gloom of public opinion polls on Truman's chances for re-election. On August 10 Stuart reported that: "The Communists continue to win the civil war. They have retained the initiative with all the advantage given by the offensive and government troops just do not seem to have the will or ability to fight." A major Red drive launched in September resulted in the taking of important cities in Manchuria and in the capture of thousands of Nationalist soldiers and an estimated 75 percent of their American equipment. Forrestal's attempt to obtain reconsideration of all-out aid drew the State Department's warning that such a step would be "a course of action of huge, indefinite and hazardous proportions." Even Vandenberg conceded that ". . . there are limits to our resources and boundaries to our miracles."

Rejection of Last Ditch Efforts To Save Nationalist China
Truman's unexpected re-election meant that the United States was not going to bail out Nationalist China. Frantic requests for more aid by Chiang, and a desperate end-of-year visit to Washington by Madam Chiang to make an emotional appeal for help elicited only expressions of sympathy. More influential was the analysis of Major General David Barr, Director of the American Military Advisory Group to the Government of China. In Mid-December he reported that: "Only a policy of immediate employment of United States Armed Forces, which I emphatically do not recommend, would enable the Nationalist Government to maintain a foothold in Southern China against a determined Communist advance." At year's end the State Department issued formal warnings to Americans to leave North China while normal transportation facilities remained available. Abandoning hope for miracles, thousands of Chinese refugees streamed to Formosa carrying large amounts of American currency and gold, while the Generalissimo and his dwindling forces remained to carry on a forlorn cause.

In the early months of 1949 the National Security Council emphasized the folly of any major effort to save Nationalist China. In January the NSC recommended that the United States should regard "efforts with respect to China as of lower priority than efforts in other areas where the benefits to U.S. security are more immediately commensurate with the expenditure of U. S. resources." A few weeks later the NSC suggested that: "It is even questionable whether we have anything to gain from political support of any of the remaining anti-communist public figures in China. They are likely to prove only slightly less impotent than Yugoslav royalists."

Although American aid totaling more than $1.5 billion since V-J day (table, p. 49) had been ineffective — much of it falling into the hands of the Communists — a last ditch effort was made in the new Democratic controlled Congress in 1949 to save Nationalist China. Employing the rhetoric of the China Lobby, young Congressman John F. Kennedy (D., Mass.) complained that "what our young men have saved, our diplomats and our President have frittered away." Twenty-five Republicans joined twenty-five Democratic Senators in sponsoring a bill providing Nationalist China with $1.5 billion in credits for economic and military aid.

But the administration opposed this futile gesture to a terminally ill patient. Dean Acheson, the new Secretary of State, pointed out that such a huge loan "would embark this government on an undertaking the eventual cost of which would almost surely be catastrophic." He claimed that "The Chinese government forces have lost no battles during the past year because of lack of ammunition and equipment, while the Chinese Communists have captured the major portion of military supplies, exclusive of ammunition, furnished the Chinese Government by the United States since V-J day."

U.S. AID, July 1, 1945 — June 30, 1963 (in millions of dollars)				
Asian Nation	Economic Aid July 1, 1945 – June 30, 1950 only	Military Grants 1945-1963	Economic Aid 1945-1963	Total Aid 1945-1963
Nationalist China	$1,593	$3,340	$1,990	$5,330
Korea	357	1,963	3,410	5,373
Japan	1,811	1,602	2,653	4,255

Source: U.S. Department of Commerce

In a sharp counterattack Senator Knowland (R., Calif.) charged that Acheson "had pulled the rug out from under" the Chinese Nationalists. A less temperate Senator Bridges accused the Secretary of actions that "might be called sabotage of the valiant" Nationalists. The self-confident Acheson, aristocratic in appearance and manner, represented a tempting target to politicians eager to impress the folks back home. Partisan attacks on the new Secretary intensified and did not abate as long as he remained in public life.

The issue of additional aid to Chiang was overtaken by events in the spring of 1949. Mao's armies crossed the Yangtze and took Shanghai in May. The victorious Reds formed "People's Governments" for liberated areas preliminary to proclaiming formally on October 1, 1949 the People's Republic of China. The Soviet Union and its satellites immediately recognized the new government of China, but the United States refused to do so. At year's end, the Nationalists, driven from Canton and threatened in Chungking, fled to Formosa.

When the new Secretary of Defense, Louis Johnson, raised the question of the defense of Formosa, Knowland, Taft, and former President Herbert Hoover promptly advocated United States naval protection for the island. Speaking for those disillusioned with Nationalist China, Democratic Senator Tom Connally, Chairman of the Foreign Relations Committee, ridiculed Knowland's plea for aid to Formosa with the withering retort: "The Senator wants to pour money down this rat hole. . . and there at the bottom of the rat hole you'll find old Chiang, the Generalissimo who never generalis-simos." Truman, unwilling to be pushed into a policy that might involve direct conflict with Red China, asserted that the United States had no ". . . intention of utilizing its armed forces to interfere in the present situation." The President was supported by the Joint Chiefs and the NSC which had reaffirmed in August 1949 that "the strategic importance of Formosa does not justify overt military action. . . ."

The Hiss Case   Although the domestic scare over internal Communist subversion had helped the Truman administration gain support for its European policies, just the opposite happened in regard to its Asian policies. Two events early in 1949 furnished ammunition to those contending that traitors inside the government had betrayed American secrets to the Communists. In March twenty-eight year old Judith Coplon, an honors graduate of Barnard College and a Justice Department employee, was arrested and charged with being a spy for the Soviet Union. At the same time the nation was enthralled by the perjury trial of Alger Hiss, a former State Department adviser who had attended the Yalta Conference.

Testimony by Whittaker Chambers, an ex-writer for *Time*, before the House Committee on Un-American Activities combined with the relentless pursuit of evidence by freshman Congressman Richard M. Nixon (R., Calif.) had led to the indictment of Hiss in December 1948. Hiss was charged with lying when he testified that he had not given copies of classified documents from the State Department in 1938 to Chambers, who confessed that he was a Communist at the time. Like Acheson, Hiss, with an aristocratic bearing and Ivy League education, irritated men of less privileged background. But many prominent people, including John Foster Dulles, issued statements in support of Hiss. Truman denounced the Congressional investigations as a "red herring." Although this first trial of Hiss ended in a hung jury, the case played into the hands of the administration's political opponents.

In this acrimonious climate of the summer of 1949 the administration's publication of a defense of its policies in a "White Paper" on China, including Wedemeyer's report, attracted hostile comments from critics contending that a more vigorous program of American aid would have saved Nationalist China. A Gallup Poll of September showed that fifty-three percent of the American people disapproved of the way the government handled the China situation, while only twenty-six percent thought the United States "did the best it could under the circumstances."

The assault on administration policies quickened in the early weeks of 1950. In a Senate speech in January, Taft alleged that the State Department had ". . . been guided by a left-wing group who obviously wanted to get rid of Chiang and were willing to turn China over to the Communists for that purpose." Proclaiming that Acheson had lost the confidence of the American people, Knowland demanded the Secretary's resignation. When a second trial convicted Hiss of perjury, Acheson, who had known Hiss from earlier State Department days, invited a torrent of verbal abuse by saying: "I do not intend to turn my back on Alger Hiss."

The Communist victory in China following so soon after the Communist advances in Eastern Europe had made rational discussion of American foreign policy almost impossible. The American people were unprepared to accept anything but their ideal of China — a democratic, united ally maintaining postwar stability in Asia. The Coplon and Hiss cases fueled simplistic conclusions that Americans, either sympathetic to or in collusion with the Reds, had caused the loss of China. The stage was set for an obscure Republican Senator from Wisconsin, Joseph McCarthy, to whip up national hysteria with sweeping accusations of treason and communism in high places. Discord, suspicion, and fear stalked the land as events in another Asian country drew the United States into a new crisis.

THE KOREAN WAR

The Temporary Division of Korea Becomes Permanent
Lights burned throughout the night of August 10, 1945 in the Pentagon office of John J. McCloy, Assistant Secretary of War, where the State, War, and Navy Department's Coordinating Committee (SWNCC) studied a pressing problem. A day earlier the dropping of the second atomic bomb, this time on Nagasaki, had made imminent the end of the war in the Pacific. Assigned the task of drafting plans for accepting the surrender of Japanese forces throughout the Pacific area, SWNCC found few guidelines for Korea, ruled by Japan since 1910. In the Cairo Declaration of 1943 Roosevelt, Churchill, and Chiang Kai-shek had promised Korea its independence "in due course.." At Teheran a few days later Stalin agreed. In February 1945 at Yalta the Big Three approved general terms for a temporary international trusteeship over Korea, but no specific plans were made for the liberation of Korea.

The Committee (SWNCC) bogged down that evening in debate between military and political points of view. War Department officials pointed out that the United States, with its nearest available troops located in Okinawa, six hundred miles from Pusan, largest port on Korea's southern coast, would be hard pressed to achieve the State Department's goal that American forces receive the Japanese surrender throughout the major part of Korea. McCloy finally asked Colonel C. H. Bonesteel of the War Department's General Staff and Dean Rusk, Assistant Secretary of State for Far Eastern Affairs, to frame a proposal that would harmonize political desires and military capabilities. By morning the two men produced a plan making the United States responsible for liberating Korea south of the 38th parallel, where almost two-thirds of the Korean population lived, with the Russians responsible for the area north of that line of latitude. Approved by the Joint Chiefs and accepted by the Soviets, this plan was sent to General Douglas MacArthur, Commander of United States forces in the Pacific theatre, for implementation.

As in Europe, geography worked against the United States. Sharing a common border with Korea for about fifty miles, the Soviet Union had a major naval base at Vladivostok, only one hundred miles from two large seaports in North Korea. The Soviets exploited this advantage of proximity and made amphibious landings in Korea on August 10, only two days after declaring war against Japan. Soviet troops, accompanied by two Korean divisions trained in Siberia, advanced rapidly to reach the 38th parallel within two weeks. Not until September 9 did American forces accept the surrender of Japanese forces south of the 38th parallel.

The fact that Koreans disagreed about future political organization of their country caused immediate problems. A large, vocal group of older, better educated, and well-to-do Koreans in Seoul, the capital city, had strong attachments to a provisional government in exile in China. Headed by seventy-year-old, Princeton educated Dr. Syngman Rhee and closely associated with the Chen clique of the KMT (p. 43), this Korean faction stood for an independent, united Korea. Professing commitment to democratic principles, Rhee's supporters urged American officials to expedite his return to Korea. An opposition group led by "radicals," who had already organized a People's Republic in the South, complicated matters by establishing ties with Communists in North Korea. In this internal struggle for power, the United States found it impossible to remain neutral. Before year's end Rhee was allowed to return. He promptly formed a Democratic Council, and demanded withdrawal of all occupying forces and an independent Korea.

In the North the Russians placed Korean Communists in positions of authority and began training and equipping a People's Army that grew to 125,000 men by early 1948. Kim Il-Sung, a young Korean Communist, was allowed to form a government that immediately undertook a program of distributing farm land to landless tenants. Whereas the United States intended to restore Korea to complete independence in America's own democratic image, the Soviet Union aimed to create another Communist nation that would strengthen Soviet power and influence in Asia.

By late September 1945 American officials in Korea protested the lack of Russian cooperation in the administration of Korea and in sending essential commodities such as coal, fertilizer and lumber to the agricultural South. Reports also indicated that the Communists were dismantling machinery and power plants for shipment to Russia. Most disquieting, according to Secretary Byrnes, was the fact that ". . . the thirty-eight degree parallel has become in reality a closed border."

Confident that democratic groups in South Korea could organize an acceptable government and unite the nation with popular support, MacArthur counseled abandonment of the trusteeship idea and withdrawal of American and Russian forces. But Harriman advised the President that ". . . far from insuring Soviet paramountcy, a trusteeship would probably mean [the] U.S.S.R. having but one of three or four equal votes." Truman agreed and supported trusteeship as the most practical way to unite Korea. Efforts of a Joint Soviet-American commission in the spring of 1946, however, were unproductive because each side maneuvered to set up a Korean government friendly to its interests.

Although discouraged by the absence of progress, the administration was assured by the JCS that ". . . from the standpoint of military security, the U.S. has little strategic interest in maintaining the present troops and bases in Korea. . . ." In September 1947 Washington referred the Korean problem to the United Nations. The latter responded by calling for the withdrawal of all military forces as soon as practical. But when the General Assembly voted 40 to 6 in November to establish a nine-nation U.N. Commission in Korea to supervise election of representatives to a Korean National Assembly, the Soviets denied it permission to enter North Korea.

The Russians and Americans proceeded to establish separate Korean governments. In May 1948 U.N. supervised elections in the South chose a National Assembly that adopted a constitution in July for the Republic of Korea. On the third anniversary of V-J day, August 15, American military authorities turned over the government of South Korea to Syngman Rhee, President of the new Republic of Korea. Meanwhile, North Korean Communists under Soviet supervision adopted a constitution for the People's Democratic Republic of Korea and claimed jurisdiction over all Korea.

The fate of postwar Germany, rigid division of the nation, now befell Korea.

The American Defense Perimeter In The Pacific   Inside the Truman administration a debate over continued presence of American troops in Korea was influenced by a top secret NSC report in April 1948 that warned: "The United States should not become so irrevocably involved in the Korea situation that an action taken by any faction in Korea or by any other power in Korea could be considered a casus belli [act of war] for the United States." When the Soviets evacuated the last of their 45,000 soldiers from North Korea in December 1948, the United States responded by reducing its military garrison to 16,000 at the end of the year.

Washington continued to assign highest priority to Europe. With Congress absorbed in debates over foreign aid, the North Atlantic Treaty, and China, the executive branch tried to avoid domestic controversy over its Korean policy. Help came from General MacArthur who reported to the NSC in March 1949 that "... complete withdrawal of U.S. troops from Korea was justified and would not adversely affect our position in Korea." A few days later Truman ordered withdrawal by June 30, 1949 of the remaining American soldiers in Korea, except for a regimental combat team of about 500 men — left to help train the Korean army. Late in the year the NSC confirmed the desirability of such action with the assertion: "It is essential that a successful strategic defense in the 'East' be assured with a minimum expenditure of military manpower and material in order that the major effort may be expended in the West."

In the circumstances it was not surprising that Truman found Congress reluctant to appropriate funds to aid South Korea. When he asked for $60 million in the 1950-51 budget, Republicans combined with renegade Democrats in the House to reject the request by one vote. Only after Acheson agreed to spend $10.5 million in aid to Formosa did Congress agree to a comparable appropriation for Korea.

Still ambiguous was America's responsibility to South Korea in the event of an attack from the North. Encouraged by the positions taken privately by MacArthur and the NSC, Acheson in a January 1950 speech indicated that America's defense line in the Pacific, extending from the Philippines through Japan, excluded both Formosa and Korea. Responsibility for areas beyond that line such as Formosa and Korea rested with the United Nations. Since the end of World War II American strategy in the Pacific had emphasized the importance of keeping Russia out of Japan. An industrialized and technologically advanced Japan was considered vital to peace and stability in the Pacific, whereas the smaller and less developed Formosa and Korea seemed relatively unimportant to American interests. In early May 1950 Senator Tom Connally admitted that Korea was not "very greatly important" in the defense strategy of the United States and surmised that the Communists were going to over-run Korea when they got ready just as they "probably will over-run Formosa."

Republican critics, however, castigated Acheson and the administration for writing off Formosa, although they expressed little concern about Korea. Senator Knowland resurrected a popular analogy by charging that "Munich certainly should have taught us that appeasement of aggression, then as now, is but surrender on the installment plan." As the verbal assault droned on, the administration was bolstered by a June 19, 1950 secret CIA memorandum suggesting that "The USSR would be restrained from using its troops by the fear of general war; and its suspected desire to restrict and control Chinese influence in northern Korea would militate against sanctioning the use of regular Chinese Communist units in Korea."

The Outbreak of War and U.N. Intervention In the drizzly predawn darkness of Sunday June 25, 1950 (Korean time) seven North Korean divisions and their support units illuminated the sky with an artillery bombardment all along the 38th parallel. Although shooting skirmishes had become an expected part of life for South Korean military units on the border, the sustained ferocity of this assault surprised the four divisions in the area. With many of their ablest officers on a training mission in Japan, the outnumbered and inadequately equipped South Koreans offered ineffective resistance.

Shortly after 10:00 P.M. (Central time) on Saturday June 24 a telephone call interrupted President Truman, relaxing at his home in Independence, Missouri. A tense Dean Acheson relayed the disquieting news of the North Korean attack. After a few minutes conversation the two men agreed to ask the U.N. Security Council to hold a special meeting to deal with the crisis.

On Sunday's return flight to Washington Truman reflected about other occasions when the strong had attacked the weak and "how each time that the democracies failed to act it has encouraged the aggressors to keep going ahead." The President mused that "If the Communists were permitted to force their way into the Republic of Korea without opposition from the free world, no small nation would have the courage to resist threats and aggression by stronger Communist neighbors." Dismissing the possibility that the conflict was a civil war, Truman correctly assumed that Russia had sanctioned the attack and was "trying to get Korea by default."

At 5:30 P.M.(Eastern Time) on Sunday June 25, the Security Council adopted an American resolution branding the North Korean action "a breach of the peace." The resolution also called for North Korea to withdraw its armed forces to the 38th parallel, and asked "all Members to render every assistance to the United Nations" to bring about the end of hostilities. Having boycotted the Security Council since early in the year in protest against a vote rejecting Red China's application for admission to the United Nations, the Soviet Union had no representative present to veto the resolution. Truman responded by authorizing General MacArthur in Japan to give the South Koreans whatever military supplies he could spare as an interim measure.

After North Korea failed to reply to a request to cease hostilities, the Security Council adopted a resolution on Tuesday June 27 recommending that "Members of the United Nations furnish such assistance to the Republic of Korea as may be necessary to repel the armed attack and to restore international peace and security in the area." On the same day, Truman announced that he had "ordered United States air and sea forces to give the Korean Government troops cover and support. . . . " and that he had "ordered the Seventh Fleet to prevent any attack on Formosa."

The Decision To Send American Troops When North Korean units smashed through weak South Korean defenses MacArthur reported on June 28 that "the United States would have to commit ground troops if the thirty-eighth parallel were to be restored." Following a personal inspection of the Korean front, the General informed the President he could "hold Korea with two American divisions." After consulting with advisers and Congressional leaders, Truman on June 30 authorized the Air Force "to conduct missions on specific military targets in Northern Korea, wherever militarily necessary. . . . " In addition, he ordered a naval blockade of the Korean coast and approved MacArthur's use of "certain supporting ground units." Although the immediate response to the United Nations call was disappointing, eventually fifteen nations did contribute supplies or troops before the war ended.

Through a simple exercise of Presidential power, American policy in Asia was reversed almost overnight. Truman, without seeking formal Congressional approval, extended the nation's defense perimeter in the Pacific to include territory that had been excluded so calculatedly only months earlier and committed American soldiers to defend it. The rapid movement of events had exposed the limitations of the American system of separation of powers and checks and balances when emergencies required decisive action.

Even though many Republican Congressmen had pressed for a United States guarantee of Formosa's security ever since Chiang fled to that island, several were unhappy about Truman's ordering American forces into action in Korea without a Congressional resolution. Senator William Jenner (R., Ind.) in a partisan attack charged that "The Korean debacle also reminds us that the same sellout-to Stalin statesmen, who turned Russia loose, are still in the saddle, riding herd on the American people." A more dignified Taft questioned the constitutionality of the President's executive order and blamed the administration for the trouble in Korea. He endorsed the proposal of Representative H. Alexander Smith (R., N.J.) that the White House seek a Congressional resolution approving the President's action. But Congress had taken its normal July 4th recess, and Truman was unwilling to call it back into session and wait for it to act. He justified his orders to MacArthur on his constitutional authority as Commander-in-Chief of the armed forces and cited "precedents" dating back to Washington and Jefferson

Crossing The 38th Parallel   After initial reverses forced American troops back to the environs of Pusan, MacArthur made an amphibious landing at Inchon, west of enemy-controlled Seoul (map, p. 58) to cut North Korean lines of communication and force their retreat. Within two weeks American soldiers re-captured Seoul, and by the end of September South Korean units had advanced north to the 38th parallel. A serious dilemma now faced the United Nations forces. Were they authorized to cross the parallel, and, if so, for what purpose?

With the Soviet delegate again in his seat in the U.N. Security Council, the United States turned to the General Assembly for a resolution of the problem. On October 7 the latter established a commission for the unification of Korea under a democratic government and authorized U.N. forces to cross the 38th parallel to assist in this program. Truman then gave MacArthur permission to advance on the condition that "there had been no entry into North Korea by major Soviet or Chinese Communist forces, no announcement of intended entry, nor a threat to counter our operations militarily in Korea." Chou En-lai's warning on October 2 that China would enter the war if American forces advanced north of the 38th parallel was ignored. When the United States First Cavalry Division crossed into North Korea on October 7, 1950 the goals of the United States and the United Nations had changed from merely driving the aggressor back across the 38th parallel to unifying Korea under a democratic government.

THE KOREAN WAR

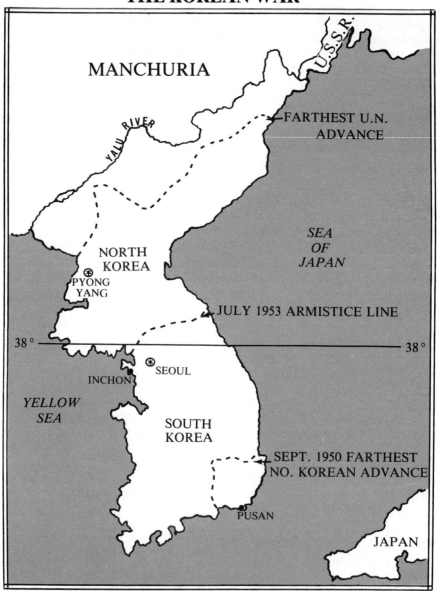

MANCHURIA

U.S.S.R.

YALU RIVER

FARTHEST U.N. ADVANCE

NORTH KOREA

PYONG YANG

SEA OF JAPAN

JULY 1953 ARMISTICE LINE

38°   38°

INCHON

SEOUL

YELLOW SEA

SOUTH KOREA

SEPT. 1950 FARTHEST NO. KOREAN ADVANCE

PUSAN

JAPAN

The MacArthur-Truman Controversy Buoyed by the popular support for destroying North Korea's ability to attack South Korea again, but also worried about a possible expansion of the war, Truman in mid-October flew to Wake Island to confer with MacArthur. The Commanding General of the United Nations forces advised the President that there was little chance of either Chinese or

Soviet intervention and confidently predicted that all Communist resistance in Korea would end by Thanksgiving.

When U.N. units advanced northward toward the Yalu River in late October, however, Chinese "volunteers" suddenly attacked U.S. Marines and South Korean troops some fifty miles south of the Chinese border. MacArthur assured Washington that full scale Chinese intervention appeared unlikely and that heavy casualties had forced the Chinese to withdraw after their first attack. He continued his drive to the Yalu in what he believed would be the "final offensive" leading to victory. But in less than a month his offensive was stopped and reversed by an army of 300,000 Chinese soldiers. Outnumbered and outfought, United Nations troops had to make a costly 275 mile retreat back to the 38th parallel. Early in the new year the United States and its allies pushed through the General Assembly a resolution condemning Communist China as an aggressor, but there was no rush to aid the United Nations cause with soldiers.

The unexpected set-back in Korea eroded public support for the administration, and the mid-term November 1950 elections sharply cut the Democrats' majority in both Houses of Congress. A late December Gallup Poll revealed that only thirty-eight percent of the people thought that the government was doing a good or fair job in Asia, while only twenty percent of those who could identify Dean Acheson had a favorable impression of him. The war in Korea became, in the eyes of the President's opponents, "Mr. Truman's War."

The seventy-one year old MacArthur experienced no such loss in prestige nor in self-confidence. Highly critical of official policy that "tied his hands," MacArthur proposed air attacks on the "enemy's privileged sanctuaries" in China, a blockade of China, and the use of Chinese Nationalist troops in a diversionary attack on the mainland. He contended that such action would destroy Red China's military potential. Taking a very different view of the situation, the Joint Chiefs advised Truman to reject MacArthur's plan as dangerously expanding the war in Asia and exposing Western Europe to a Communist attack.

Although the President adopted a JCS recommendation to seek an end to the war by re-establishing the 38th parallel as the boundary between North and South Korea, MacArthur continued to speak out for his proposals. He disregarded directives ordering all public officials in the war zone to clear with Washington statements about American war policies. Convinced that his views were sound and should be heard, the General in a series of interviews to American and foreign correspondents, implied that the administration's policies were preventing him from achieving a triumph over Communism in Asia. In March 1951 he wrote to Joseph Martin (R., Mass.), Minority Leader of the House, that:

It seems strangely difficult for some to realize that here in Asia is where the Communist conspirators have elected to make their play for global conquest, and that we have joined the issue thus raised on the battlefield; that here we fight Europe's war with arms, while the diplomats there still fight it with words; that if we lose this war to Communism in Asia, the fall of Europe is inevitable; win it and Europe most probably would avoid war and yet preserve freedom. As you pointed out, we must win. There is no substitute for victory.

After Martin read the letter in the House of Representatives in early April, Truman, supported by the Joint Chiefs, removed MacArthur from all of his commands for insubordination. The President believed that his constitutional authority as Commander-in-Chief had been challenged by MacArthur and that control of the military by elected civilian officials was in jeopardy. In his *Memoirs* Truman claimed that: "Even before he [MacArthur] started his ill-fated offensive of November 24, he still talked as if he had the answer to all questions. But when it turned out that it was not so, he let all the world know that he would have won except for the fact that we would not let him have his way."

An hysterical popular reaction followed the announcement of the firing of MacArthur. A flood of telegrams to Congress ran ten to one against Truman. House Republicans urged that MacArthur be called to testify, and Martin hinted that impeachments might be sought. Senator Jenner exclaimed that ". . . this country today is in the hands of a secret inner coterie which is directed by agents of the Soviet Union. . . . our only choice is to impeach President Truman and find out who is the secret invisible government." McCarthy used the occasion to call the President a "sonofabitch" who must have made his decision while he was "drunk on bourbon and benedictine."

Frustrated with the unending war in Korea and the "general foreign mess," the masses turned to MacArthur for clear, easy answers. The General, who had spent the last fourteen years in the Orient, was welcomed home as a hero by enthusiastic crowds in San Francisco, Washington, and New York. An audience of millions listened to and watched on television his emotional address to a Joint Session of Congress.

Senate hearings on the government's policy in East Asia, however, revealed that the nation's military experts had opposed

MacArthur's recommendations and that his analysis had focused narrowly on Asia only. After a renewed offensive in Korea under General Matthew Ridgway recovered territory back to the 38th parallel and stabilized the front, the clamor against the administration lessened.

Although Truman's popularity continued to decline to a low of only twenty-four percent approval and sixty-one percent disapproval, polls indicated that the public strongly believed that stopping Communism in Europe was more important than stopping it in Asia. When a Gallup Poll in July 1951 showed a majority approving a truce at the 38th parallel, it was clear that MacArthur, despite his great personal prestige, had not proved his case.

Ending The Korean War As the uproar over the firing of MacArthur subsided, private discussions with the Russians at the U.N. led in July 1951 to cease-fire negotiations between Ridgway and the Chinese Communists. The talks stalled over China's demand that all foreigners leave Korea and that Formosa be returned to the People's Republic of China. When the Reds abandoned these demands late in the year it was agreed that the demarcation line in Korea would be the battle line on the date of the armistice. But a new snag arose over the repatriation of prisoners of war (P.O.W.'s). After discovering that many of the 170,000 prisoners captured by U.N. forces did not want to return to North Korea or China, the Americans refused forced repatriation as demanded by the Communists. Truman declared that: "We will not buy an armistice by turning over human beings for slaughter or slavery." Vigorous Communist protests against the American position blocked progress in negotiations in the spring of 1952 as the American people geared up for the presidential election.

The Korean War, with American casualties (dead, wounded and missing) climbing over the 100,000 mark, became a major issue even before the nomination of candidates and Truman's withdrawal from the race. Public disenchantment with the failure of Truman to produce either a victory or peace in Korea meant that the new president must assign the highest priority to settling the Korean issue. Eisenhower's pledge to go to Korea caught the public fancy, and in December, as President-elect, he fulfilled this commitment by journeying to Korea for a first hand look. His appraisal of the military situation convinced him that the United States ' . . . could not stand forever on a static front and continue to accept the casualties without any visible results." If satisfactory terms ending the war could not be obtained, Eisenhower believed that the United States would have to take off the wraps and use the weapons necessary for a military victory.

Once in office, Eisenhower discovered that Mao expected better peace terms because of Republican campaign promises to end the war. Although the new President rejected pressure from the military to use tactical nuclear weapons to break the deadlock, he did encourage Dulles to drop a hint that "in the absence of satisfactory progress, the United States would no longer be responsible for confining hostilities to the Korean peninsula." Early in February 1953 the administration removed the Seventh Fleet from the Formosa Straits in a gesture of "unleashing" Chiang Kai-shek. At the end of the month the Communists abandoned their long held position on forced return of all prisoners and expressed a willingness to repatriate seriously sick and wounded prisoners of war at once, and to negotiate other issues. Eisenhower accepted, talks resumed, and the Communists agreed to repatriation of prisoners of war willing to return. On July 27, 1953 an armistice ended more than three years of fighting.

CONTAINMENT IN ASIA

South East Asia Treaty Organization   In his first State of the Union Message, Eisenhower proclaimed that: "The freedom we cherish and defend in Europe and in the Americas is no different from the freedom that is imperiled in Asia." Having employed such arguments for so long, Republican stalwarts realized that, once in power, they had to rectify what they called "past mistakes" and turn back the Communist threat in Asia. Party leaders were also eager to obtain guarantees that never again would the United States find itself fighting Communist aggression, as in Korea, without strong allies. Eisenhower had a strong mandate from his party to develop "a dynamic Asian policy." The time appeared propitious to forge an "iron ring of universal containment" to safeguard East Asia as effectively as NATO protected Western Europe. Mutual security treaties, according to this point of view, would not only gain allies against future aggressors, but would also deter aggression. Precedents had already been set in 1951 by the Truman administration's mutual defense treaty with the Philippines, by the Anzus Treaty with Australia and New Zealand, and by a mutual defense treaty with Japan. Dulles himself, as special Ambassador, had negotiated each of these treaties.

As its first step, the Eisenhower administration drafted a mutual defense treaty with South Korea in January 1954. To strengthen this new ally the United States began to provide financial support to the Rhee government that would soon amount to seventy-five percent of the latter's military budget and about half of its civil budget.

The Manila Conference in September 1954 produced the next part of the administration's Pacific plan — the Southeast Asia Treaty Organization (SEATO) — which had been advocated by Dulles during the crisis that preceded the French defeat in Vietnam (pp. 113-8). By this pact the United States agreed with Britain, France, the Philippines, Australia, New Zealand, Pakistan, and Thailand that:

> . . . aggression by means of armed attack in the treaty area against any of the Parties or against any State or territory which the Parties by unanimous agreement may hereafter designate, would endanger its own peace and safety, and agree that it will in that event act to meet the common danger in accordance with its constitutional processes.

An accompanying protocol designated Cambodia, Laos, and the free territory under the jurisdiction of the State of Vietnam as being included in the treaty area to be defended. While emphasizing the deterrent objective, Dulles carefully pointed out that SEATO was not a replica of NATO since no supporting military force was created or contemplated.

It was also noteworthy that Formosa, China's offshore islands, and Hong Kong, geographically the most vulnerable to Chinese Communist aggression, were not included in the area explicitly defended by SEATO. Skeptics quickly pointed out that only Pakistan and Thailand of the signatories were really Asian nations and that their defense was hardly vital to the United States. Some journalists speculated that the major motive behind the new treaty was the creation of a legal device to sanction U.S. intervention in Indochina if the Communists threatened to expand their control.

Mutual Defense Treaty With Nationalist China   To coincide with the arrival of Dulles in the Philippines to complete the negotiations for SEATO, Mao-Tse-tung initiated heavy artillery bombardment of the off-shore island of Quemoy occupied by nearly 50,000 Nationalist soldiers. "A horrible dilemma," according to Dulles, confronted the American government. Defense of the offshore islands would involve the United States directly in China's civil war, while failure to act might be interpreted by the Communists as a signal that an attack on Formosa would not provoke a forceful American reaction. The Joint Chiefs, except for General Ridgway, favored defending the islands and aiding the Nationalists in attacking the mainland. Although Eisenhower believed that "concessions were no answer," he resisted the advice of the military on the grounds that

"We're not talking now about a limited brushfire war. We're talking about going to the threshold of World War III."

The Formosa Straits crisis led to the final step in the grand plan for containing Communism in Asia. In December 1954 the United States and Nationalist China signed a Mutual Defense Treaty. The two nations agreed that an armed attack on either would be considered a threat to the other. although the treaty included the Pescadore Islands, it left optional the defense of the off-shore islands. A week after signing the treaty, Chiang in a secret agreement pledged not to attack the mainland without prior agreement of the United States. In Eisenhower's words this security treaty with Nationalist China "rounded out the far Pacific security chain. . . ." Whereas Acheson's defense perimeter of 1950 had been drawn in the water so that the United States could hold it with superior sea and air power, Dulles extended the line to land masses of the Asian continent, the defense of which would require massive American land forces or the use of nuclear weapons. Proponents rejoiced that Communism would now be contained in Asia as in Europe. Critics warned that the Asian policy, confusing quantity for quality in the number of American allies, had acquired for America "severe liabilities and few assets."

Brinkmanship   When the Chinese Communists probed American intentions by launching attacks early in 1955 on offshore Tachen Island, Eisenhower turned to Congress for authority to use armed forces for "protecting Formosa and the Pescadores against armed attack," and "related positions . . . now in friendly hands. . . ." The President alone would judge whether an attack on the off-shore islands was preliminary to an assault on Formosa. Although a few Democrats questioned this vague resolution and such a blanket grant of power to the executive, the House by a vote of 410 to 3 approved the President's request. After beating back an amendment that would have excluded Quemoy and Matsu, the Senate passed the Formosa Resolution by 83 to 3 on January 28, 1955. Senator Hubert Humphrey (D.-Minn.) pointed out that rejection "would be to undermine the President's authority completely and totally." He failed to point out that Congress was establishing a precedent in acquiescing to a broad grant of power to the President to conduct foreign affairs.

Washington deliberately kept the Formosa Resolution, as it came to be called, ambiguous in order to keep the Chinese Communists in the dark as to what the United States would do in the event of an attack on Quemoy or Matsu. In response to questions about American intent, Dulles hedged: "It cannot be assumed that the defense would be static and confined to Taiwan itself or that the aggressor would enjoy immunity." Privately he told the President: "If we defend Quemoy and Matsu, we'll have to use atomic weapons. They alone will be effective against the mainland airfields." At a press conference a few days later Eisenhower appeared to sanction the use of nuclear weapons as "a bullet against strictly military targets for strictly military purposes." Such statements playing on the ambiguity in the Formosa Resolution distressed many Americans and prompted Churchill to advise Eisenhower that America should give Chiang "its shield but not the use of its sword."

A new storm developed when Dulles, according to an interview published in *Life* Magazine in January 1956, revealed that his skillful diplomacy in averting war in the Formosa Strait was the third such occasion on which he had saved the day. The author of the article claimed that Dulles had used the nuclear threat to persuade the Chinese Reds to agree to an armistice in Korea in 1953 and that he had threatened United States military action if the Chinese Communists intervened in the Indochina War in 1954. The Secretary was quoted as saying: "The ability to get to the verge without getting into the war is the necessary art. If you cannot master it, you inevitably get into the war. If you try to run away from it, if you are scared to go to the brink, you are lost." Howls of indignation arose at home and abroad. Adlai Stevenson, Eisenhower's opponent in 1952 and again in 1956, exclaimed that he was "shocked that the Secretary of State is willing to play Russian roulette with the life of the nation." Several members of Congress demanded that Dulles resign because of his irresponsible and tactless words. A new word, "brinkmanship," heated the political atmosphere and captioned cartoon and editorial.

Rejection of Rapprochement with Communist China   In the weeks prior to this furor over "brinkmanship" Eisenhower and his advisers had to assess conciliatory gestures made by Peking whose relations with the U.S.S.R. had deteriorated. In mid-summer 1955 Mao initiated limited diplomatic contacts with the United States in Geneva. But Washington, having bombarded the public for years with admonitions of the wickedness of the Chinese Reds, could hardly afford to soften its opposition to any deals with them without risking the loss of political support at home. Dulles as usual took the high moral position and closed the door to Chinese overtures with the statement that "under present conditions, neither recognition, nor trade, nor cultural relations, nor all three together would favorably influence the evolution of affairs in China." In April 1958 the United States suspended the occasional diplomatic talks with the Chinese Communists in Geneva. Its task done, the China Lobby relaxed.

Defending its long time policy of non-recognition of Red China, the State Department released in August 1958 a memorandum declaring that ". . . the Soviet bloc, of which Communist China is an important part is engaged in a long-range struggle to destroy the way of life of the free countries of the world and bring about the global dominion of Communism." Official assumptions had not changed. Monolithic Communism remained the enemy. Between 1957 and 1961 the percentage of Americans, according to Gallup polls, who thought that Communist China should be admitted to the United Nations never climbed higher than twenty percent. In 1958 Chinese Communist bombardment of off-shore islands still occupied by Nationalist Chinese strengthened American suspicions that leaders of the People's Republic of China intended to expand its domain.

Anti-Americanism in Japan   Meanwhile, pressure developed in Japan for changes in that nation's relationship with the United States. The willingness of Eisenhower to re-negotiate the Mutual Security Treaty of 1952 on terms more favorable to Japan failed to satisfy the more ardent anti-American groups who opposed any military presence by American troops. Three months of turbulent debate in the Japanese Diet in the spring of 1960 preceded ratification of a new mutual security pact. Japanese labor federations and student organizations contended that Japan would be drawn into a war fighting for Chiang against mainland China. In the midst of this unrest in Japan, Eisenhower set out on a Pacific tour with a visit to Japan scheduled for mid-June. The President's advisers believed that a successful foreign visit was needed to regain some of the luster lost by Khrushchev's cancellation of a summit conference due to the U-2 incident (p. 29). Unfortunately three U-2's were based in Japan, and the announcement of Eisenhower's proposed visit set off riots and demonstrations in principal Japanese cities. Fear of uncontrollable violence caused the cancellation of the President's visit to Japan after he had reached Manila.

As the Eisenhower administration came to an end, American policy in Asia continued to function in the context of the U.S. — U.S.S.R. cold war. Primary attention continued to be centered on Western Europe. Although some signs of a rift between China and the Soviet Union had appeared, Americans continued to regard Mao's China as part of the international conspiracy headquartered in Moscow. Developments in parts of the world other than Europe and Asia tended to reinforce such beliefs which precluded any lifting of the bamboo curtain that isolated China until 1972.

Chapter Three

The United States and The Third World

"We have a natural sympathy with those everywhere who would follow our example."

John Foster Dulles, 1954

". . . we must strengthen the cause of freedom throughout all Latin America, creating an atmosphere where liberty will flourish, and where Cuban Communism will be resisted, isolated, and left to die on the vine."

John F. Kennedy, 1960

"The division of the planet between rich and poor could become as grim as the darkest days of the cold war."

Henry Kissinger, 1975

THE LESSER DEVELOPED NATIONS AND THE COLD WAR

The Third World　South of the industrialized nations of North America, Europe, and Asia, over one hundred countries occupy slightly more than half of the world's land surface and contain almost half of the world's population. Three-fourths of these countries, with mostly non-white populations, were once colonies of western nations who exported Christianity, white supremacy, and industrial products while extracting valuable raw materials. A lack of modern technology and heavy reliance on agriculture contributed to keeping these countries underdeveloped economically. A high birth rate and widespread illiteracy also retard progress. Millions live in primitive conditions where inadequate diet, poverty, and disease reduce life expectancy to about half that of inhabitants of developed countries.

Instability and violence have characterized political evolution in the lesser developed nations. Few have established enduring democratic governments. Even fewer, only four as of 1979, live under communist dictatorships. Rather, most have been governed by corrupt and oppressive military dictatorships vulnerable to coups by other military juntas. The upper classes, opposed to social and economic change, have relied on the military to perpetuate the status quo.

Except for the nations of Latin America, older and more advanced in general because of longer western influence, the lesser developed nations have tended to remain unaligned or neutral in the Cold War. The French label, "Tiers Monde," or Third World, defines the whole area as outside the arena in Europe and Asia where East and West jostled for domination immediately after World War II. Yet within a decade the rivalry between Communist and Democratic nations had spread to the Third World.

Attitudes Toward the West. Although attracted by the principles of the Declaration of Independence and delighted with the promises of the Atlantic Charter, many Third World peoples had ambivalent feelings about the United States. They praised America's postwar stance in granting independence to the Philippines and in encouraging the British to withdraw from India. But racism in the United States and American reluctance to pressure its allies to relinquish Asian and African colonies tarnished the American image. In addition, costly struggles by native leaders to free their peoples from tenacious western control built up resentment against the West.

Communism and the Third World Seeking to capitalize on widespread discontent and disaffection with the West in the Third World, the Soviet Union exported Marxist propaganda against "the imperalists" and recruited native leaders to organize national communist movements. In 1955, Khrushchev initiated Soviet military aid programs to several countries in the Third World. Thus, within a decade of the end of World War II the Cold War had spilled over into Latin America, the Middle East, Africa, and Southeast Asia.

The United States and the Third World In his Inaugural Address on January 20, 1949 President Harry Truman recommended as the fourth point in his foreign policy ". . . a bold new program for making the benefits of our scientific advances and industrial progress available for the improvement and growth of underdeveloped areas." Point Four assumed that communism flows from poverty and discontent and that technical aid would promote economic development and an improvement in living standards that would make communism unattractive. Although Truman asked for a modest $45 million in the first year of Point Four aid, Congress reluctantly appropriated only $27 million. To coordinate and administer assistance programs to Third World Nations Congress in 1950 passed the Act for International Development (AID). But as the focus of the Cold War switched from Europe following the outbreak of the Korean War, the United States funneled more and more aid to the Third World as the table below illustrates.

Distribution of U.S. Economic and Technical Aid			
Years	Average annual amt. ec. and tech. aid	Percent to Europe	Percent to Third World
1949-52	$3.4 billion	86%	14%
1953-57	1.8	25%	75%
1958-61	1.85	6%	94%
1962-66	2.3	0	100%
1967-71	2.2	0	100%
1972-76	3.37	0	100%
Source. Agency for International Development (A..I.D.)			

THE UNITED STATES AND LATIN AMERICA IN THE COLD WAR

Different Needs and Goals   With almost $3 billion of private American capital invested, American consumers the main market for Latin American goods, and American industry the principal supplier of imports, the United States dominated the Latin American economy at the end of World War II. More important to the United States than economic interests, Latin America's geographic location involved it intimately with the security of the United States. The Caribbean area, where Cuba at one point is separated from Florida by less than 100 miles of water and where dozens of islands lie in the traffic lanes of ships using the Panama Canal, had special strategic importance for the United States. Late in World War II, concern about the security of the Western Hemisphere prompted the United States to ratify with nineteen American republics (all except Axis-oriented Argentina) the Act of Chapultepec. Binding for the duration of the war, this regional security arrangement declared that an attack by any nation upon any American state would be considered

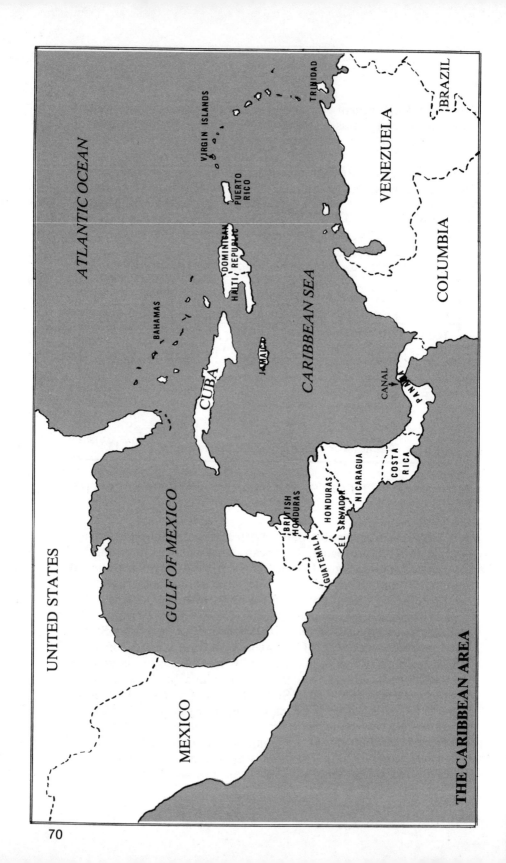

THE CARIBBEAN AREA

an act of aggression against all and endorsed the "use of armed force to prevent or repel aggression."

Following the war, different priorities led to misunderstandings and friction between the United States and Latin America. Responding to its assessment of the needs of the domestic economy, the Truman administration allowed special wartime purchase arrangements with Latin American nations to lapse and reduced orders for their products. Although hemispheric defense appeared secure against outside threats, Latin American economic problems and political instability remained. Some Americans stressed the need to furnish direct economic aid to prevent such conditions from attracting revolutionary ideology and Communist infiltration. The prevailing American view, however, was that if Latin Americans practiced Yankee virtues of hard work, self-reliance, and frugality, they would solve their problems. Washington answered Latin American requests for direct assistance with lectures about the need for proper management of their resources and for being hospitable to the investment of private capital. American business and government appeared indifferent, if not hostile, to large scale industrialization.

Having expanded production of raw materials to meet wartime demand, Latin Americans resented the abrupt decline in orders, reduction in credit, and much higher prices for American goods. As unemployment increased and inflation accelerated, discontent and anti-American nationalism blossomed. Latin American spokesmen wanted a long term commitment of American economic aid and the freedom to use that aid as they saw fit.

The Rio Pact, 1947.   As the Cold War evolved, the United States moved to safeguard the Western Hemisphere through an autonomous regional security system as projected in the Act of Chapultepec and in Articles 51 and 52 of the U.N. Charter. In September 1947 an Inter-American Conference in Brazil produced the Rio Pact whereby each contracting nation reaffirmed "that an armed attack by any State against an American State shall be considered an attack against all the American States." In addition, the treaty provided that if the territory or political independence of any American State should be threatened "by an aggression which is not an armed attack, or by any extra-continental or intra-continental conflict, or by any other fact or situation. . ." the parties agreed to ". . . meet immediately in order to agree on measures which must be taken. . . ." Championed by Vandenberg in the Senate, the Rio Pact, ratified with only one dissenting vote, became the first peacetime military pact of the United States and the model for NATO.

The Organization of American States   Three months later at

Bogotá, the Ninth Pan-American Conference drafted the charter of the Organization of American States (OAS) establishing machinery for dealing with aggression against an American nation. The United States delegation also pushed through a resolution that condemned "international communism or any other totalitarian doctrine" as being "incompatible with the concept of American freedom."

But only a trickle of United States foreign aid, about $160 million per year, or less than three percent of its total for all nations, reached Latin America between 1946 and 1952 (see p. 78). Marshall at the Bogotá Conference admitted that there would be no Marshall Plan for Latin America. "It is beyond the capacity of the United States government itself," he said, "to finance more than a small portion of the vast development needed." Private capital, fearful that Latin American regimes might nationalize industrial and commercial enterprises, likewise dribbled southward very sluggishly, except for investment in Venezuelan oil.

The Eisenhower-Dulles Policy   Although the bombast of the 1952 election campaign, featuring charges of neglect of Latin America, promised otherwise, the Republican triumph did not usher in major changes in the nation's Latin American policy. Economic aid was increased, but the major concern remained the security of the Western Hemisphere against Communist penetration in any form. To guarantee such security Eisenhower and Dulles became deeply involved in the internal affairs of two Latin American states in the Caribbean area — Guatemala and Cuba.

Intervention in Guatemala, 1954   On May 15, 1954, a Swedish cargo ship outbound from Stettin, Poland docked at Puerto Barrios, Guatemala laden with 1,900 tons listed in the manifest as "hardware and optical goods." Unloaded at night in great secrecy, the cargo actually consisted of 15,000 cases of rifles, machine guns and other military equipment manufactured in Czechoslovakia and consigned to the Guatemalan government.

The arms had been purchased by the administration of Colonel Jacobo Arbenz Guzmán, elected President in November 1951 on a platform pledging major land reforms in a nation where two percent of the three million people owned 70 percent of the land. Guatemala's economy had long been dominated by the American-owned United Fruit Company whose banana plantations furnished an important part of the nation's foreign exchange. Early in 1953 Arbenz expropriated over 200,000 acres of uncultivated land owned by United Fruit and began a program of land distribution among the landless peasants. He offered to compensate United Fruit by paying $600,000, the assessed value of the land for tax purposes, but the company demanded $15 million.

In late 1953 the new United States Ambassador, John Peurifoy, reported that "unless the Communist influences in Guatemala were counteracted, Guatemala would within six months fall completely under Communist control." Although no known Communists held cabinet posts in the government, Arbenz openly accepted the Communists as a legitimate national party (estimated 3000 members) and used Communist leaders to administer educational and agrarian reforms.

In this setting the CIA arranged the covert "Operation El Diablo" to overthrow the Arbenz government. With the help of United Fruit Company executives, the CIA enlisted exiled Colonel Carlos Castillo Armas to lead a coup. Secret headquarters were established in Honduras, with a training center on an island off the Nicaraguan coast. Arbenz, early in 1954, accused the United States of intervention in internal affairs of Guatemala and opened negotiations with the Soviet Union for arms.

Washington moved promptly to isolate the Arbenz government. At the Tenth Inter-American Conference in Caracas in March 1954, extreme United States pressure forced adoption of an OAS resolution proclaiming that "the domination or control of the political institutions of any American state by the international Communist movement. . . would constitute a threat to the sovereignty and political independence of the American states, endangering the peace of America."

The arrival of the arms from Czechoslovakia in May drew a sharp protest and compensatory United States arms shipments to Nicaragua and Honduras. CIA agents speeded up the plans for overthrowing Arbenz. On June 18, 1954 about 150 armed men led by Castillo Armas crossed the Guatemalan border from Honduras and were joined by some 500 supporters. Aided by an air cover of four old World War II P-47 Thunderbolts, supplied by the United States and flown by American pilots employed by the CIA, the invaders advanced into Guatemala meeting little resistance. The most stirring battle took place in the United Nations in New York as a result of Guatemala's demand for Security Council action. While the United States parried the thrust by Guatemala and the Soviet Union in the U.N. by claiming OAS jurisdiction, Guatemala's regular army defected and joined the rebels. By June 27 the government had collapsed, and Arbenz had fled.

Three days later John Foster Dulles proclaimed that "The people of the United States and the other American Republics can feel tonight that at least one great danger has been averted." The Secretary went on to announce that "The ambitious and unscrupulous will be less prone to feel that Communism is the wave of their future." Guatemala's dictatorship speedily disfranchised seventy percent of the population, suspended all constitutional liberties, and returned confiscated land to the United Fruit Company. Latin America seemed relatively secure from Communist intervention, and American interests were safe again. It had all been so easy and inexpensive — covert aid to a native group committed to overthrow a regime deemed unfriendly to American interests. This successful venture later served as a precedent for further Latin American activities by the United States.

The Anti-Nixon Demonstrations   The overthrow of a legitimately elected government by a coup engineered clandestinely by the United States did not sit well with many Latin Americans. Anti-Americanism smoldered from Mexico to Argentina. Increased economic and modest military aid during the next three years (see p. 78) failed to appease those critical of both Unites States' obsession with fighting Communism and America's failure to do much to solve Latin America's serious problems. This hostility erupted during Vice President Nixon's Latin American "good will" trip in May 1958. Protesters in Lima, Peru and in Bogotá, Colombia stoned, booed, and spat upon the Vice-President's motorcade. In Caracas, Venezuela an angry mob threatened to overturn the automobile in which Nixon was riding. Blaming the demonstrations on Communists, Nixon reported to Eisenhower that "the threat of Communism in Latin America is greater than ever before." Subsequent events in Cuba soon made most Americans concerned about that threat.

Friction With Castro's Cuba, 1959-1960   On January 1, 1959 followers of Fidel Castro's 26th of July Movement took over the streets of Havana, Cuba, following the sudden flight of Fulgencio Batista, the repressive military dictator of Cuba since 1933. One week later the bearded thirty-two year old leader of the victorious revolutionaries, after more than three years of guerrilla warfare, entered the capital city to a tumultuous welcome. Within a few weeks he committed himself to a radical social revolution designed to terminate the domination of Cuba by the United States.

Castro and his followers had many reasons for feeling unfriendly toward the United States. Until 1958 the United States had sold arms to Batista and maintained a military training mission in Cuba. Following Batista's downfall, his supporters had found a hospitable haven in the United States, and thousands of refugees had fled to Florida. Americans had invested over $1 billion in Batista's Cuba, supplied Cuba with three-fourths of its imports, and purchased about 60 percent of Cuba's exports. Cuba's revolutionary leaders resolved to change all that. In May 1959 an Agrarian Reform Law expropriated large land holdings and divided them among landless peasants.

American investors and businessmen were outraged, even though Castro promised compensation in Cuban bonds, and called upon the government to act. Reflecting the feeling of American investors in Cuba, the *Wall Street Journal* observed that "This revolution may be like a watermelon. The more they slice it, the redder it gets." When Castro visited the United States at the invitation of the American Society of Newpaper Editors in April 1959, Eisenhower refused to meet with him and rejected his request for arms. Castro then turned to the Soviet Union and obtained a credit of $100 million. Renouncing the Rio Pact, he made speech after speech against "Yankee imperialism."

Worried about Cuba's drift toward Communism, Eisenhower made a fateful decision early in 1960. He ordered Allen W. Dulles, head of the CIA, to direct the funding, training, and equipping of a military force of Cubans-in-exile to liberate Cuba from Castro. Over the next several months at secret bases in friendly Guatemala, the CIA prepared several hundred Cubans for an invasion of their homeland.

In late June 1960 Castro seized American oil refineries in Cuba without offering compensation. When Eisenhower retaliated by suspending the balance of Cuba's 1960 quota of sugar imported by the United States, Castro nationalized without compensation all 36 sugar mills owned by Americans and additional property valued at about $750 million. Vice President Nixon called Castro "either incredibly naive about Communism or under Communist discipline." In October the administration imposed an embargo on exports to Cuba, covering everything except food and medicine.

The Bay of Pigs Disaster, 1961   Despite press speculation about clandestine military preparations of anti-Castro Cubans, Democratic presidential candidate John F. Kennedy castigated the Republicans for "policies of neglect and indifference" that let Cuba "slip behind the Iron Curtain." Kennedy promised that if elected he would take strong measures to rid the hemisphere of Communism. Late in the heated campaign against Nixon, Kennedy, apparently unaware of specific CIA plans, suggested that: "We must attempt to strengthen the non-Batista democratic forces in exile, and in Cuba itself, who offer eventual hopes of overthrowing Castro." Twitting the Republicans, Kennedy observed that "Thus far these fighters for freedom have had virtually no support from our government." A furious Nixon, convinced that Kennedy knew of the CIA plan, scored his opponent for "most dangerously irresponsible recommendations."

By the time the CIA, shortly after the election, had briefed President-elect Kennedy on the invasion plan, relations with Cuba had deteriorated to the breaking point. A joint Soviet-Cuban communique in mid-December 1960 expressing Socialist solidarity convinced leaders of both political parties that Castro was pro-Communist and a serious threat to American interests. Seventeen days before Kennedy was inaugurated, Eisenhower broke diplomatic relations with Cuba.

With Pentagon approval, Allen Dulles, the CIA director, pressured the new President to proceed with the invasion. Dulles reminded Kennedy that he [Dulles] had stood there in front of Eisenhower's desk in 1954 and told him that he was certain of the success of the CIA supervised Guatemalan revolution against Arbenz. Now, argued Dulles, "the prospects for this plan are even better than they were for that one." It appeared to Kennedy that, if he failed to act, Castro might become "a much greater danger than he is today." Moreover, a veto of an attempt to depose the Cuban leader might furnish ammunition to Kennedy's political opponents at home while encouraging the Russians to regard it as a sign of weakness.

Although Senator Fulbright (D., Ark.) warned the President that: "To give this activity even covert support is of a piece with the hypocrisy and cynicism for which the United States is constantly denouncing the Soviet Union in the United Nations and elsewhere," Kennedy gave the go-ahead. To reassure anxious allies and a public confused by rumors, the President pledged on April 12 that ". . . there will not be, under any conditions, any intervention in Cuba by United States armed forces."

Three days later eight B-26 medium bombers, disguised with Cuban air force markings and piloted by refugee Cubans, took off from Nicaraguan air bases to destroy Castro's small air force. To present this raid to the world as an attack by pilots defecting from the Cuban air force, one B-26, riddled with bullet holes, flew directly from Nicaragua to Florida. Not only did the raid fail to destroy Castro's planes, but the cover story failed to deceive the prying eyes of reporters, who became suspicious when denied permission to interview the pilot.

Despite this early bungle, the operation was allowed to proceed. Just before midnight on April 17, a flotilla of small ships approached the southern coast of Cuba, east of the Bay of Pigs. The

1,400 CIA trained Cubans on board included just 150 professional soldiers. Crammed into fourteen-foot fiberglass boats, the advance group floundered on coral reefs and lost equipment and supplies in the darkness. It was almost 4:00 A.M. before the first "liberator" landed. Until ammunition ran out four days later, the invaders inflicted heavy casualties on Castro's forces. But as befits an ill-conceived plan, everything went wrong. The underground uprising did not occur, Castro's planes sank or drove away supply ships, and the expected second air strike was canceled by Kennedy, who feared it would put the United States in an untenable position before the bar of world opinion. By April 21 Castro's men were rounding up the survivors, and Kennedy was accepting responsibility for the fiasco. Not only had the operation failed to pave the way for the overthrow of Castro, but it had also given him and other American opponents the opportunity to point a morally accusing finger at the United States.

The Alliance for Progress   Kennedy decided that a different policy was needed to encourage economic and social progress in Latin America as a barrier against the spread of Castroism. In his campaign Kennedy had referred to a new "Alliance for Progress" with Latin America to demonstrate "that man's unsatisfied aspiration for economic progress and social justice can best be achieved by free men working within a framework of democratic institutions." At Punte del Este, Uruguay in August 1961, twenty American republics, with only Cuba abstaining, drafted a charter for an Alliance for Progress. It pledged "To improve and strengthen democratic institutions . . . to accelerate economic and social development. . . to encourage programs of comprehensive agrarian reform. . . ." For its part the United States offered to provide $20 billion over the next twenty years. Latin America seemed finally to have its version of the Marshall Plan.

Operation Mongoose   Washington next moved against Cuba. At a second Inter-American Conference at Punte del Este five months later, Cuba was expelled from the OAS by a fourteen to six vote after strong American urging. OAS members also agreed not to sell arms to Cuba and to prepare collective defense against Communist penetration of the hemisphere. One final step remained — the elimination of Castro himself. To this end Operation Mongoose was devised and placed under the direct supervision of Attorney-General Robert Kennedy. According to William Moyers, later an adviser to President Johnson, the CIA assumed that the goal made permissible a covert plan to assassinate the Cuban leader. In September 1961 the Cuban press reported that several Cubans, alleged agents of the

Graph — U.S. Economic Aid to Latin America, Fiscal Yrs., 1949-1974

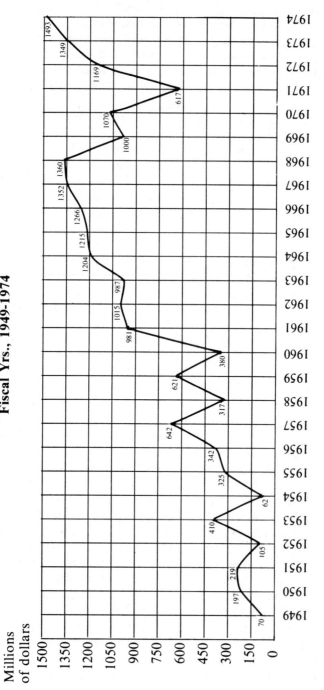

Millions of dollars

Source: A.I.D.

CIA, had been arrested for an attempt on Castro's life. No confirming evidence has been made public to date.

When Castro declared himself a Marxist-Leninist in December 1961, the rift with the United States appeared beyond repair. Although the Kennedy administration had isolated Cuba in the Western Hemisphere, Cuba had drawn ever closer to the Soviet Union.

The Cuban Missile Crisis, 1962   On Monday October 22, 1962 Americans tuned in television or radio sets to hear an address by the President. Since late summer the news media had carried alarming reports of a Soviet missiles and arms build-up in Cuba, and the nation sensed that a crisis was at hand.

Kennedy revealed that the Soviet Union was installing missiles in Cuba capable of carrying nuclear warheads to Washington, D.C., the Panama Canal, and other prime targets in North and South America. Somberly he explained that he had ordered the United States Navy and Air Force to impose a strict "quarantine" on all offensive military equipment under shipment to Cuba. He pledged that it would be the nation's policy "to regard any nuclear missiles launched from Cuba against any nation in the Western Hemisphere as an attack by the Soviet Union on the United States, requiring a full retaliatory response upon the Soviet Union." The United States also introduced a resolution in the Security Council calling for "the prompt dismantling and withdrawal of all offensive weapons in Cuba, under the supervision of U.N. observers, before the quarantine can be lifted."

The crisis had developed with dramatic speed. Late in August two American U-2 reconnaissance planes photographed in Cuba sites for surface-to-air missiles which military experts regarded as defensive. On August 31 Republican Senator Kenneth Keating of New York claimed that he had evidence of Russian troops and rocket installations in Cuba. Richard Nixon, campaigning for the California Governorship, used the opening to accuse Kennedy of appeasing both Castro and Khrushchev. Fearful that Soviet activities in Cuba might be the forerunner of a new move on West Berlin, Kennedy hoped to downplay the Cuban situation. But in order to protect his own political flank he asked Congress for authorization to call up 150,000 reservists.

On September 11, Tass, the official Soviet news agency, claimed that "The armaments and military equipment sent to Cuba are designed exclusively for defensive purposes. . . ." At a press conference two days later Kennedy underscored the difference between defensive and offensive missiles with the warning that:

If at any time the Communist build-up in Cuba were to endanger or interfere with our security in any way. . . or if Cuba should ever. . . become an offensive military base of significant capacity for the Soviet Union, then this country will do whatever must be done to protect its own security and that of its allies.

Not until Sunday October 14 did a U-2 photograph evidence of the construction of Soviet medium-range missile bases. Two days later Kennedy met with an Executive Committee of the National Security Council (ExCom) and decided to proceed in strictest secrecy until both the facts and the United States response could be announced. Round-the-clock meetings were held by the ExCom for the next four days. Additional U-2 photos revealed a total of six 1000 mile range missile sites and excavations for three 2200 mile range missiles. Suggestions of direct private negotiations with Castro as well as a proposal to turn the matter over to the United Nations were quickly dismissed by the ExCom as totally unacceptable. Ambassador to the United Nations Adlai Stevenson's suggestion of a deal agreeing to withdraw United States missiles from Turkey in exchange for the withdrawal of the Russian missiles from Cuba was ridiculed by the hard-liners. Finally, after rejecting both a "surgical" air strike to knock out the missiles and a full scale military intervention proposed by the Joint Chiefs, the ExCom decided on a blockade as a "more limited, low-key military action than the air-strike." According to Presidential Adviser Ted Sorensen, Kennedy "liked the idea of leaving Khrushchev a way out, of beginning at a low level that could then be stepped up." From OAS members, European allies, and Congressional leaders of both parties, the administration received overwhelming support.

For five days following the President's speech, the world marked time waiting for deliverance from a threatened holocaust. Parents frantically telephoned sons and daughters to return home from school, college, and even jobs so that families would be together in the event of nuclear war. Other Americans rushed to summer hideaways far from urban centers; some hastened to stock their fallout shelters with basic necessities. The armed forces were placed on war alert. Polaris nuclear submarines took up positions at sea within range of targets inside the U.S.S.R., while the Strategic Air Command kept fleets of long-range bombers, loaded with nuclear weapons, in the air round the clock.

At sea twenty-six ships of a United States naval force established a blockade line five hundred miles east of Cuba. The fleet had orders to "disable but not sink" any Russian ship that attempted to continue on course toward Cuba. But on Wednesday morning, October 24 the Navy informed Washington that the Russian ships nearest Cuba had apparently stopped or altered course.

Tension continued, however, because the danger of the missiles still remained. New U-2 photos revealed that work on the sites was going ahead at full speed and that all of the medium range missiles would be operational within a few days. Kennedy massed in Florida the largest invasion force since World War II and readied plans for a bombing strike. Then, at the height of the crisis a letter from Premier Khrushchev expressed a willingness to negotiate the removal of the missiles in return for lifting the quarantine and an American pledge not to invade Cuba. A second Khrushchev letter, more belligerent in tone, added a demand for the removal of American Jupiter missiles from Turkey.

In his reply Kennedy concentrated on the terms suggested in the first letter. He agreed that in return for "cessation of work on missile sites in Cuba and measures to render such weapons inoperable, under effective international guarantees," the United States would lift the quarantine and give assurances against an invasion of Cuba. On Sunday October 28 Khrushchev, accepting Kennedy's terms, agreed to remove the missiles. Nuclear war had been averted. As Secretary of State Dean Rusk put it, we were "eyeball to eyeball, and they blinked first."

The 1963 Test Ban Treaty and A Thaw In The Cold War Three crises in twenty-four months — Berlin, Cuba, and Laos (p. 122) — appeared to induce Moscow to reappraise its policies. Late in November 1962 Khrushchev responded favorably to a Kennedy proposal for a test-ban treaty, and the way was prepared for discussions. In early June 1963 Kennedy in a commencement address at American University described peace as "the necessary rational end of rational men" and appealed to Soviet leaders to take steps necessary to relax international tensions. After months of negotiations a treaty to cease atmospheric testing of nuclear weapons was signed, in July 1963. Later that summer a special teletype circuit linking Moscow and Washington, "the hot line," was installed to provide instant communications in the event of a grave crisis. To many Americans these developments signaled a warming trend in the Cold War.

Continuing Problems in Latin America Serious problems, however, continued to beset United States relations with Latin America. Although Washington poured in aid and private capital (see graph, p. 78), the Alliance for Progress floundered. Projected economic growth rates were not achieved, in large measure due to failures by the Latin Americans themselves. Most Latin American countries still had unfavorable balances of trade, and political instability remained widespread. Inefficiency, injustice, and corruption invited revolutionary activity. The Cuban "solution" appeared contagious and difficult to contain.

Intervention in the Dominican Republic, 1965   About fifty miles east of Cuba in the Caribbean Sea lies the island of Hispaniola divided into two nations — Haiti and the Dominican Republic. Political turmoil and economic crises plagued the latter nation following the May 1961 assassination of General Rafael Trujillo, ruthless and corrupt dictator for thirty years. Washington attempted without success to assist in the development of a constitutional government that might serve as a "showcase for democracy" in the Caribbean region. Although Americans had limited economic interests in the Dominican Republic, the United States did have a vital interest in preventing any situation threatening its own security. Above all, domestic political reality required that any American administration must prevent the establishment of a second Communist state in the Caribbean.

When Washington received word on April 25, 1965 of growing disorder inspired by opponents of the government of President Cabral, President Lyndon Johnson ordered a naval task force, including a marine battalion, to sail to the vicinity of the Dominican Republic. On the next day, the American chargé d'affairs, William Connett, cabled that rebels supporting the return of former President Juan Bosch had seized the Presidential palace. Bosch, elected President in 1962 on a radical reform platform, had been ousted by a military junta ten months later. Connett warned Washington that the political philosophy of groups supporting Bosch foreshadowed danger of a Communist government, and that an American "show of force" might be useful. On April 28 United States Ambassador W. Tapley Bennett wired Washington that the situation was "deteriorating rapidly" and that "American lives are in danger." He urged "armed intervention. . . to prevent another Cuba."

Stressing the need to protect and evacuate American civilians, Johnson, on April 28, without first consulting the OAS, authorized the landing of 500 marines, the first American combat-ready troops to enter a Latin American country since 1925. Later that day an urgent message from Ambassador Bennett warned: "All indications point to the fact that if present efforts of forces loyal to the government fail, power will be assumed by groups clearly identified with the Communist party." Johnson ordered the landing of an additional 1500 marines and the sending of paratroops from the 82nd

Airborne Divison. Within a week the United States had 23,000 troops on the island as the OAS attempted to arrange a cease-fire. The President explained to an aide, "I do not intend to sit here with my hands tied and let the Communists take the island."

When pressed by newsmen for evidence of the Communist role, the State Department supplied a list of fifty-eight alleged Communists said to be active in the revolt. Later investigations by reporters disclosed three names appeared on the list twice, while some of the fifty-five were out of the country or in jail. In a nationwide radio and TV address on May 2, 1965 Johnson defended his action by contending that: ". . . what had begun as a popular democratic revolution, committed to democracy and social justice, very shortly moved and was taken over and really seized and placed into the hands of a band of Communist conspirators." Many Americans, however, were skeptical. For instance, *The New York Times* complained: "Little awareness has been shown by the United States that the Dominican people — not just a handful of Communists — were fighting and dying for social justice and constitutionalism."

Elections held finally on June 1, 1966 resulted in victory for Joaquin Balaguer, who ruled with an iron hand in Trujillo fashion until his defeat in the 1978 election. American intervention had neither saved the people of the Dominican Republic from oppressive rule, nor had it won the plaudits of sister republics in Latin America. But Lyndon Johnson had made sure that no political rival could accuse him of lacking the will to meet Communists head-on. He had also strengthened his own confidence in the efficacy of military force to smash Communist threats — a faith later tested severely in Vietnam.

Intervention in Chile, 1964-1973   At a June 1970 meeting of the top-secret "Forty Committee," a special interagency group that controlled covert operations of the federal government, Henry Kissinger said: "I don't see why we need to stand by and watch a country go Communist due to irresponsibility of its own people." President Nixon's National Security Adviser was referring to the September Presidential election in Chile where Salvador Allende, a sixty-one year old Socialist, was the candidate of left-wing parties in a three-man race.

That Chile was a concern of the United States was not a new development. A long, narrow, sliver-shaped country on the southwest coast of South America, Chile suffered from economic conditions that seemed to encourage revolution. The wealthiest five percent of the population received more than twenty-five percent of the total income, while the poorest half got less than sixteen percent.

Disturbed by Allende's support from Communist groups and by his platform calling for seizure of property owned by such American corporations as International Telephone and Telegraph, Anaconda Copper, and Kennecott, both the Eisenhower Administration in 1958 and the Johnson administration in 1964 aided Allende's more conservative opponents. In the 1964 campaign, according to Director William Colby, the CIA spent $3 million to defeat Allende.

Kissinger's appeal in 1970 produced an allocation of five hundred thousand dollars by the Forty Committee for an anti-Allende operation. Both Anaconda and ITT also made substantial contributions, and Chile's largest newspaper received CIA funds to aid the cause of Allende's rivals. Shortly before the election Kissinger warned that: "There is good chance that he (Allende) will establish over a period of years some sort of Communist government" which could lead to "massive problems for us and for democratic forces and pro-U.S. forces in Latin America." Reviving the domino theory, Kissinger cautioned lest the "contagious example" of Chile "infect" such NATO nations as Italy and France with strong Communist parties.

Despite the best efforts of American intrigue and money, Allende received about 40,000 more votes than his nearest competitor in 1970, but only thirty-six percent of the total vote. He, however, would not become President unless elected in October by the Chilean Congress. So American efforts to prevent his election continued. An internal ITT memorandum of September 18, 1970 indicated that U.S. Ambassador to Chile, Edward Korry, had received from Washington "maximum authority to do all possible — short of a Dominican Republic-type action — to keep Allende from taking power." According to Congressman Michael Harrington (D., Mass.) the Forty Committee authorized $350,000 "to bribe the Chilean Congress." But the latter followed tradition and elected the highest vote getter — Allende. He thereby became the first avowed Marxist to win election to the highest office in a Western Hemisphere nation.

The Nixon administration, however, was unwilling to accept the result, especially after Allende nationalized the $1 billion holdings of American copper mining companies and offered "inadequate" compensation. Nixon secretly ordered the CIA to "get rougher" to undermine Allende. According to a 1975 report of a Senate Select Committee on Intelligence Activities, the United States government "remained in intelligence contact with the Chilean military, including officers who were participating in coup plotting." Under Kissinger's direction, the Forty Committee furnished

$5 million for a "destabilization" program that included strikes, demonstrations, sabotage and anti-government propaganda in the Chilean press. Military aid to the Chilean armed services jumped from less than $1 million in 1970 to over $12 million in 1972. In the autumn of 1973 Chilean army officers staged a coup that resulted in the murder of Allende and the installation of a new, conservative dictatorship. Congenial to American corporate investment in Chile, the new government gained immediate recognition by the United States.

Critics of covert United States participation in the overthrow of the legitimate government of Chile pointed to a disturbing pattern. In Guatemala, the Dominican Republic, and Chile Washington had assisted in putting into power authoritarian regimes willing to subordinate immediate aspirations of their own people to the interests of the United States. Many Latin Americans saw the United States as their oppressor rather than as a partner in democracy and rising expectations.

The Panama Canal Treaties, 1978   The 1903 Treaty that gave the United States "in perpetuity, the use, occupation and control" of the ten mile wide Panama Canal Zone was a long-standing source of friction between the United States and Latin America. Panamanians never liked the treaty that excluded them from living in the Canal Zone unless employed by the U.S. government. They resented the relatively small economic return to Panama, the total American control of all activities in the Zone, and the contrast between the luxurious American standard of living there and the poverty in Panama itself.

A crisis erupted in January 1964 when rioting broke out after a group of American students at Balboa High School in the Canal Zone raised an American flag in front of the school contrary to a 1962 agreement. Four U.S. soldiers and twenty Panamanian rioters died. After breaking relations with the United States, Panama brought its case to the U.N. and to the OAS. With broad bipartisan support, President Johnson committed the United States to negotiate a new treaty. But in 1970, General Torrijos, Panama's new leader, rejected as inadequate treaties drafted in 1967 that would have abrogated the 1903 Treaty and provided for eventual Panamanian sovereignty in the Zone and ownership of the canal.

Supported by sister Latin American republics, Panama brought her cause before a special U.N. Security Council meeting in Panama City in the spring of 1973. After the United States vetoed a Security Council resolution calling for the two nations to negotiate a "just and equitable treaty," Secretary of State Kissinger explained that the United States wished to deal with Panama bilaterally, without outside pressure. In early 1974 Kissinger and Panamanian Foreign Minister Juan Tack agreed on general principles ending the concept of perpetuity, transferring jurisdiction in the Canal Zone to Panama and continuing American responsibility for defense of the canal.

Three years of hard negotiations ensued, midst a rising clamor from American opponents of any "Panama Canal giveaway," before specific phrasing of two treaties was agreed on in August 1977. The first treaty gave Panama immediate territorial jurisdiction over the Canal Zone while the United States retained responsibility for operating and defending the canal until the year 2000. The second treaty guaranteed the permanent neutrality of the canal after control passed to Panama. In addition U.S. and Panamanian warships would be entitled to go to the head of the line.

Although every American President from Truman to Carter supported a new canal treaty, a heated debate followed. A torrent of well-organized protest flowed from those who agreed with former California Governor Ronald Reagan's pronouncement: "We bought it, we paid for it, and they can't have it." Public opinion polls throughout 1977 and early 1978 indicated that a majority of citizens disapproved of the treaties. Opponents stressed the danger of a Communist take-over of the canal and the threat to the nation's security. They especially disliked General Torrijos whom they regarded as sympathetic to Communism.

The Carter administration, nevertheless, worked vigorously and effectively to convince enough Senators to muster the necessary two-thirds vote. Supporters worried that if the United States failed to ratify the treaties acts of violence and sabotage might close the canal. At length the Senate in April 1978 approved the Panama Canal Treaties with one vote to spare. An elated President Carter noted:

> This is a day of which Americans can always feel proud. . . .
> These treaties can mark the beginning of a new era in our relations not only with Panama but with all the rest of the world.
> They symbolize our determination to deal with the developing nations of the world, the small nations of the world, on the basis of mutual respect and partnership.

An important step had been taken to counter the imperialist image and the "colossus of the North" reputation that had plagued the relations of the United States and Latin America for so long. But many Americans continued to deplore the "give-away" of the canal.

THE UNITED STATES AND THE MIDDLE EAST

The First Israeli-Arab War, 1948-1949   Ten minutes after Israel proclaimed its independence on May 14, 1948 the United States extended de facto recognition to the new nation. Before the day ended five Arab nations — Egypt, Lebanon, Syria, Iraq, and Jordan — attacked Israel with the intent to destroy the Jewish state. The ancient conflict between Arab and Jew in Palestine placed the United States in a very difficult situation. Sympathetic with the Jewish desire for a national state, especially after the horror of Nazi extermination policies, yet understanding legitimate Arab nationalism after a long domination by western colonialism, Americans faced a dilemma. There was no clear choice between right and wrong.

In the turbulent Middle East the United States desired stable political conditions that curbed expansionist nationalism and Communist penetration while preserving national independence and territorial boundaries. It was important to maintain ready access to Mid-East oil, about 60 percent of the proven oil reserves in the world. The Arab-Israeli conflict threatened these American objectives, especially since the Soviet Union supported Israel by a prompt shipment of arms from Czechoslovakia. Kremlin leaders had long sought to replace Britain as the dominant influence in the Middle East (see p. 11).

Complicating the problem for the United States was its "special relationship" with Israel. Many elected officials had a large constituency with strong personal interests in and emotional attachments to the new Jewish state. Washington felt a steady pressure to give special consideration to Israel's well being. No Arab nation had a similar lobby. Truman, in his 1948 campaign, responded to this political reality by successfully stalling until after the election a U.N. Security Council vote to apply sanctions against Israel, if she did not give up all territorial gains in the Negev.

Dispute over this territory captured by Israel delayed a ceasefire until early January 1949. The United Nations' plan for the partition of Palestine was one of the victims of the war. Even more ominous, the war had rendered homeless almost one million Palestine Arabs. In an effort to stabilize conditions pending a permanent solution, the United States in 1950 joined Great Britain and France in a Tripartite Declaration. The three nations agreed to provide arms to Israel and the Arab states for internal security and self-defense only, and to oppose "the use of force between any of the states in that area." But American friendship for Israel continued, and at year's end the Export-Import Bank granted Israel a new loan of $35 million.

The Iranian Crisis, 1951-1953   As the uneasy truce between Israel and the Arab states held, events in Iran, a non-Arab nation, enabled the United States to strengthen its Middle East position. In 1951 Mohammed Mossadeq led a nationalist movement that reduced the Shah, Iran's monarch, to a figurehead role and nationalized the Anglo-Iranian Oil Company owned by British investors. Efforts by the Truman administration to resolve differences between Iran and Britain failed. When Prime Minister Mossadeq in the spring of 1953 appealed to the United States for economic aid and increased purchases of Iranian oil, Eisenhower replied that Americans would oppose such actions while the Anglo-Iranian dispute remained unsettled. Concerned that "Iran's downhill course toward Communist-supported dictatorship was picking up momentum," Eisenhower approved a CIA covert operation, led by a grandson of Theodore Roosevelt, that toppled the Mossadeq government. The United States secretly provided guns and military equipment to the Shah's forces. Not only did the coup install Iranian leadership friendly to American interests in the Middle East, but it also opened the door to an agreement to set up a new oil consortium in which five major American oil companies acquired a 40 percent interest. Such a clear victory for American diplomacy was not achieved so easily elsewhere in the Middle East.

The Baghdad Pact, 1955   Obsessed by fear of Communist expansion, Secretary of State John Foster Dulles envisioned a defense pact to do for the Middle East what NATO had done for Western Europe. Despite relative Soviet inaction in the area, and Malenkov's peaceful coexistence gestures, Dulles in 1954 promoted an anti-Soviet security agreement between Turkey and Pakistan. A year later his treaty was expanded into the Baghdad Pact with Britain, Iran, and Iraq joining.

This action, carrying out the British concept of a "northern tier defense line," antagonized the new Egyptian President, Gamal Abdel Nasser, who desired to lead the region into a Pan-Arab, nonaligned bloc. Haunted by the humiliating defeat in the 1948 war, Nasser saw the need to overcome internal weaknesses and to build Arab military strength. Disagreeing with Dulles, Nasser saw neutrality in the Cold War as essential to Arab goals.

Arms Build-up, 1954-1956   In 1954 Nasser approached the United States for arms. When Washington priced at the Egyptian leader's list of defense requirements at $27 million in cash, he made inquiries to the Russians. Dismissing a Soviet offer to Nasser as pure bluff, Dulles refused to modify the American position. Nasser's opposition to the Baghdad Pact irked the Secretary of State, who viewed neutralism as immoral and a transitional stage leading to Communist control.

Nasser had become the champion of Arab nationalism by blockading Israeli shipping through the Suez Canal and on all goods destined for Israel. In late 1953 he also began to restrict Israeli commerce in the Straits of Tiran to prevent use of Israel's key port — Elath at the head of the Gulf of Aqaba (map, p. 97). Circumventing the 1950 Tripartite Agreement, Nasser in October 1955 concluded a deal with Czechoslovakia — bartering arms for cotton. Israel at once sought arms to balance Communist bloc aid to Egypt. Rebuffed by the United States, who stood by the 1950 Agreement, Israel negotiated a $50 million purchase of French jet planes and tanks.

These Middle East developments in an election year created political problems for the Republican administration. Democratic candidates for the presidency in 1956, sensing a good issue, supported Israel's request for $63 million in arms and questioned the wisdom of the Republican decision to fulfill a Saudi Arabian order of 1955 for eighteen American tanks. Adlai Stevenson, hoping to be re-nominated, urged the sale of arms to "enable the Israeli to prevent war by defending themselves." Senator Estes Kefauver, the front-runner in early Democratic primaries, charged that the United States had enabled the U.S.S.R. "to take another giant step" by becoming a "party of interest in the Middle East." The 1956 Democratic platform blamed Eisenhower policies in the Middle East for "unnecessarily increasing the risk that war will break out in this area."

The Suez Crisis, 1954-1956 Although the arms build-up created a dilemma for Eisenhower, Nasser's ambitions offered an opportunity to direct Egypt's energies to peaceful pursuits. Not long after coming to power in September 1953, Nasser had approached Washington about financing the Aswan Dam, a gigantic power and irrigation project on the upper Nile with a projected price tag of $1.3 billion. Late in 1955 the United States tentatively agreed to a cash grant of $56 million and a loan of $200 million from the World Bank with the possibility of additional grants.

Early in the spring of 1956 opposition to financing the Aswan Dam began to appear in the United States. Nasser hurt his own cause by recognizing Red China and negotiating with the Soviets for increased trade and economic aid. Although warned by Eugene Black, President of the World Bank, that "Hell might break loose" if the United States withdrew its offer of aid, Dulles on July 19 told the Egyptian Ambassador that the offer was withdrawn. Eisenhower later explained that Nasser "gave the impression of a man who was convinced that he could play off East against West by blackmailing both."

One week after the American snub, Nasser shocked the West by nationalizing the Suez Canal. British Prime Minister Anthony Eden immediately cabled Eisenhower that his government believed it "... must be ready, in the last resort, to use force to bring Nasser to his senses." The President cautioned his allies "as to the unwisdom even of contemplating the use of military force at this moment." A mid-August London Conference of twenty-two Suez canal-using nations to decide upon a course of action had, according to Eisenhower, "all the aspects of an unfriendly poker game." In September the British and French grudgingly accepted an American proposal to create an international Suez Canal Users' Association to supervise traffic through the canal. Nasser would have none of it, so the crisis continued. The American people, however, did not view the situation as warranting strong action against Nasser. A Gallup Poll taken in late September revealed that fifty-five percent opposed the sending of American troops even if England and France did.

Although Dulles insisted that the Suez issue be treated separately from the Arab-Israeli conflict, the British, French and Israelis did not agree. Without informing the United States, they proceeded with plans to drive Nasser from power and regain control of the canal. Late in October, eight days before the American presidential election, Israel initiated a surprise attack on Egypt. Routing Nasser's forces, the Israeli quickly advanced to the canal. Two days later the British and French, claiming the need to intervene to safeguard the canal and separate the combatants, began to bomb Egyptian air bases and parachuted troops to capture Port Said. An irate Eisenhower, already concerned about the crisis in Hungry (p. 30), instructed Dulles — "All right, Foster, you tell 'em that, goddamn it, we're going to apply sanctions, we're going to the United Nations, we're going to do everything that there is so we can stop this thing."

On October 31 the President said he believed that the Israeli, British and French actions were "taken in error." He promised that "there will be no United States involvement in these present hostilities." Stevenson, once again the Democratic candidate for President, obliquely criticized Eisenhower by quoting from the *New York Times*: "The United States has lost control of events in areas vital to its security." The administration's resolution in the Security Council demanding that Israeli forces withdraw to their own territory was vetoed by Britain and France. With Communist bloc support the General Assembly adopted an American resolution condemning the action of the three powers, demanding an immediate cease-fire, and proposing a U.N. truce team to maintain peace in the area. Within a week a cease-fire was in effect, hastened no doubt by a United States move that cut off Britain's and France's supply of oil from Latin America and by Soviet threats against the two powers. United Nations forces took over British and French positions in Egypt, and the Israelis withdrew.

Although the United States had won the appreciation of the Arab world, the anomaly of acting in conjunction with the Soviet Union against Britain, France, and Israel distressed most Americans. Shaken by the Suez War which shattered Britain's stabilizing presence while strengthening Nasser's position and Soviet influence in the Arab world, Eisenhower and Dulles resolved to develop a stronger policy in the Middle East. The Third World was becoming the focal point of the Cold War.

The Eisenhower Doctrine, 1957 Two days after his triumphant re-election Eisenhower asserted that the United States had to be "ready to take any kind of action. . . that will exclude from the area (Middle East) Soviet influence." The President believed that: "The Soviet objective was, in plain fact, power politics: to seize the oil, to cut the canal and pipelines of the Middle East, and thus seriously to weaken western civilization." As for Nasser, the President thought that, "If he was not a Communist, he certainly succeeded in making us very suspicious of him." To administration leaders revolutionary Arab nationalism as practiced by the Egyptian leader seemed indistinguishable from Communism. The fact that the Soviet Union had switched sides to champion the Arabs in their dispute with Israel strengthened that impression.

Early in January 1957 Eisenhower asked Congress to authorize the Executive to employ "the armed forces of the United States to secure and protect the territorial integrity and political independence of such nations, requesting such aid, against overt armed aggression from any nation controlled by International Communism." He did not intend to get trapped in a situation, as Truman had in Korea, without advanced Congressional authorization to respond with force to Communist aggression. The President also requested $200 million for military and economic aid for the Middle East. Although Senator Fulbright questioned giving a "blank check" to an executive branch that included "a current Secretary of State who greets the dawn with a boast about his triumphs, and meets the dusk with scare words of panic, saying that the Nation will be ruined unless it unites to ratify the mistakes he made during the day," Congress complied with Eisenhower's request.

Dubbed the Eisenhower Doctrine by the press, this corollary to the Truman Doctrine attracted a mixed reception in the Middle East. The Arab response ranged from open hostility by Egypt, Syria, and Saudi Arabia to warm endorsement by Lebanon and the northern tier of states — members of the Baghdad Pact. To convince the Arab world of the fairness and desirability of the Eisenhower Doctrine, Washington pressured Israel to comply with a U.N. resolution requiring withdrawal of her forces to pre-October 1956 lines. Fearing U.N. sanctions, Israel gave in after the United States announced it would support a U.N. Emergency Force in the Gaza Strip to prevent Egyptian attacks and would work to assure free passage through the Gulf of Aqaba. But the Arabs remained skeptical. The Eisenhower Doctrine appeared to support a status quo in the Middle East, whereas Arab leaders were committed to change — the elimination of Israel and promotion of Pan-Arabism.

Aid To Jordan, 1957 In April 1957 when riots in Jordan, allegedly stirred up by Nasser, threatened King Hussein's rule, Eisenhower sent the Sixth Fleet to the Eastern Mediterranean and extended $30 million in aid to the beleaguered Jordanian government. The State Department explained the President's actions as necessary "because of the threat to . . . Jordan by international Communism, as King Hussein himself stated." Critics quickly charged that this first application of the Eisenhower Doctrine overlooked the fact that the real issue was not Communist interference, but Naser's effort to unite the Arab world.

Intervention in Lebanon, 1958 A year later, concern that President Chamoun of Lebanon might circumvent the six year constitutional limitation on his term precipitated street violence and protests in Beirut. Chamoun, a Christian, was regarded as an obstacle to Arab unity by the United Arab Republic, the newly formed union of Egypt and Syria. The U.A.R. aided the Lebanese Arab insurrectionists who formed a United National Opposition Front. As a counter to the U.A.R., the State Department encouraged King Faisal of Iraq and Hussein of Jordan to join their countries in a federal state, the Arab Union. When on May 13, 1958 Chamoun asked the United States what it would do if he requested military help, Washington replied that the United States would honor such a request if conditions warranted it. Eisenhower later explained that "Behind everything was our deep-seated conviction that the Communists were primarily responsible for the trouble, and that President Chamoun was motivated only by a strong feeling of patriotism." Strong Soviet support for the U.A.R. and repeated Communist denunciations of the Eisenhower Doctrine gave credence to the President's position.

In June Chamoun brought his case against the U.A.R. to the United Nations. But before a U.N. Observation Group could report, an event in neighboring Iraq worsened the crisis. A pro-Nasser unit of the Iraqi army assassinated King Faisal on July 14 and overthrew the government. Chamoun immediately asked the United States for assistance against possible threats to his regime. Sniffing a Communist plot behind the Iraqi coup, Eisenhower, after consulting with Congressional leaders, ordered marines to Lebanon to protect 2500 Americans living there. He wanted to dispel any sentiment in the Middle East "that Americans were capable only of words, that we were afraid of Soviet reaction if we attempted military action."

Greeted by the curious stares of "sunbathers and Coca-Cola vendors," a combat-ready marine contingent waded ashore at high tide on Red Beach, south of Beirut, in mid-afternoon on July 15. As the marines landed Eisenhower told the nation that "What we now see in the Middle East . . . " is ". . . the same pattern of conquest with which we became familiar during the period of 1945 to 1950." In the President's mind "the question was whether it would be better to incur the deep resentment of nearly all of the Arab world (and some of the Free World) and in doing so risk general war with the Soviet Union or to do something worse — which was nothing."

Within three days three marine battalions with tanks and armored amphibians had landed in Lebanon. On July 19 an army battle group arrived from Europe. At the end of the month over 15,000 U.S. troops were in Lebanon in a show of force designed to impress the Soviet Union. The latter condemned the American landing as "a direct act of war and piracy," but made no military moves. A crisis hardened American public appeared somewhat skeptical about the situation according to a Gallup Poll that showed only forty-two percent approving the sending of troops into Lebanon.

After the Soviet Union had blocked Security Council efforts to resolve the crisis, Eisenhower, Khrushchev, and other world leaders agreed early in August to a U.N. General Assembly meeting on the Middle East. In Lebanon, meanwhile, Chamoun bowed out of the race, preparing the way for a new government. By the end of October all American forces had been removed as demanded by a General Assembly resolution. Not a single casualty was suffered, and apparently not a single shot had been fired at an enemy, but the Soviets had learned that the Eisenhower Doctrine was no paper tiger.

A fragile truce prevailed in the Middle East for a decade as Nasser reaffirmed his neutral position in the Cold War and worked for Arab unity under Egyptian leadership. The Communist bloc saw the Arab cause as their own because they viewed the elimination of Israel as the elimination of the West from the Middle East. American leaders committed the nation to maintain an arms balance so that Israel could defend herself.

The Six Days War, June 1967   A telephone awakened the President in his White House bedroom at 4:35 A.M. on June 5, 1967. Lyndon Johnson heard the grave voice of Walt Rostow, his National Security Adviser, saying that war had broken out in the Middle East with a surprise Israeli attack against Egypt. A few minutes before 8:00 A.M. Johnson received on that telephone a message heard for the first time by an American President. The Secretary of Defense, Robert McNamara said: "Mr. President, the hot line is up." Johnson hastened to the Situation Room where he took a message from Aleksei Kosygin, Chairman of the Council of Ministers of the U.S.S.R., explaining Soviet intent to work for a cease-fire and urging the United States to exert influence on Israel. Johnson replied that "we would use all our influence to bring hostilities to an end. . . ." To stop the fighting before Israel's victory reached proportions that might tempt Soviet leaders to intervene to save their Arab friends became the major concern. In six days Israeli forces occupied all of Palestine including the old city of Jerusalem, the entire Sinai Peninsula to the banks of the Suez Canal, and the Golan Heights of Syria. The magnitude of the Israeli victory was at once humiliating to the Arabs and embarrassing to the Soviets.

On June 10 Kosygin informed Johnson on the hot line that unless Israel halted all military operations within the next few hours, the U.S.S.R. would take "necessary actions, including military." In his *Memoirs*, Johnson noted that: "The room was deathly still as we carefully studied this grave communication." Deciding that he had to warn the Kremlin that "the United States was prepared to resist Soviet intrusion in the Middle East," the President issued orders to the Sixth Fleet to move within fifty miles of the coast of Syria. Soviet monitors in the eastern Mediterranean would be sure to report this action to the Kremlin. As in the Dominican Republic incident, Lyndon Johnson was determined to stand up to the Communists. But he carefully assured Kosygin that he "had been pressing Israel to make the ceasefire completely effective and had received assurances that this would be done." A tenuous armistice soon reduced fighting without stopping it. Later in the month Kosygin, on a visit to the United Nations in New York, met with Johnson at Glassboro, New

Jersey. Unable to agree on any substantive matters, the two leaders did reaffirm the need for a prompt and durable cease-fire in the Middle East and the right of every state to live in peace.

The Six Days War of June 1967 made clear to Washington that keeping Israel strong enough to hold off any Arab coalition reduced the risk of a Middle East war that might necessitate United States involvement. Aid to Israel was increased in 1968, and before leaving office the Johnson administration approved the sale of fifty F-4 Phantom jet fighters to Israel. Although supportive of United Nations efforts to achieve an accord, Washington refused to pressure Israel to withdraw from occupied territory.

The Yom Kippur War, October 1973   A week after his inauguration, Richard Nixon said of the Middle East: "I consider it a powder keg, very explosive. It needs to be defused." Early in 1970 Secretary of State William P. Rogers persuaded the Arabs and Israelis to accept a total cessation of military actions. But high expectations for a United States sponsored peace agreement collapsed when Israel balked at Arab terms. Under pressure from ardent nationalists, Nasser then turned to Moscow for help. He received not only surface-to-air missiles (SAMs), tanks, and late model supersonic MIGs, but also thousands of Russian "technicians and military advisers."

Nixon responded by delivering the Phantom jets promised under Johnson and by approving an additional $500 million in aid to Israel. And that was just the beginning. By the end of its first term the Nixon administration had furnished to Israel more military and economic aid than all previous administrations combined. Instead of being defused, the powder keg was refilled.

U.S. Aid To Middle East, 1946-1976 (in millions)					
	1946-52	1953-1961	1962-67	1968-72	1973-1976
Israel Economic Military	86.5 0	507.2 0.9	262.8 136.4	289.6 985.0	1,228.8 4,590.2
Egypt Economic Military	12.3 0	302.3 0	580.5 0	1.5 0	856.5 0
Source: Agency for International Development (A.I.D.)					

On October 6, 1973, the day of Yom Kippur, the most solemn Jewish holiday, the explosion occurred. Egyptian infantry launched a surprise attack on Israeli fortifications in the Sinai and drove forward. Simultaneously three Syrian armored divisions attacked the Israeli lines on the Golan heights.

Preoccupied with accumulating Watergate revelations and perhaps lulled by progress in détente with the Soviet Union, Washington was completely surprised. The Nixon administration may also have misread the fact that Anwar al-Sadat, who was elevated to the Presidency by Nasser's death in September 1970, had ordered the Russian technicians and advisers out of Egypt in 1972 and had even approached the United States to exert influence on Israel. But, having lost hope of achieving his goal of Israeli withdrawal to pre-1967 boundaries and under heavy domestic pressure, Sadat turned to a military solution.

When Israel sustained heavy losses before gaining the initiative in the October War, Nixon ordered an all-out airlift of military supplies to Israel from the United States as well as from NATO bases. The President also asked Congress for an emergency $2.2 billion in military aid for the hard-pressed Israelis. In retaliation the Arab-dominated OPEC (Organization of Petroleum Exporting Countries) imposed an oil embargo. An acute shortage of petroleum soon threatened the economies of Western Europe and Japan that now demonstrated that their interests in the Middle East were economic by expressions of sympathy for the Arabs and criticisms of American policies. But the uproar from its allies was mild in comparison to the storm of protest from angry Americans who faced long lines at filling stations, reduced fuel oil deliveries during a cold winter, and lay-offs because of plant shutdowns. The United States and much of the West soon faced an acute energy shortage, and the Arabs bore the brunt of the blame.

Eager to end the fighting before Israel could mount an effective offensive, Leonid Brezhnev, the Soviet leader, approached Washington to cooperate in bringing about a cease-fire. Kissinger desired to end the fighting before either side suffered a clear defeat so that he could institute negotiations for a final Mid-East settlement. On Brezhnev's invitation the Secretary of State flew to Moscow on October 20. In two days the two men worked out a cease-fire formula and provisions for the start of negotiations. But when the cease-fire failed to hold, both Sadat and Brezhnev proposed the immediate sending of American and Soviet troops to stop the fighting. After Washington rejected this idea, Brezhnev informed Nixon that the Soviet Union might find it necessary to take "appropriate"

THE MIDDLE EAST IN 1978

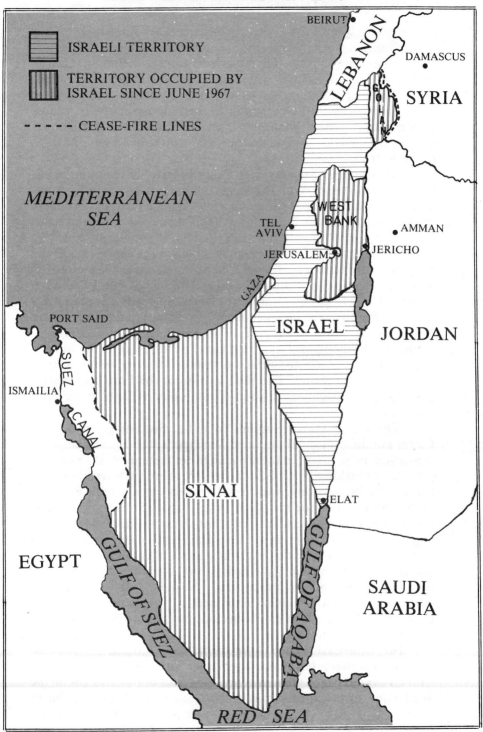

action by itself with the "gravest consequences" for Israel.

In the midst of a "firestorm" over the firing of the special Watergate prosecutor, Nixon put American forces, including nuclear strike units, on global alert as evidence of United States determination to prevent unilateral Soviet action. The crisis passed when the belligerents agreed on October 25 to the sending of a U.N. peacekeeping force. Israel consented only after Nixon and Kissinger warned they would suspend deliveries of arms if Israel continued its military drive.

The Kissinger Step By Step Peace Effort   In the months following the October War, Kissinger embarked on "shuttle diplomacy" to obtain permanent peace in the Middle East. In the course of almost two years he logged over 300,000 miles in travel and thousands of hours of negotiations. Praised as "a man of miracles" by President Sadat, Kissinger brought about disengagement on the Suez front in January 1974, as well as an effective cease-fire. His diplomacy led to the lifting of the oil embargo in March 1974 and to increased American economic aid to Israel, Egypt, and Jordan. Despite the turmoil of the impeachment proceedings that culminated in Nixon's resignation in August 1974, Kissinger produced in September the Sinai Accord by which Israel withdrew from the western part of the Sinai and accepted a demilitarized zone occupied by a U.N. Emergency Force. For the duration of the Ford administration, Kissinger continued his step-by-step plan without achieving a break-through.

The Camp David Summit Meeting, September 1978   The Carter administration abandoned Kissinger's step-by-step personal mediation in favor of a total package settlement of all issues. A precedent-breaking visit of Sadat to Jerusalem in November 1977 and face to face meetings with Israeli leaders eased Middle East tensions and offered hope for peace. After negotiations stalled, President Carter invited President Sadat and Prime Minister Menachem Begin of Israel to a meeting at Camp David in September 1978. Two weeks of discussions ended with the signing of two documents providing a comprehensive settlement of the issues and "a framework for the conclusion of a peace treaty between Israel and Egypt." Although difficult problems remained, a promising step toward peace in the Middle East had been made possible by the good offices of the United States.

The Mid-East Peace Agreement, 1979   When an impasse developed between Israel and Egypt over "linkage" of a peace treaty with an overall peace plan resolving the status of Palestinians on the West Bank of the Jordan and in the Gaza Strip, President Carter again mediated. He flew to Egypt and to Israel in March 1979 and negotiated the agreement of President Sadat and Prime Minister Begin to sign a peace treaty as the first step. The opposition of most of the Arab World to the Egypt-Israel Treaty raised the spectres of possible Soviet involvement and of a revival of an anti-Western oil policy by the Arab nations. But in the interest of stability and peace between the ancient enemies, Carter took these risks and agreed to furnish extensive military aid to both Israel and Egypt. In Washington's eyes a balance of power between nations friendly to the United States and those armed and backed by the Soviet Union seemed to offer the best guarantee of long range peace in the Middle East.

Iranian Revolution, 1979 The sense of relief following the Egypt-Israel Treaty was tempered by disastrous developments in another Middle Eastern nation — Iran. Simmering discontent with the regime of Shah Mohammed Reza Pahlavi, who had been returned to power in 1953 with covert American assistance (p. 88), erupted into violence in the summer of 1978. Riots and demonstrations against the government by both leftist and rightist groups became a regular occurrence in Iranian cities. American support of the Shah and official pronouncements that Iran was "the island of stability in one of the more troubled areas of the world" rested on an inaccurate assessment of the depth and breadth of opposition to the Shah's policies. When the embattled Shah finally fled in mid-January 1979, the United States announced support of the caretaker government appointed by the Shah. Within a month that regime was toppled by the backers of the seventy-eight year old Ayatollah Khomeini who was committed to the establishment of an Islamic Republic in Iran. Violent anti-American demonstrations, including a storming of the American Embassy in Teheran, forced the evacuation of Americans from Iran and temporarily shut down production of Iranian oil. A key bulwark against the Soviet Union in the Middle East had disappeared at a time when much of the Arab world resented America's policies.

THE UNITED STATES AND AFRICA

Relative Neglect, 1945-1960 Although over ten percent of its own population claimed African ancestry, the United States had little interest in Africa. With only four independent nations in 1945, Africa remained the province of Europe. American trade and investment were relatively small, and strategic concerns were even smaller. In the early stages of the Cold War, American leaders, fearing that premature independence might open the door to Communism, favored European interests in Africa over those of the Africans. In the words of Assistant Secretary of State George McGhee in 1950, Africa was a place "where in the broadest sense — no crisis exists. . . in which no significant inroads have been made by Communism. . . ." And Washington intended to keep it that way.

The strong nationalism that infected other Third World areas and led to East-West involvement arrived late in Africa. Fragmented by over two thousand different languages or dialects, Africa had no national units when imperialists took over in the nineteenth century. When Eisenhower became President there were still only five free nations in Africa, and the United States had fewer foreign service officers in all of Africa than in West Germany alone. Washington remained more concerned about nationalist revolutions creating a power vacuum that the Soviets might exploit than about legitimate aspirations of the people of Africa.

But under the pressure of African developments American policy began to change during the second Eisenhower term. When Kwame Nkrumah led Ghana to independence in 1957 Black Africa was reborn. By the end of 1960 twenty-two nations, including sixteen in September and October, had gained independence since the end of World War II. Washington recognized the need to soften its warnings about premature independence and to acknowledge that colonialism was ending. A new Bureau of African Affairs under its own Assistant Secretary of State was established. Vice President Nixon made a month long visit of Africa on the occasion of Ghana's celebration of its independence. Loans and grants to Africa were increased. Yet the administration could not turn its back on European allies still holding territory in Africa. Its ambivalence appeared in a May 1959 statement by Joseph Satterthwaite, Assistant Secretary of State for African Affairs: " We support African political aspirations where they are moderate, non-violent and constructive and take into account their obligations to and interdependence with the world community. We also support the principle of continued African ties with Western Europe." This desire to have it both ways was soon put to the test in the Congo.

The Congo Civil War, 1960-1964   Within two weeks after gaining its independence from Belgium in late June 1960, The Republic of the Congo was disrupted by tribal civil war. Moise Tshombe refused to accept the jurisdiction of the central government and declared the secession of Katanga Province. Belgian business interests immediately convinced their government to aid Katangan rebels with paratroopers. Tshombe also hired white soldiers from Rhodesia and South Africa. When asked by President

Joseph Kasavubu of the Congo to intervene, Eisenhower suggested reference of the problem to the United Nations. The Security Council responded to the Congo's request with a call for the withdrawal of Belgian troops and by approving a peacekeeping force that would not take sides in the civil conflict.

In support of the U.N. the United States agreed to supply the airlift, food, and equipment needed to preserve order. Eisenhower and his advisers believed that the new Congo Republic would be unable to support itself and would be susceptible to Communist penetration if it lost Katanga — its richest province with sixty percent of the world's cobalt and ten percent of its copper and tin. Complicating the problem was the defection of Premier Patrice Lumumba who broke with Kasavubu, established a separate government in Stanleyville, and turned to Khrushchev for aid to drive from Katanga the Belgians and their "white mercenaries." To Eisenhower Lumumba was "radical and unstable" and "a Communist sympathizer if not a member of the Party."

Washington's support of the U.N. peacekeeping plan angered both ends of the political spectrum in the United States. Some Americans saw Tshombe and Katanga as the only safe anti-Communist bulwark in the Congo. The fact that Great Britain and France abstained on the U.N. resolution while the Soviet Union supported it, demonstrated, they argued, that the United States was abandoning its allies as in the Suez crisis. But other Americans, including leaders of the Black community, saw Lumumba, "the black Messiah," as the only hope for ridding the Congo of colonialism. They contended that America's interests would be best served by "New Africa" not by "Old Europe." African policy became a campaign issue in 1960 when Kennedy charged that under the Republicans "we have lost ground in Africa because we have neglected and ignored the needs and aspirations of the African people."

Although campaign rhetoric had promised otherwise, Kennedy's African policy, in Sorensen's words, "was largely an extension of the Eisenhower policy" aimed at keeping the Russians out of an independent and united Congo. Three weeks after his inauguration Kennedy received news that Lumumba had been killed, allegedly as he tried to escape from the custody of Tshombe's soldiers. A new crisis loomed when the U.S.S.R. after recognizing Antoine Gizenga, Lumumba's Vice Premier, as head of the Congo, introduced a resolution calling for the withdrawal of all U.N. troops from the Congo. Determined to avoid another Laos or Cuba, Kennedy immediately pledged support for continued U.N. presence in the Congo and for the government of Kasavubu. The State

Department explained that the United States policy was one of "sanitary intervention" to contain radicalism in central Africa.

The administration's support of the U.N. peacekeeping force and its refusal to back Katanga drew the fire of Republican Senator Barry Goldwater who charged that the United States was "condoning aggression by international machinery and paving the way for a Communist takeover in the Congo." The American Committee for Aid to Katanga Freedom Fighters, promoted by a Belgian public relations expert, lobbied hard against Kennedy's policy.

Although the Katanga secession ended in February 1963, Gizenga continued the conflict against the central government. When the U.N. forces withdrew in 1964 the Johnson administration sent both a military mission to train Congolese soldiers and military equipment. The CIA furnished Cuban Bay of Pigs veterans as pilots and paratroopers to aid the government now directed by its new Premier, Moise Tshombe. In November 1964 rebel seizure of 1300 foreigners as hostages led to a successful American air rescue operation. But much of Africa viewed the American action as imperialist intervention to aid Tshombe and his white mercenaries.

In late December 1964 the General Assembly passed a resolution calling for a cease-fire and an end to outside intervention in the Congo's domestic affairs. The United States had spent $400 million to preserve Congo unity and to keep Communism out. The cost in Third World good will was not so easily measured.

The Rhodesian Problem   Engrossed in the Vietnam War abroad and in the Great Society at home, the Johnson administration assigned a low priority to Africa following the cease-fire in the Congo. But Africa would not go away. In English-speaking South Africa racism joined nationalism on center stage and demanded American attention.

In November 1965 white leaders of Southern Rhodesia declared independence of Great Britain and set up a government totally controlled by the white minority representing only four percent of the population. Black nationalists reacted by organizing to fight for a black nation — Zimbabwe. In the midst of a campaign to obtain equal rights for American blacks, the Johnson administration could hardly support white supremacy in Africa. But Washington faced strong pressure to keep open the supply of strategic minerals, especially chrome ore, from Rhodesia. Taking a middle road, the government endorsed a U.N. sponsored arms embargo and denounced racism in any form in any place while continuing limited trade with Rhodesia. When the Security Council voted a total trade embargo in 1968, important American industries expressed concern. Making an exception to the U.N. embargo on grounds of national security, Congress in 1971 passed the Byrd Amendment to permit the importation of strategic materials from Rhodesia. Later both the Nixon and Ford administrations called for its repeal, but the amendment was not removed until the Carter administration in 1978.

Although the United States continued to support the movement for an independent Zimbabwe and served as "an honest broker among the contending parties," little progress toward a peaceful settlement was made. When the State Department warned in mid-1978 that "Soviet and Cuban intervention is a strong possibility if the conflict continues. . . " there was no clamor from Congress or the public for direct American intervention. A token effort at establishing an integrated government, initiated by the white leadership in Rhodesia in 1978, attracted little enthusiasm from the Carter administration.

Problems in Southern Africa   Meanwhile in the Republic of South Africa (RSA) and in Namibia, its mandate since 1920, the United States faced an even more difficult balancing act. There the ruling white minority maintained a policy of rigid separation of the races known as apartheid. In 1958 the Eisenhower administration supported a U.N. resolution expressing "regret and concern" about apartheid on the grounds that it violated the U.N. Charter, but American capital continued to flow freely into RSA. The Kennedy administration in 1961 opposed economic sanctions against South Africa, but a year later Kennedy banned the sale of arms to the RSA.

Although Richard Nixon visited thirty-one different countries as President of the United States, he never set foot in Africa during his administration, and he never expressed great sympathy for the cause of the native population. During his presidency a secret "Tar Baby" policy relaxed the standing embargo on arms sales to South Africa and to Portugal trying to hold on to its African colonies. Dozens of American corporations continued to invest in South African subsidiaries, while large banks extended loans to the South African government despite the efforts of students at a score of American schools and colleges to discourage the practice. By 1976, $1.5 billion, about forty percent of American investment in Africa, was invested in the Republic of South Africa. The pursuit of profits remained more important than the promotion of democracy and justice.

The sudden collapse of Portuguese rule in Angola and Mozambique in 1974 complicated America's problems in southern Africa. Soviet-backed Cuban troops arrived to aid leftist African groups and to strengthen Marxist oriented governments. Angola became a

SOUTHERN AFRICA IN 1978

Date is the year of independence

base for guerrillas seeking to dismember Zaire (formerly the Congo) and to bring down the oppressive white regimes in Rhodesia and the Republic of South Africa. President Ford secretly furnished aid to the anti-communists until Congress discovered it and cut off funds. By early 1976 the Soviet-backed faction controlled the Angolan movement.

At stake, in addition to the strategic resources of southern Africa, was the sea passage around the southern tip (Cape of Good Hope), the route for more than sixty percent of Western Europe's oil from the Persian Gulf. If the Communists gained control of that route and the horn of Africa overlooking the Red Sea and the entrances to the Suez Canal, America's NATO allies would be weakened seriously. But if the United States attempted to maintain stability by supporting white regimes, it risked its moral leadership of the cause of human rights.

A Continuing Challenge.   President Jimmy Carter in June 1978 expressed the complexity of America's task in the Third World when he described the American goal as an Africa "free of the dominance of outside powers, free of the burdens of poverty, hunger and disease." At the end of 1978 that lofty goal seemed far distant as Black Africa, after twenty years of independence, remained torn by ideological conflict and economically dependent on its former colonial masters. The dangers of race war and growing Communist influence worried thoughtful Americans.

Chapter Four

The Vietnam War

"The wicked are wicked, no doubt, and they go astray and they fall, and they come by their deserts; but who can tell the mischief which the very virtuous do?"
—William Makepeace Thackeray

"Once on the tiger's back we cannot be sure of picking the place to dismount."
—George W. Ball, 1964

A Fateful Step   Nine Senators and seven Representatives, the Congressional leadership of both parties, hastened to the White House in response to an emergency summons from the President of the United States. The heat and humidity of the early August day had moderated only slightly as the eight Democrats and eight Republicans assembled in the cabinet room. Forgotten for the moment was the Presidential election campaign just getting under way. After perfunctory greetings, Secretary of Defense Robert S. McNamara, businesslike as usual, described in detail North Vietnamese torpedo boat attacks earlier in the day on two American destroyers in the Gulf of Tonkin. Although no Americans were injured and no American ships damaged, the Secretary said that the United States must respond or face further violations of its rights. He then outlined the government's plan for immediate retaliatory air strikes against North Vietnamese naval bases.

A grave President Lyndon B. Johnson, who had come directly from a meeting of the National Security Council, next read a statement that he planned to deliver later that evening to the American people. He asked the sixteen leaders to back a Congressional resolution of support for the administration's entire position in Southeast Asia. Admitting that the nation "might be forced into further action," the President said: "I do not want to go in unless Congress goes in with me." After reminding his listeners that Congress had supported President Eisenhower in this way in both the Lebanon and Formosan crises, Johnson asked each person for a "frank opinion." The fifteen men and one woman expressed "wholehearted endorsement of both the government's course of action and of the proposed resolution." Later that evening of August 4, 1964, after United States aircraft carriers had launched the first of sixty-four bombing strikes in reprisal, the President appeared on television to inform the nation of the crisis and of the "limited and fitting" American response. The next day in a speech at Syracuse University, Johnson defended his action with the words: "The world remembers, the world must never forget that aggression unchallenged is aggression unleashed. . . . there can be no peace by aggression and no immunity from reply."

After just two days of deliberation Congress gave Johnson what he requested. In an election year, rare is the Congressman who opposes presidential foreign policy measures widely regarded as in the national interest. On August 7, 1964 only two members of Congress warned against the executive's use of his power as Commander-in-Chief to carry on a war when the constitution delegated the power to declare war to the legislature. A passive House of Representatives by a unanimous 416 to 0 vote and the Senate by a 88 to 2 vote approved the "Gulf of Tonkin Resolution." The astute Johnson had prevailed upon the highly respected J. William Fulbright, Chairman of the Senate Foreign Relations Committee to steer the resolution through the Senate. Only Senators Wayne Morse (D., Ore.) and Ernest Gruening (D., Alaska) voted in the negative.

Morse suspected that the PT Boat attacks were provoked by the shelling of North Vietnamese islands by South Vietnamese naval vessels on Friday July 31 and by a shooting encounter between the American destroyer Maddox and North Vietnamese ships two days later. Doubts about the legality, necessity, or desirability of American reprisal raids also appeared in the Security Council of the United Nations where only Nationalist China and Britain supported the United States.

The Congressional Resolution authorized the President "to take all necessary measures to repel any armed attack against the forces of the United States and to prevent further aggression." In addition, the resolution stated that "the United States is . . . prepared, as the President determines, to take all necessary steps, including the use of armed force, to assist any member or protocol state of the Southeast Asia Collective Defense Treaty requesting assistance in defense of its freedom." Upon signing the resolution on August 10, Johnson announced: "To any armed attack upon our forces, we shall reply. To any in Southeast Asia who ask our help in defending their freedom, we shall give it." A new phase in the long Vietnam War was about to begin.

DEEP ROOTS AND MANY BRANCHES: ORIGINS OF THE VIETNAM WAR

Creation of Democratic Republic of Vietnam, 1945   By 1964 twenty-eight million Vietnamese had endured military strife for almost two decades. In the latter stages of World War II nationalist Vietnamese, the Vietminh, had carried on a guerrilla struggle against the Japanese who occupied Indochina (the states of Laos, Cambodia, and Vietnam). Leader of the Vietminh was the fifty-five year old Ho Chi Minh, who as a young man in exile in Paris in the 1920's became a Leninist, helped to found the French Communist Party, and then served as a Comintern agent in Europe for fifteen years before the outbreak of World War II. He then returned to Vietnam to liberate his native land from foreign aggressors.

As World War II drew to a close the United States had no set plan for the future of Indochina. President Roosevelt's idea of a Pacific Charter corresponding to the Atlantic Charter and leading to independence for subject peoples got a cool reception from British and French leaders. The need for wartime unity and postwar cooperation in Europe precluded any strong stand by Washington against colonialism. Thus the United States left to France the decision about the future of Indochina. But in Hanoi on V-J Day, September 2, 1945 Ho Chi Minh, having liberated North Vietnam from the Japanese, declared the independence of the Democratic Republic of Vietnam in a document paraphrasing parts of the United States' Declaration of Independence.

United States Dilemma in Indochina   French determination to re-establish control over Indochina, despite strong opposition of Vietnamese nationalists, placed the United States in a difficult position. Practical considerations conflicted with idealistic principles. After fighting broke out between the returning French forces and the Vietminh, the State Department in October 1945 tried to resolve the dilemma by declaring that: "it is not the policy of this government to assist the French to re-establish their control over Indochina by force. . . ."

Nor would it be the United States policy to assist the Vietminh.

When Ho asked in 1946 for United States support at the United Nations for a resolution guaranteeing Vietnam the same free status recently granted the Philippines, he received no answer. Repeated requests for American economic and technical aid to help rebuild Vietnam's shattered economy attracted the same stony silence.

Although consistently urging France to make meaningful concessions to Vietnamese nationalism, the Truman administration refrained from intervening in the conflict. Absorbed in the promotion of European recovery and in blocking Communist expansion there, Truman chose to avoid a potentially divisive policy such as insisting on French withdrawal from Indochina. The United States could hardly subordinate its interests in Europe to an idealistic stance in an area of the world that appeared relatively insignificant to American interests. But while reassuring the sensitive French that the United States did not question their sovereignty over Indochina, Washington did not bestow a blank check. As early as October 1945 the State Department warned that "the willingness of the United States to see French control re-established assumes that French claim to have the support of the population of Indochina is borne out by future events."

America's apprehensions and aspirations, however, tied her to the French in Indochina. Acheson admitted the nation's lack of options in December 1946 instructions to the American diplomatic representative in Hanoi: "Keep in mind Ho's clear record as [an] agent [of] international Communism, [the] absence [of] recantation, [his] Moscow affiliations . . . . Least desirable eventuality would be establishment [of] Communist-dominated Moscow-oriented state [in] Indochina. . . ." Two months later Secretary of State Marshall reminded the American embassy in Paris that: "We do not lose sight of the fact that Ho Chi Minh had direct Communist connections and it should be obvious that we are not interested in seeing colonial empire administrations supplanted by philosophy and political organization emanating from and controlled by [the] Kremlin." By May 1947 the State Department was advising American embassies in France and Vietnam that ". . . in respect [to] developments affecting position [of] Western democratic powers in southern Asia, we [are] essentially in the same boat as [the] French, also as British and Dutch. We cannot conceive setbacks to long range interests of France which would not also be setbacks of our own."

An obsessive fear of Communism dominated America's Southeast Asian policy, even though in mid-summer 1948 the State Department acknowledged that it had "no evidence of a direct link between Ho and Moscow but assumes it exists. . . ." The Truman administration could not take a chance that Ho might be acting independent of the Soviet Union. The success of the Chinese Communists in 1948 and early 1949 made Washington even more jittery about Indochina. A June 1949 NSC study concluded that ". . . colonial-nationalist conflict provides a fertile field for subversive Communist activities, and it is now clear that Southeast Asia is the target of a co-ordinated offensive directed by the Kremlin." If Indochina fell, the other dominoes, the Middle East and Australia, would be next according to this line of thought.

Failing to win a decisive military settlement against Ho, the French turned to a political solution. Somewhat reluctantly Paris sponsored a nationalist movement under Bao Dai, a former playboy Emperor who spent much of his time on the French Riviera. More than two years of negotiations produced in January 1950 French recognition of the independence of Bao Dai's Vietnam, and recognition of Laos and Cambodia as Associated States within the French Union. Ho Chi Minh immediately denied the legitimacy of the new Vietnam state, while the Soviet Union and People's Republic of China promptly extended recognition to Ho's Democratic Republic of Vietnam as the "only legal government of the Vietnam people."

Condemning the "surprise" recognition, Acheson asserted that: "The Soviet acknowledgment of this movement should remove any illusions as to the 'nationalist' nature of Ho Chi Minh's aims and reveals Ho in his true colors as the mortal enemy of native independence in Indochina." In early February 1950 Washington recognized the Bao Dai government. The Cold War had come to Vietnam.

The First Step: U.S. Aid to France in Indochina   When France in mid-February 1950 requested military and economic aid in prosecuting the Indochina war, sympathetic American officials stressed the seriousness of the Communist threat. Secretary of Defense Louis Johnson advised Truman that: "The choice confronting the United States is to support the legal governments in Indochina or to face the extension of Communism over the remainder of the continental area of Southeast Asia and possibly westward. . . ." A National Security Council report at the end of February pointed out that "there is already evidence of movement of arms" from Communist China to Ho Chi Minh's forces." The State Department endorsed aid to the French, and the JCS recommended immediate allocation of $15 million.

Truman and his key advisers continued to assume that it was necessary to bolster France in Asia in order to have a strong France in Europe. American Ambassador to the Soviet Union, Charles E. Bohlen, summed up this argument at a top secret briefing of the

State Department in April 1950 when he said: "As to Indochina, if the current war there continues for two or three years, we will get very little sound military development in France. On the other hand, if we can help France to get out of the existing stalemate in Indochina, France can do something effective in Western Europe."

Such arguments proved irresistible. On May 9, 1950 Truman approved $10 million in military aid for Indochina. A little more than two weeks later the State Department announced the intent to establish an economic aid mission to Cambodia, Laos, and Vietnam and recommended a "modest" appropriation of $60 million. The crucial first step of involvement in Vietnam's war was taken.

The outbreak of the Korean War in June 1950 gave a new urgency to developments in Vietnam. Even though it had become clear that Bao Dai was little more than a figurehead for the French, Truman announced on June 27 that he had "directed acceleration in the furnishing of military assistance to the forces of France and the Associated States in Indochina and the dispatch of a military mission to provide close working relations with those forces."

When Communist China entered the Korean War (p. 59) American leaders feared that the Chinese might intervene in Indochina, especially in view of the large number of Chinese troops on the border of Vietnam and the substantial aid being furnished to Ho Chi Minh. To meet this threat Washington assigned to military shipments to Indochina the second highest priority, just behind those to Korea. In addition, the National Security Council drafted a plan for the "resolute defense" of Indochina in case of a massive Red Chinese intervention.

In effect, the Truman administration had little room for maneuvering in its Southeast Asian policy. The United States could exert little pressure on France because of concern that she might reject the European Defense Community Treaty (p. 25). Moreover, given the political climate in the United States, Washington could not push for a negotiated settlement with Communists. For, as the frustrations of the Korean War mounted, administration leaders felt the stings of Senator McCarthy and his cohorts who accused the Democrats of being "the party of treason" and "soft on communism." (p. 60).

A Second Step: U.S. Military Technicians in Vietnam. Republican oratory in the successful Presidential campaign of 1952 promised a more vigorous effort to contain Communism in Asia. But the same factors that limited Truman's options in Southeast Asia still applied. For instance, whereas a June 1953 Gallup Poll indicated that twice as many Americans favored as opposed sending war materials to help the French in Indochina, eighty-five percent in a September poll opposed sending American soldiers to Vietnam.

Eisenhower proceeded with caution. True, the National Security Council proposed aid to France and the Associated States in "an aggressive military, political, psychological program, including covert operations to eliminate organized Viet Minh forces by mid-1955." And the NSC would have the United States take "necessary military action" if Red China intervened. But Eisenhower limited his action to proposals for increased military aid for Indochina in his fiscal 1954 budget. The President also agreed to send two hundred uniformed United States Air Force mechanics to Vietnam, provided that they were stationed at a safe distance from combat areas.

A Step Almost Taken, 1954   A Big Four agreement to discuss the Indochina question at a forthcoming international conference scheduled to convene in Geneva in late April 1954 disturbed American officials who felt that negotiations would end in capitulation unless the French first won a substantial military victory. The JCS warned early in March that "a settlement based upon free elections would be attended by almost certain loss of the Associated States to Communist control." Admiral Radford, Chairman of the JCS, suggested that: ". . . the United States must be prepared to act promptly, and in force possibly, to a frantic and belated request by the French for United States intervention."

As the news from the front became grim, Washington worked to keep France from negotiating with Ho Chi Minh and withdrawing from the war. But a disaster was in the making — 15,000 of France's best troops were under siege at Dien Bien Phu in northern Vietnam more than two hundred miles behind enemy lines. The administration hastened efforts to secure allied agreement to a Southeast Asia collective defense pact corresponding to NATO (p. 62). In a letter to Prime Minister Churchill, Eisenhower argued the lesson of history:

> . . . we failed to halt Hirohito, Mussolini and Hitler by not acting in unit and in time. That marked the beginning of many years of stark tragedy and desperate peril. May it not be that our nations have learned something from that lesson?

British reaction to the Munich analogy, while favorable, held that no such move should be made before the Geneva Conference.

On Saturday, April 3, 1954, as Eisenhower worked at Camp David on a speech, eight Congressional leaders received a surprise phone call from the Secretary of State to come to the Department for an extremely important meeting. Present in the fifth floor conference room in addition to Dulles were Admiral Radford and Pentagon officials. After detailing the critical status of French forces at Dien Bien Phu, Dulles indicated that the administration wanted Congress to pass a joint resolution that would permit the President to use air and naval power in Indochina. Radford supported the Secretary and proposed a single massive air strike. But under close questioning from Senators Earle Clements (D., Ky.) and Lyndon B. Johnson (D., Tex.), Radford acknowledged that no other member of the JCS agreed with him. And Dulles admitted that he had not consulted America's allies. The three Republican and five Democratic Congressmen, therefore, concurred that Dulles should first find out whether he had British and French support.

Douglas Dillon, United States Ambassador to France, meanwhile, sent word that the French Government claimed that "immediate armed intervention of U.S. carrier aircraft at Dien Bien Phu is now necessary to save the situation." At the same time the President's Special Committee on Southeast Asia recommended that the United States be ready for active participation "and without French support should that be necessary." But the meeting between Dulles and Congressional leaders had convinced Eisenhower that any American military involvement in Indochina would require a coalition with allies to pursue "united action," as well as Congressional approval and France's commitment to speed up the independence of the Associated States.

When Senator John F. Kennedy (D., Mass.) questioned whether any amount of American military aid in Indochina could defeat the Vietminh, Eisenhower defended his policies in a press conference with an explanation of the "falling domino" principle.

> You have a row of dominoes set up, you knock over the first one, and what will happen to the last one is the certainty that it will go over very quickly. So you could have a beginning of a disintegration that would have the most profound influences.

Having originated in the Truman administration, the domino theory had strong adherents in the Democratic Party, as Eisenhower well knew.

Dulles, meanwhile, had scurried off to obtain endorsement from Britain and France. In London he met a skeptical Anthony Eden, British Foreign Secretary, who saw dangers in setting up a coalition in advance of the Geneva Conference. Moreover, the British dismissed the domino theory as inapplicable to Southeast Asia. In Paris Dulles found the French eager for localized American help at Dien Bien Phu, but opposed to "united action" that might strip control of the war from France.

Having returned from Europe empty-handed, the Secretary of

State tried to set up a meeting in Washington with representatives of the United Kingdom, France, the Associated States, Australia, New Zealand, Thailand, and the Philippines to organize the projected Southeast Asia defense group. Again he was rebuffed by the British, who were influenced by India to avoid giving assent to "united action" at that inappropriate moment before the Geneva Conference. Vice President Nixon's statement on April 17 that "to avoid further Communist expansion in Asia and Indochina" the executive might have to "take the risk now by putting our boys in" had not reassured British leaders as to America's calm and reasoned approach to the problem.

Dulles returned to Paris, where on April 23 he was shown a telegram from General Navarre, French Commander in Indochina, stating that only a massive air attack could save Dien Bien Phu. Accompanied by Radford, Dulles met with Eden to urge approval of an American air strike. Although personally opposed to such action, Eden agreed to fly to London to consult with Prime Minister Churchill and the cabinet. Even before Eden returned with a flat "no," Dulles sensed that his entreaties had failed. He, therefore, informed the French that the United States could not intervene without Congressional approval and without "united action." Two days later the Geneva Conference convened.

The Geneva Conference, 1954   Pessimistic from the outset about the Geneva Conference, the Eisenhower administration found little satisfaction in the course of the deliberations. French and American differences over goals were not resolved at Geneva. A JCS recommendation that a satisfactory political settlement precede any cease-fire guided administration officials who tried in vain to convince the French to avoid concessions merely to end hostilities. A discouraged Dulles left Geneva on May 4, four days before the conference even began discussion of Indochina, and the American delegation was downgraded to an "observer mission." Washington had no intention of fueling domestic criticism by taking a prominent part in negotiations almost certain to result in placing millions of Vietnamese under Communist rule,

After the French surrender at Dien Bien Phu on May 7 foreshadowed a Communist diplomatic triumph at Geneva, Dulles advised that the United States would not approve "any ceasefire, armistice, or other settlement. . . subverting the existing lawful governments of the three aforementioned states [Laos, Cambodia, Vietnam] or of placing in jeopardy the forces of the French Union in Indochina. . . ." Washington again held out to the French the possibility of American military intervention if Congress approved and the French agreed to independence for the Associated States. But French leaders were committed to a negotiated settlement. Washington was also given pause by public coolness to military intervention. At the height of the Geneva Conference almost three-fourths of those polled by Gallup expressed opposition to sending troops to Indochina, while only eighteen percent believed that the United States would stop the spread of Communism by fighting in Indochina.

The final Declaration of the Geneva Conference, signed on July 21, 1954, established a truce between North Vietnam and France while dividing Vietnam temporarily at the 17th parallel with a demilitarized zone separating North and South Vietnam. Ho agreed to withdraw his troops north of that line, and France was to move its forces south and remain until requested to withdraw by the Vietnam parties. General elections supervised by an international commission were to be held in Vietnam within two years, while elections were to be held in Laos and Cambodia in 1955. The Geneva Accords also prohibited any military alliances and the establishment of any foreign military base in either zone of Vietnam.

Refusing to join in the Declaration of the Conference, the United States issued a unilateral declaration affirming that it would "refrain from the threat or the use of force to disturb them (the agreements)" and that "it would view any renewal of the aggression in violation of the aforesaid agreements with grave concern. . . ." The American statement also noted that "In the case of nations now divided against their will, we shall continue to seek to achieve unity through free elections supervised by the United Nations to insure that they are conducted fairly."

Nor did the new South Vietnamese state, granted independence by France on June 4, 1954 after seventy years of French rule, sign the Accords. South Vietnamese delegates opposed the partition of Vietnam as "deeply wounding the national sentiment of the Vietnamese people." Poorly understood at the time, the Geneva Accords contained fatal flaws — American disassociation, opposition of South Vietnamese leaders, and reliance on a weakened France to carry out the agreements.

The Next Step: United States Support of the Diem Regime. As the Geneva Conference debated the fate of Vietnam, an ardent nationalist, Ngo Dinh Diem (Ning-ow Ze-yuh Zee-emm), arrived in Saigon early in July 1954. Having lived in self-imposed exile since 1933 to protest French rule, the ascetic Diem belonged to Vietnam's feudal aristocracy. A Roman Catholic in a predominantly Buddhist country, he returned home after living for the past

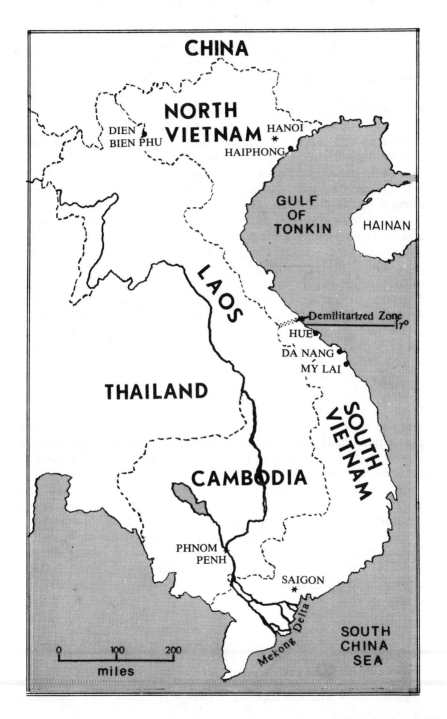

CHINA

NORTH
VIETNAM

DIEN
BIEN PHU

HANOI

HAIPHONG

GULF
OF
TONKIN

HAINAN

LAOS

Demilitarized Zone
17°

HUE

DA NANG

MY LAI

THAILAND

SOUTH
VIETNAM

CAMBODIA

PHNOM
PENH

SAIGON

SOUTH
CHINA
SEA

Mekong Delta

0   100   200

miles

four years at Maryknoll seminaries in New York and New Jersey.

Appointed Premier by Bao Dai, Diem moved at once to consolidate his control of the power structure and to get rid of the hated French. He repudiated the Geneva agreements as signed by a foreign military command "in contempt of Vietnamese national interests" and not binding on his government. He refused to consult with the North Vietnamese and even rejected economic relations and postal exchanges with Ho's government. The 17th parallel became a rigid line dividing Vietnam into two hostile countries.

Diem gained solid backing in Washington. On August 17, 1954, Eisenhower directed that aid to Indochina henceforth be given directly to the Associated States rather than through the French. After approving a NSC recommendation that the United States assume the burden of defending South Vietnam, the President in a letter to Diem in October offered American aid to assist "in developing a strong, viable state, capable of resisting attempted subversion or aggression through military means." In return, Diem was expected to undertake needed political and economic reforms. American officials, meanwhile, continued to refuse to have any dealings with Ho Chi Minh, even though there was some speculation in the press that he might become an Asian Tito, independent of control by either Moscow or Peiping.

Problems developed almost immediately for Diem and the United States. Over 800,000 refugees from the North, a majority of them Catholic, crowded into the South. Diem's authoritarianism and nepotism aroused serious opposition in the army and among municipal leaders. In March 1955 when a number of sect leaders joined in a United Front of Nationalist Forces, fighting broke out between them and Diem's forces. Popular support from the masses for Diem did not develop. And Diem's outspoken criticism of the Geneva Accords coupled with his repeated refusals to prepare for elections that would lead to the unification of Vietnam angered a French Government obligated to carry out those agreements. French leaders urged Washington to help in replacing the "irresponsible" Diem. But Eisenhower had no enthusiasm for elections according to the Geneva formula. In his *Memoirs* he confessed that:

> I have never talked or corresponded with a person knowledgeable in Indochinese Affairs who did not agree that had elections been held as of the time of the fighting, possibly 80 percent of the population would have voted for the Communist Ho Chi Minh as their leader. . . .

However, at a SEATO meeting in February 1955 both Britain and

France warned the United States that SEATO nations would not be obligated to act if the South Vietnamese refusal to hold the required elections resulted in an attack by North Vietnam. Washington could be left without allies in Southeast Asia — exactly the opposite of what Dulles and Eisenhower had worked to achieve.

Some pressure evolved within the administration to accept the French position and abandon Diem. The new American Ambassador to South Vietnam, General J. Lawton Collins cabled early in April 1955 that ". . . it is my considered judgment that the man lacks the personal qualities of leadership and the executive ability successfully to head a government that must compete with the unity of purpose and efficiency of the Viet Minh under Ho Chi Minh."

Several factors, however, continued to work for Diem. Dulles became very reluctant to make a move, especially since Congress, where Diem had powerful supporters, was debating the Mutual Security Bill. Diem's initial military success against his domestic opponents, followed by his avowal to reconstitute the government and proceed with reforms, heartened his defenders. Senator Hubert Humphrey told the Senate that: "Premier Diem is the best hope we have in South Vietnam. He is the leader of his people. He deserves and must have the whole-hearted support of the American Government and our foreign policy." Belatedly the JCS observed that "the government of !Prime Minister Ngo Dinh Diem has shown the greatest promise of achieving the internal stability essential for the future security of Vietnam."

Reinforced by such backing, Dulles told the French that: "Diem is the only means US sees to save South Vietnam and counteract revolutionary movement underway in Vietnam. . . . Whatever US view has been in past, US must support Diem whole-heartedly." The Secretary's arguments convinced the reluctant French to keep their Expeditionary Corps in South Vietnam until a National Assembly could be elected and a strong Vietnamese state established.

French Withdrawal   Buoyed by almost unqualified American support, Diem moved against his opposition. He arrested and imprisoned without due process thousands of known and suspected Communists. He centralized administration by eliminating the autonomy of South Vietnam's 2500 villages. After winning 98.2 percent of the vote against Bao Dai in a "rigged" referendum in October 1955, Diem proclaimed the establishment of the Republic of Vietnam with himself as president. Before the end of the year he terminated economic and financial arrangements with France and withdrew South Vietnamese representatives from the French Union

Assembly. Encouraged by American officials, he refused to talk to the Viet Minh and insisted on election conditions totally unacceptable to the Communists. Dulles was delighted, for he believed that "while we should certainly take no positive step to speed up present process of decay of Geneva Accords, neither should we make the slightest effort to infuse life into them."

Diem's policies made the French position untenable, and in 1956 they began to evacuate the last of their troops. Into the vacuum left by the departing French rushed the United States to safeguard a defenseless South Vietnam against any Communist threat. In May the administration added 350 men to its Military Advisory Group that worked to equip and train a South Vietnamese army of 150,000 men. Washington also assumed full cost of the military training, that averaged $85 million in each of the next five years. In 1956 the NSC instructed United States agencies to "assist Free Vietnam to assert an increasingly attractive contrast to conditions in the present Communist zone. . . ."

A NEW WAR AND ESCALATING U.S. INVOLVEMENT, 1955-1964

Viet Cong Insurgency   The July 1956 Geneva deadline for elections throughout Vietnam passed without any move to enforce the agreement. Despite the pleas of Ho Chi Minh, the international community accepted the reality of two Vietnams as it had accepted two Germanys and two Koreas. But, unlike free West Germany and South Korea, the new Republic of Vietnam lacked a strong military deterrent force and contained within its boundaries a hostile minority, the Viet Minh, capable of carrying on the struggle for unity with Communist North Vietnam. The potential for renewed conflict lurked in the countryside.

But Vietnam did not loom large among international concerns through most of the second Eisenhower term. More pressing problems in Europe, Latin America, and the Middle East after 1955 crowded Vietnam almost out of any mention in Eisenhower's *Memoirs*. Peaceful coexistence also appeared to have encouraged a measure of complacency. Public opinion polls between 1955 and 1961 showed a steady increase in the percentage of Americans who believed that the United States and Soviet Union could live peacefully together.

Dispatches from American officials in Vietnam, however, expressed concern about Diem's failure to win broad popular support. They also criticized the fact that after five years of alleged land reform, fifteen percent of the population still owned seventy-five percent of the land. Yet, Washington remained reluctant to pressure Diem as long as no threat appeared to undermine Vietnam's security. The Eisenhower administration continued to support Diem with substantial economic aid (see graph below), three-fourths of which went for military expenditures with the bulk of the benefits reaching the upper middle classes only.

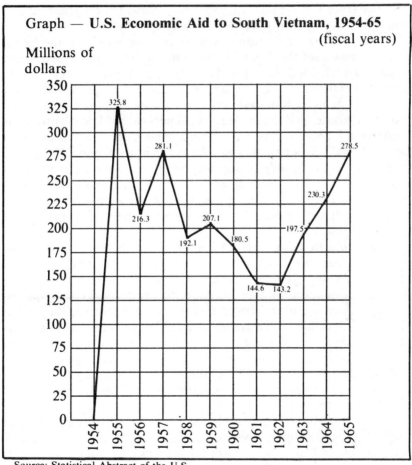

Graph — **U.S. Economic Aid to South Vietnam, 1954-65**
(fiscal years)

Source: Statistical Abstract of the U.S.

No change in American policy occurred even when dissident South Vietnamese began in 1957 to rebel against the government of Diem. Although many of the rebels were farmers wanting land reform and former government officials opposed to autocratic rule,

Diem's government applied indiscriminately the term "Viet Cong" (Vietnamese Communist) to all political opponents. Intolerant of dissent or criticism, Diem stepped up the campaign to eliminate all domestic opposition. An increase in assassinations, kidnappings and acts of terrorism by the Viet Cong prompted the United States Military Assistance Advisory Group to report in July 1957 that "... the Communists have been forming front organizations to influence portions of anti-government minorities." By 1959 the Viet Cong had evolved from a secret political movement to overthrow Diem into an open military operation to defeat the Republic of Vietnam.

Large-scale infiltration of troops and supplies from the North finally persuaded the Joint Chiefs to propose a counter-insurgency plan in March 1960. But State Department officials resisted. Believing that Diem's authoritarianism caused the insurgency, they favored pressuring him to make reforms. The Defense Department, however, contended that military weakness caused Diem's problems and that a build-up of military force against Communist subversion was needed. The debate was won by the Pentagon, and in June 1960 the American Advisory Group was more than doubled to a total of 685 men. But in its remaining weeks in office the Eisenhower administration did not implement a counter-insurgency plan. In the election campaign more pressing issues overshadowed differences about Vietnam policies.

Trouble in Laos   Before leaving office Eisenhower told his successor that the "Laos mess" was so bad that "you might have to go in there and fight it out." An anti-Communist, pro-American faction in Laos backed by over 300 American military advisors was losing to a Soviet Union backed faction of Communists, the Pathet Lao, and neutralists. American officials on the scene advised that only United States troops could save the pro-American faction from defeat. Kennedy went through the motions of preparing for war by moving the Seventh Fleet to the Gulf of Siam and flying 500 marines into Thailand to convince the Communists of the desirability of a peaceful settlement.

Early in May 1961 a ceasefire was arranged. During prolonged negotiations to set up a government, fighting erupted again. Finally in October 1961 the parties agreed in principle to a coalition government under neutralist Souvanna Phouma. Ironically, a similar neutralist coalition had been toppled with CIA assistance in 1958 when the pro-American government, now being abandoned in 1961, was put into power. Although it was risky to accept the new coalition because it might not work and might raise doubts about the credibility of the American commitment to anti-Communists, Kennedy had little choice. American intervention in Laos had cost over 300 million dollars and left that nation with a very shaky peace and a devastated countryside. Throughout the rest of the Kennedy administration the threat of a Communist take-over in Laos haunted American leaders.

The Counter Insurgency Program in Vietnam   The situation in Vietnam did not look much brighter to the new administration. In December 1960 the newly created National Liberation Front of South Vietnam (NLF) backed by North Vietnam stepped up guerrilla activity against the Diem regime. Although the NLF hinted a willingness to negotiate a settlement, Kennedy scorned the overtures. For a president elected by a very narrow margin, any deal with Communists that expanded their influence was politically unthinkable.

Kennedy was inundated with advice, Journalist Walter Lippmann, Ambassador to India John K. Galbraith, and retired General Douglas MacArthur all pointed out the difficulties of foreign troops putting down a nationalist insurgency, especially on the Asian continent. Enroute to Vienna for talks with Khrushchev (p. 33), Kennedy stopped in Paris on May 31, 1961 for a courtesy call on President De Gaulle. The old French leader cautioned the young American President against rekindling the war that had cost the French so dearly. "I predict to you," said De Gaulle, "that you will step by step be sucked into a bottomless military and political quagmire despite the losses and expenditures you may squander."

Kennedy's own advisers thought differently, although they disagreed over specific strategy. In April 1961 a Pentagon task force recommended an increase in the Military Assistance Advisory Group and deployment of 3600 additional American troops to Vietnam to train two new divisions of the Army of the Republic of Vietnam (ARVN). In May Kennedy sent Vice President Lyndon Johnson on a fact finding tour with instructions to reassure Asian leaders that the United States could be counted on to support them. After Laos and the Bay of Pigs (p. 75) the administration needed a demonstration of will and strength. Impressed by Diem, whom he proclaimed "the Winston Churchill of Southeast Asia," Johnson reported to Kennedy that local leaders "do not want American troops involved in Southeast Asia other than on training missions." But the Vice-President added: "We must decide whether to help these countries to the best of our ability or throw in the towel in the area and pull back our defenses to San Francisco and [a] 'Fortress America' concept."

Even before receiving Johnson's report Kennedy had decided

to go ahead with a counter insurgency program. Intrigued by the idea of employing guerrilla tactics against guerrillas, the President authorized the sending of 400 Special Forces troops, the Green Berets, to Vietnam. These troops were instructed to: "Infiltrate teams under light civilian cover to southeast Laos to locate and attack Vietnamese Communist bases and lines of communication. In North Vietnam, using the foundation established by intelligence operations, form networks of resistance, covert bases and teams for sabotage and light harassment."

When increased guerilla attacks by the Viet Cong in early fall 1961 gained them control of most of the southern delta, pressures mounted within the administration to send American ground forces. To look into the "feasibility" of such a move, Kennedy in October sent to Vietnam General Maxwell Taylor, Army Chief of Staff and Walt W. Rostow, White House Aide. In a report combining optimism with urgency, Taylor and Rostow recommended that the United States "put in a task force consisting largely of logistical troops. . . a U.S. military presence in Vietnam capable of assuring Diem of our readiness to join him in a military showdown with the Viet Cong or Viet Minh."

Defense Secretary McNamara and Secretary of State Dean Rusk countered that a decision on the introduction of combat forces could be deferred and that Diem should be pressured to "mobilize" all his resources and "overhaul" his military command structure in return for additional American support forces such as helicopters and communication systems. Kennedy embraced this proposal because, according to his adviser Arthur M. Schlesinger, Jr., the President did not want to send more troops to Vietnam. As recalled by Schlesinger, Kennedy said: "Then we will be told we have to send in more troops. It's like taking a drink. The effect wears off, and you have to take another."

Actually Kennedy had increased American military involvement to the extent that by the end of 1961 the size of the American military force in Vietnam had tripled since inauguration day. By his actions Kennedy moved the United States from an adviser relationship to a limited partnership with South Vietnam. And for the first time American servicemen lost their lives in the Vietnam war — a total of eleven in 1961.

The Strategic Hamlet Program Early in 1962 Washington came up with a new twist to counter insurgency — the Strategic Hamlet Program to "pacify" rural Vietnam and develop support among the peasants for the central government. This operation involved clearing Viet Cong insurgents from an area and resettling the population in villages to be defended by ARVN troops. Confidence in the eventual success of this program encouraged, in July 1962, secret adoption of a plan for phased withdrawal of United States Forces from Vietnam over a period of three years and a reduction in military aid. The war was to be won or lost by the South Vietnamese.

But the optimism that launched the Strategic Hamlet Program evaporated as peasants resisted resettlement while Diem exploited it to extend his control. And in June 1963 belief that cooperation with Diem was possible went up in flames on the streets of Saigon. A Buddhist monk, protesting Diem's oppressive measures, set himself afire before a horrified crowd as cameras recorded the event for the next day's television in the United States. After Diem declared martial law and ordered attacks on Buddhist pagodas, Washington concluded that it could no longer tolerate Diem's continuation in power. "To sink or swim with Ngo Dinh Diem" as one correspondent put it, was not in the American interest.

Overthrow of Diem Government   With the full knowledge and even encouragement of American authorities, a group of South Vietnamese generals plotted the overthrow of Diem. Kennedy's new Ambassador to Vietnam, Henry Cabot Lodge, cabled Rusk late in August: "We are launched on a course from which there is no respectable turning back, the overthrow of the Diem government." On November 2, 1964 Diem and his brother Nhu, who had supervised the attacks on the Buddhists, were seized by the conspirators and murdered. Shocked by the killings, Washington was reviewing its Vietnam policy when twenty days later in Dallas an assassin's bullet snuffed out the life of President John F. Kennedy.

Johnson's Hesitant Steps   The new President, Lyndon B. Johnson, pledged to "keep our commitments from South Vietnam to West Berlin" and to carry out all of the late President's policies. A few days after taking the oath of office, Johnson informed Lodge: "I am not going to lose Vietnam. I am not going to be the President who saw Southeast Asia go the way China went."

Relatively inexperienced in foreign affairs despite his long service in Congress, Johnson solicited advice from "wise experts of established reputation." He discovered that neither political stability nor military success smiled on the new Vietnamese regime. Defense Secretary McNamara returned in December 1963 from a hurried trip to Vietnam with the gloomy report that: "Current trends, unless reversed in the next 2-3 months, will lead to neutralization at best and more likely to a Communist-controlled state." A pessimistic Senator Mansfield, Majority Leader, advised withdrawal of American advisory forces from Vietnam and acceptance of a division of the country similar to that in Korea. On the other hand, a CIA report, that admitted "a serious and steadily deteriorating" situation, implied that more military involvement might save the day.

Gradually a hesitant President inched away from a political solution toward a military one. A McNamara-Taylor mission to Saigon in March 1964 confirmed that the military situation "has unquestionably been growing worse" and that Hanoi's involvement in the insurgency, "always significant, has been increasing." They urged that the United States "reiterate that it will provide all the assistance and advice required to do the job regardless of how long it takes." Late in March Johnson signed a top secret National Security Advisory Memorandum instructing United States forces "to be in a position on 72 hours notice to initiate. . . 'Retaliatory Actions' against North Vietnam, and to be in a position on 30 days' notice to initiate the program of 'Graduated Overt Military Pressure' against North Vietnam." What had been regarded as an internal struggle in South Vietnam had become, in the administration's eyes, a war between "free" South Vietnam and a Communist aggressor, North Vietnam. Moreover, the Vietnam conflict, in McNamara's words, was "a test case of U.S. capacity to help a nation meet a Communist war of liberation." Lyndon Johnson intended to be ready for that test.

But in a presidential election year and with Great Society programs such as civil rights and anti-poverty legislation to enact, Johnson did not want to go beyond beefing up the pacification program with more economic aid and advisory troops. Temporarily deferring phased withdrawal, the President in May 1964 increased the American military force in Vietnam to over 17,000 men. In June he appointed General William C. Westmoreland as Commander of American forces in Vietnam. But U.S. troops were still not authorized to engage in combat against the North Vietnamese enemy. More advisory troops were sent in July, and naval patrols in offshore waters of North Vietnam were expanded. The Gulf of Tonkin incident in August came as no great surprise to the Pentagon or the White House.

Holding His Fire   Five days after the adoption of the Gulf of Tonkin Resolution, President Johnson, with one eye on the American electorate and a sideward glance at Hanoi, projected an image of firmness with restraint. He told the American Bar Association: "No one should think for a moment that we will be worn down, nor will we be driven out, and we will not be provoked into rashness. . . ."

Throughout the campaign Johnson occupied this high ground, and his political acumen paid off. The American people came to perceive him as the peace candidate and Barry Goldwater, who advocated full scale air attacks on North Vietnam, as the war candidate. A Gallup Poll released three weeks after the passage of the Tonkin Gulf Resolution listed seventy-one percent as believing that the United States was handling affairs in Vietnam "as well as to be expected." Johnson spurted into a long lead and won the highest percentage of the popular vote ever received by a President.

Unknown to the general public, however, the Defense Department and CIA in September drew up plans "to respond as appropriate against North Vietnam in case of an attack on U.S. units or of any 'special' North Vietnamese-Viet Cong action against South Vietnam." The Pentagon assumed that bombing strikes against North Vietnam "would be required at some proximate future date . . . ." to discourage Hanoi's underwriting the insurgency. Convinced by the unanimous endorsement of his advisers, Johnson approved the plan.

When the Viet Cong attacked an American base north of Saigon just two days before the November election, Johnson followed the advice of civilian advisers and refused to authorize an "eye for an eye" air strike advocated by the JCS and the new American Ambassador to Vietnam, General Maxwell Taylor. Nor did the newly reelected President retaliate when on Christmas Eve another Viet Cong raid killed two and wounded fifty Americans. But even Johnson's civilian aides began to counsel that "calculated doses of force" would be needed to bring Hanoi to the bargaining table.

In his January 1965 State of the Union Message President Johnson reviewed the reasons for the United States presence in Vietnam as ". . . first, because a friendly nation has asked us for help against Communist aggression. Ten years ago we pledged our help. Three Presidents have supported that pledge. We will not break it. Second, our own security is tied to the peace of Asia." For the next four years Lyndon Johnson stuck by that argument.

ESCALATION OF THE VIETNAM WAR, 1965-1968

Operation Rolling Thunder   Disturbed by the political instability and military ineffectiveness of South Vietnam, Ambassador Taylor reported early in January that: "We are presently on a losing track and must risk a change. . . . To take no positive action now is to accept defeat in the fairly near future." John McCone, CIA Director, advised the bombing of targets in North Vietnam.

Johnson was on the spot. The intelligence community had furnished evidence of large scale infiltration of military units from North Vietnam. American officials in Saigon did not think that the South Vietnamese Government could prevent a Communist takeover without direct participation by American military forces. The American people were becoming restless and unhappy about Viet Cong killings of American servicemen unable to fight back. A public opinion poll in late January 1965 revealed that fifty percent thought that the United States should use its military forces to stop such attacks, whereas only twenty-eight percent opposed such action. Reluctantly the President authorized use of American planes against the Viet Cong, but only in support of Vietnamese troops when Westmoreland considered it absolutely necessary.

Another Viet Cong attack on an American base on February 6 killed eight Americans and wounded sixty. This incident convinced National Security Adviser McGeorge Bundy, in Saigon on a fact-finding mission when the attack occurred, that the United States must respond. With a solid consensus supporting him, Johnson decided to hit back with an air strike against North Vietnam to "convince the leaders in Hanoi that we were serious in our purpose and also that the North could not count on continued immunity if they persisted in aggression in the South."

On February 7 forty-nine U.S. Navy jets bombed North Vietnamese barracks and staging areas forty miles north of the 17th parallel. The next day Johnson decided to carry out "continuing action" against North Vietnam until she stopped her aggression. "We have kept our guns over the mantel," said the President, "and our shells in the cupboard for a long time now. And what was the result? They are killing our men while they sleep in the night. I can't ask our American soldiers out there to continue to fight with one hand tied behind their backs." After more than ten years of only military aid and advice to South Vietnam, the United States committed its air power to the war against North Vietnam. By using air power only, the President hoped to avoid the use of American ground forces. Lyndon Johnson made war in order to make peace, or in his words, "I saw our bombs as my political resources for negotiating a peace."

American involvement in the war increased throughout the spring without much public awareness. Johnson's Great Society programs focused public attention on the effort to make America a better place for all its citizens. But, behind the scenes the Commander-in-Chief was busy with the Vietnam War. Early in March he approved the use of napalm to make the bombing attacks more effective, and Johnson himself participated directly in hours of discussion to choose each target to be bombed. After repeated requests from Westmoreland, two Marine Battalion Landing Teams of 1500 men, the first regular American combat troops to be sent to Vietnam, arrived in March 1965 to protect the American air base near Danang. But, for the time being, Johnson, with Taylor's backing, resisted the proposal of the JCS to send two United States divisions and one South Korean division for combat action against the Viet Cong in South Vietnam.

The Final Step: Commitment of U.S. Ground Forces   To the dismay of the administration, the bombing seemed to increase rather than decrease the attacks on American installations. The Communists, ironically, not the United States, controlled the escalation of the war. After the Viet Cong blew up the American Embassy in Saigon killing twenty persons, Johnson secretly authorized on April 2, 1965 participation of marines in combat to protect nearby South Vietnamese units if necessary. He also decided to add 20,000 men to support American forces already in South Vietnam. With the Gulf of Tonkin Resolution on his desk, the President believed he had no need to consult Congress nor explain his actions openly to the public.

Johnson, however, still hoped to avoid that last step leading to ground fighting and American casualties. In a speech on April 7, 1965 he signaled Hanoi that the United States "remains ready... for unconditional discussions" and that he would seek $1 billion in reconstruction funds for all of Vietnam immediately after peace was established. The North Vietnamese ignored the overture and refused to discuss or negotiate until all American troops had been withdrawn from Indochina — a condition unacceptable to Washington.

Fresh from his "anti-Communist" success in the Dominican Republic (p. 82), Johnson in May 1965 instituted a bombing pause as evidence of his desire to negotiate, but the Viet Cong attacks continued. After eight days without a North Vietnamese response he resumed bombing missions against selected North Vietnamese targets, but he still resisted the JCS advice to begin large-scale strategic bombing to destroy the industrial base of North Vietnam. The President wanted to be able to pull back if Red China reacted with threats to retaliate, so he kept Hanoi and its port city of Haiphong off-limits.

By mid-summer 1965 American policy-makers realized that bombing North Vietnam would not do the job by itself. The flow of men and supplies from North Vietnam to the insurgents in the South had to be cut off on the ground if Viet Cong attacks were to be stopped. Without fanfare U.S. troops began to engage in combat against Viet Cong guerrillas, and a gradual build-up of the American military force continued. Westmoreland embarked on "search and destroy" missions that relied on helicopters to bring devastating fire power to hit the enemy. In his judgment, such tactics stood "a good chance of achieving an acceptable outcome within a reasonable time in Vietnam."

The Song of Doves   As the American involvement escalated throughout 1965 a different voice, faint and uncoordinated at first, echoed across America. A one day moratorium to protest the war, at the University of Michigan in March 1965, set an example which spread to dozens of college campuses that spring. In May a National Teach-In to protest the war took place in the nation's capital. In October citizens in towns and villages across the nation held peace demonstrations. Later in the fall over thirty thousand persons joined in a peace march in Washington.

Within the administration Under Secretary of State George Ball made dovish noises. Questioning the effectiveness of bombing, he said, "I have great apprehensions that we can't win under these conditions." Ball even argued that Vietnam was not vital to the security of the United States, and he suggested that the nation "cut its losses" by withdrawing. Doubts also infected upper echelons in the Defense Department. During another pause in the bombing between Christmas Eve 1965 and the end of January 1966 Assistant Secretary of Defense John McNaughton wrote a secret memo warning that: "We have in Vietnam the ingredients of an enormous miscalculation. . . . We are in an escalating stalemate." Retreating from his early hard-line position, McNamara advised the President in 1966 that "even with the recommended deployments, we will be faced early in 1967 with a military standoff at a much higher level."

Dissenting voices were also heard in Congress. Senator Mansfield warned of a larger war involving Red China if the United States continued to expand its commitment. An even more pessimistic Senator Morse predicted that: "A United States military stronghold in Vietnam can only be maintained by perpetual war." And Senator Fulbright, having second thoughts about the wisdom of the Gulf of Tonkin Resolution, said in June 1965 that "It is clear to all reasonable Americans that a complete military victory in Vietnam, though theoretically attainable, can in fact be attained only at a cost far exceeding the requirements of our interest and our honor." Seven months later, the Senate Foreign Relations Committee, chaired by Fulbright, held public hearings on the Vietnam War. Several Senators challenged the administration's new argument that the United States was obligated according to the SEATO treaty (p. 62) to come to the aid of South Vietnam.

The Whir of Hawks   The pro-war faction, led by the Joint Chiefs and Walt W. Rostow, answered the doves with statistics demonstrating military progress and with arguments for an expansion of American military pressure to force North Vietnam to the bargaining table. Characteristic of the argument of the hawks was Ambassador Maxwell Taylor's testimony before the Fulbright Committee hearings early in 1966. "We are not being licked," claimed Taylor. "We are looking for these people and destroying them at the greatest rate that has ever taken place in the history of the struggle." Administration spokesmen relied heavily on the "body count" of enemy dead to document the success of American arms.

The hawks had strong allies in a Congress that continued to pass military appropriation bills requested by the Administration. To vote against supplying necessary resources to American combat soldiers was unthinkable to most Congressmen, even to those troubled about the war. And to back down under Communist pressure was un-American and disloyal, as Richard Nixon argued. In a letter to the *New York Times* in October 1965 he ventured that "victory for the Vietcong. . . would mean ultimately the destruction of freedom of speech for all men for all time not only in Asia but the United States as well. . . ."

Although the tide of opposition to the war was clearly rising, a majority of the American people tended to believe their political and military leaders. Public opinion polls consistently showed throughout 1965 and 1966 that a clear majority supported the administration, even in bombing North Vietnam. Such backing encouraged officials to send more ground troops, to increase draft calls, and to continue the bombing. Johnson regarded his action as a reasonable middle course short of total commitment of the nation's military power. By fighting a limited war in Vietnam, he believed that America could avoid World War III, bring about a negotiated peace, and have both "guns and butter." Opponents of the war he dismissed contemptuously as "Nervous Nellies" unwilling to see a tough job through to the end. But his policy, unless it produced measurable gains, risked antagonizing both those who thought the United States should pull out and those who believed in total victory. Thus there was a necessity for a spate of optimistic slogans emanating from Washington — Rostow saw a "light at the end of the tunnel"; Westmoreland claimed "the enemy's hopes are bankrupt"; and Taylor held "the cause in Vietnam is being won."

To Escalate or Not To Escalate?   But more bombings, an increase in the "body count" of enemy dead, and more property destroyed did not appear to weaken the Viet Cong. Nor did the bombing of North Vietnam's oil-storage facilities in July and August 1966 "bring the enemy to the conference table" or "cause the insurgency to wither" as so confidently predicted by the military. In fact, a secret Defense Department study by forty-seven scientists reported to McNamara in September that Operation Rolling Thunder, the heavy bombing of North Vietnam, "had no measurable direct affect" on North Vietnam's capability to make war. McNamara counseled the President to stop the bombing and negotiate a political settlement. In November 1966 he told Johnson that there is "no evidence" that additional troops as requested by Westmoreland, "would substantially change the situation."

As the war dragged on with expanded bombing attacks and ground fighting, Westmoreland as usual requested more troops — this time a whopping 200,000. In addition, the Joint Chiefs pressured for the mobilization of reserves and "an extension of the war" into Laos and Cambodia. But Johnson, perhaps persuaded by Bundy's argument against ground escalation in 1967 and 1968 before a presidential election, authorized only a modest increase. Bundy may also have struck a sensitive chord with his suggestion that ". . . what we must plan to offer as a defense of administration policy is not victory over Hanoi, but growing success —and self-reliance — in the south."

The Anti-War Movement in High Gear   In May 1967 a discouraged McNaughton confided to his Chief, Secretary McNamara, that "a feeling is widely and strongly held that 'the Establishment' is out of its mind. . . ." McNaughton sensed a change in public attitude toward the war and a growing polarization of the nation. Television brought into American homes nightly the horrors of modern war in vivid detail. The killing of innocent civilians, including women and children, and the devastation of the countryside distressed even many who had supported the war. So did mounting American casualties that in 1967 reached 100,000 dead, wounded, or missing. (See table p. 138.) Public opinion polls, that in January 1965 had shown only twenty-eight percent believing that the United States had made a mistake in sending troops to Vietnam, revealed in July 1967 that forty-one percent thought so. Moreover, in the latter poll only forty-one percent approved the sending of another 100,000 soldiers, and for the first time less than half of those polled thought that the United States should continue the bombing.

The protest movement accelerated throughout the spring and summer of 1967. In April more than 125,000 persons demonstrated in New York for an end to the war, while 30,000 marched in San

Francisco. Muhammed Ali was stripped of his heavyweight boxing crown and imprisoned for refusing to be drafted. Hundreds of young men fled to Canada, Sweden, and other foreign havens to escape induction. Others defied the law and outraged patriots by burning their draft cards and even the American flag. Thousands of young persons, male and female, participated in Vietnam Summer of 1967 organizing teach-ins, sit-ins, and demonstrations against the war. An October citizens march on the Pentagon emphasized the intensity of the peace movement. Chanting "Hey, hey, LBJ, how many kids have you killed today?" anti-war demonstrators paraded in front of the White House where the President remained a virtual prisoner. For months Johnson avoided public appearances except at military bases where a safe, friendly reception was assured. Efforts by supporters of the war to rally people behind the flag seemed to attract less attention and enthusiasm. The nation was badly divided, and so was the national government.

Secretary of Defense McNamara's doubts reflected the division. He confessed to McNaughton that "The picture of the world's greatest superpower killing or seriously injuring 1000 noncombatants a week while trying to pound a tiny, backward nation into submission on an issue whose merits are hotly disputed, is not a pretty one." In November 1967 he submitted his resignation without recriminations, and early in the new year joined the growing ranks of former members of the Johnson administration.

The Shock of The Tet Offensive   The failure of American military and political leaders to diagnose the realities in Vietnam was exposed early in 1968 when the Viet Cong violated the customary cease-fire marking the Tet, Vietnam's Lunar New Year holiday. On January 31, 1968, the first day of Tet, Viet Cong units launched a coordinated offensive against thirty-six major cities, scores of towns and villages, and a dozen American bases, including even the United States Embassy in Saigon. So unprepared were South Vietnamese military commanders that nearly half of the South Vietnamese soldiers had holiday leaves.

Two days after the Tet offensive began, Johnson at a press conference claimed that the enemy attack had been "anticipated, prepared for and met," and that the enemy had suffered militarily "a complete failure." General Westmoreland, who had vainly attempted to stir the South Vietnamese to prepare for a major enemy offensive, believed that the enemy had decided "to go for broke" in hopes of fostering "American disenchantment with the war." He claimed that the Viet Cong had suffered "a catastrophic military defeat."

But the Tet offensive shocked the American people. Pictures of

American corpses in the garden of the American Embassy in Saigon and nightly television pictures of hard fighting in and bombing of South Vietnamese cities over several weeks to dislodge the Viet Cong punctured optimistic official statements and cast doubt on the credibility of the nation's leaders. Opponents of the war found new strength. In their eyes an American military officer unwittingly dramatized the futility of the war when he explained the destructive artillery and air attacks on Ben Tre, a small South Vietnamese city, with the remark "It became necessary to destroy the town to save it." Senator Robert F. Kennedy (D., N.Y.) brushed aside Johnson's and Westmoreland's claims with the observation "It is as if James Madison [had claimed] victory in 1812 because the British only burned Washington instead of annexing it to the British Empire." Even within the administration some officials, such as Assistant Secretary of Defense Alain Enthoven, recognized the failure of American policies. "Our control of the countryside," he pointed out, "is essentially at the pre-August 1965 levels."

Nevertheless, strong voices were raised against abandoning the war. Richard Nixon, gearing up for another run for the presidency, contended, a few days after the Tet offensive began, that "the only effective way" to bring Hanoi to the peace table was to " prosecute the war more effectively." Administration leaders cautioned that defeatism at home played into the hands of the enemy. The chorus of opposition to the war was nurtured, according to Johnson, by "emotional and exaggerated reporting of the Tet offensive in our press and on television." An optimistic Westmoreland reported that enemy losses in the Tet attack provided "an opportunity to seize the initiative and materially shorten the war."

But Westmoreland's request for 200,000 more men was widely viewed as evidence of the desperate nature of the American military position, rather than as a logical move to expand operations against a weakened enemy. Johnson turned down the request because it would necessitate calling up the inactive reserves. Such a step, it was feared, would increase domestic opposition to the war and make it more difficult to open negotiations with Hanoi. Westmoreland was learning, as MacArthur had in Korea, that an American military victory "in the classic sense," ending in the surrender of the enemy, was impossible because the American people were unwilling to pay the heavy price of all-out war.

Reverberations from Tet also resounded through the snow-banks of New Hampshire where the nation's first Presidential primary of 1968 was held in early March. Although President Johnson won the Democratic primary, the narrow margin of his victory over the anti-war candidate, Senator Eugene McCarthy (D., Minn.) startled the nation. Public opinion polls also showed a sharp decline in the President's standing. The forty percent that in late January approved Johnson's handling of the war dwindled by early March to only twenty-six percent. On March 31, just two months after the start of the Tet Offensive, the President announced on national television that he would halt the bombing north of the 20th parallel and that he would not be a candidate for re-election.

Peace Talks in Paris Within a few days Hanoi responded favorably to Johnson's initiative, and peace talks began in Paris in May. But little progress was made during spring and summer sessions. The North Vietnamese insisted on the unconditional cessation of all bombing and "other acts of war" by the United States. American officials replied that they could not comply until North Vietnam ceased its military operations against South Vietnam. Some observers suspected that Hanoi was stalling until after the American election in hopes of a change in the American position. But, just before the election, North Vietnam agreed to include South Vietnam in the talks, and Johnson responded by ordering a halt in all bombardment of the North.

The maneuvering in Paris spilled over into the political debate in the presidential campaign. Vice-President Hubert Humphrey, the Democratic candidate, was burdened by his association with the unpopular Johnson administration and by the brutal suppression of anti-war demonstrators by Mayor Daley's police during the nominating convention in Chicago. Far behind the Republican nominee, Richard Nixon, in the polls, Humphrey revitalized his campaign late in September by pledging to stop all the bombing if elected. Nixon, coasting on the lead, merely indicated that he had a secret plan "to end the war and win the peace." With a margin of less than one percent of the popular vote, Nixon was elected.

VIETNAMIZATION OF THE WAR

Revival of an Old Approach Nixon, like his immediate predecessors in the White House, opposed any peace settlement that left the Communists in control of all of Vietnam. He, too, did not intend to become the first president to lose a war. A separate, free South Vietnam had to be preserved. But he realized, as he confided to aides during the campaign, "that there's no way to win the war." So the problem remained — "how to end the war without losing it."

To achieve that goal the new Chief Executive and his National Security Adviser, Henry Kissinger, a former Harvard professor, proposed to "Vietnamize" the war by the slow withdrawal of American troops and their simultaneous replacement with American equipped and directed South Vietnamese forces. During the transition period the United States could renew the bombing if Hanoi tried to take advantage of the withdrawal. After a "decent interval" the responsibility for fighting the Communists and defending the territory of South Vietnam from aggression would be shouldered by the South Vietnamese themselves.

Remarkably similar to Kennedy's "phased withdrawal," the Nixon-Kissinger plan was neat, tidy, and politically astute. Domestic opponents of the war would be quieted as American boys returned home, casualties declined, and the draft ended. Avid hawks would be reassured by the commitment to stay in Vietnam until the government of South Vietnam was strong enough to stand on its own. And a solid base at home could be constructed from the so-called "silent majority" — the average, middle-class, white, patriotic, law-abiding citizens who detested the "hippies," draft-dodgers, and war protesters. This grand scheme would enable the United States to honor its commitments, deny the Communists victory in Vietnam, save the "dominoes," halt the decline of American power and prestige, and guarantee Nixon's re-election in 1972.

The Nixon Doctrine   As the first step Nixon announced in early June 1969 "the immediate redeployment from Vietnam of a division equivalent of approximately 25,000 men." A month later during a trip to Southeast Asia the President embellished his strategy by announcing "the Nixon Doctrine." In a press conference on Guam, Nixon proclaimed that hereafter problems of internal security and military defense "will be handled by, and the responsibility for it taken by, the Asian nations themselves. . . ." No longer would the United States bear almost single handedly the burden of containing Communism in Asia.

Neither Vietnamization nor the peace talks proceeded smoothly. The Paris negotiations remained deadlocked. And the Viet Cong continued hit and run attacks in South Vietnam to which the administration felt obligated to respond with counterblows, or in the words of a Pentagon spokesman, "protective reactions" by American bombers. Equally discouraging were manifestations that American programs, instead of strengthening South Vietnam's will and capability, had weakened both. General Thieu's government relied more and more on American aid and less on Vietnamese resources. With withdrawals of American troops dependent on South Vietnam's ability to defend itself, the United States had in effect become "the satellite of its own satellite." South Vietnam's needs and desires increasingly controlled America's actions.

Nixon's policies also led to angry confrontations with opponents of the war. Critics contended that Vietnamization merely "changed the color of the corpses." A huge anti-war demonstration in Washington in October 1969 elicited from the President the warning that: "If a vocal minority, however fervent its cause, prevails over reason and the will of the majority, this nation has no future as a free society." He denounced demands by anti-war leaders for an arbitrary cut-off date for withdrawal of all troops as "defeatist." As the emotional rhetoric intensified, the polarization of American society hardened.

The United States Commitment To Vietnam, 1960–1972		
U.S. Troop Levels (as of Dec. 31)	United States Aid to South Vietnam (in millions)	
	Economic	Military
1960 — 900	1960 — $180.5	
1961 — 3,200	1961 — 144.6	
1962 — 11,300	1962 — 143.2	
1963 — 16,300	1963 — 197.5	
1964 — 23,300	1964 — 230.3	
1965 — 184,300	1965 — 278.5	— 297.0
1966 — 385,300	1966 — 337.0	— 862.0
1967 — 485,000	1967 — 568.0	— 1,204.0
1968 — 536,100	1968 — 537.0	— 1,055.0
1969 — 475,200	1969 — 414.0	— 1,608.0
1970 — 334,600	1970 — 477.0	— 1,693.0
1971 — 156,800	1971 — 576.0	— 1,883.0
1972 — 24,200	1972 — 455.0	— 2,383.0
	1973 — 502.0	— 3,349.0
	1974 — 654.0	— 941.9

Source: *Statistical Abstract of The United States*

| U.S. Casualties | | The Draft |
Killed	Wounded	
1961 — 11 — 3		1955 — 215,000
1962 — 31 — 78		1960 — 90,000
1963 — 78 — 411		1963 — 74,000
1964 — 147 — 1,039		1964 — 151,000
1965 — 1,369 — 6,114		1965 — 103,000
1966 — 5,008 — 30,093		1966 — 340,000
1967 — 9,378 — 62,025		1967 — 299,000
1968 — 14,582 — 92,820		1968 — 340,000
1969 — 9,414 — 70,216		1969 — 265,000
1970 — 4,221 — 30,643		1970 — 207,000
1971 — 1,381 — 8,936		1971 — 156,000
1972 — 300 — 1,221		1972 — 27,000
1973 — 237 — 60		

Source: *Statistical Abstract of The United States*

My Lai Massacre   To make matters worse for Washington, revelations in November 1969 that American soldiers in March 1968 in the aftermath of Tet had massacred over three hundred civilians, mainly women and children in the village of My Lai, set off a wave of horror and shame. So disturbing was the incident that a poll taken in St. Louis indicated that only twelve percent of those who had heard the story about My Lai believed that it was true. But demands for an investigation and for punishment of those responsible kept the issue before the nation for months and caused further division over the war.

More Troop Withdrawals   Nixon held fast to his contention that total withdrawal before South Vietnam could defend itself would mean defeat. In his January 1970 State of the Union Message he added another reason for staying, with the warning that: "When we assumed the burden of helping South Vietnam, millions of South Vietnamese men and women placed their trust in us. To abandon them would risk a massacre that would shock and dismay everyone in the world who values human life." Three months later he announced the projected withdrawal of 150,000 in addition to the 50,000 already withdrawn to date in 1970. It would be possible to pull out that large a number within the next twelve months, the President said, because ". . . we finally have in sight the just peace we are seeking. . . ." Having heard such optimistic statements from high officials so many times, skeptics shook their heads in disbelief.

Invasion of Cambodia   In the meantime, the administration put into operation a new tactic that expanded the war and renewed the turmoil at home. In a move that caught the American people by surprise, American and South Vietnamese forces crossed the border into Cambodia (map, p. 117) at the end of April to destroy Viet Cong supplies and sanctuaries through which military supplies and troop reinforcements funneled into South Vietnam. President Nixon, in a national television address, explained that: "This is not an invasion of Cambodia. . . . Once enemy forces are driven out of these sanctuaries and once their military supplies are destroyed, we will withdraw." Appealing for popular support of this action, he said: "If, when the chips are down, the world's most powerful nation, the United States of America, acts like a pitiful, helpless giant, the forces of totalitarianism and anarchy will threaten free nations and free institutions throughout the world." On the next day American planes carried out the heaviest bombing attacks on North Vietnam since Johnson announced a cessation on November 1, 1968.

Denouncing this escalation of the war by the so-called "incursion" into neutral Cambodia, students on campuses of hundreds of colleges and scores of schools demonstrated against the war and against the President. The national protest spread to Washington where 100,000 marched in opposition to the war. Hundreds were arrested by municipal police and National Guardsmen. An angry President dismissed the young demonstrators as "bums. . . blowing up the campuses," while he praised "the kids" fighting in Vietnam as "the greatest." Such language fed the storm. On May 4 National Guardsmen, called out to maintain order on the campus of Kent State University in Ohio, shot to death four students and wounded eight.

Stirred to action by the national uproar over the "incursion" into Cambodia and the killing of the students, Senators George McGovern, (D., So. Dak.) and Mark Hatfield (R., Ore.) pushed for an "end-to-the-war" amendment to a regular appropriations bill. This amendment would ban expenditure of funds for war in Vietnam unless Congress declared war. Even though Nixon claimed on June 3 that "the great triumph" in Cambodia had "eliminated an immediate danger to the security of the remaining Americans in Vietnam" and enabled him to speed up troop withdrawal, Congressional opposition to his policies did not subside. In June an amendment, sponsored by Senators John Cooper (R., Ky.) and Frank Church (D., Ida.), banning further United States combat air activity over Cambodia passed the Senate, but was defeated in the House. The Senate, concerned about excessive executive power, also voted to terminate the Gulf of Tonkin Resolution of 1964 that had given the Chief Executive "carte blanche" to deploy American combat forces in Southeast Asia. But when Nixon pulled American troops out of Cambodia at the end of June and announced a speed up of troop withdrawals from Vietnam for the rest of the year, emotions cooled. Conveniently overlooked was the fact that Communist forces increased their control to more than half of Cambodia and had the Cambodian pro-western government under heavy siege.

Throughout the summer and fall of 1970 efforts to secure North Vietnam's agreement to a cease-fire and peace terms failed, as Hanoi still insisted on the preliminary withdrawal of all American forces. Instead of negotiating a truce, the North Vietnamese continued to move men and supplies into the South. When military intelligence estimated in mid-October that North Vietnamese infiltrations had exceeded American withdrawals, Nixon ordered renewed large-scale bombing of the North.

A DIPLOMATIC REVOLUTION

Opening Relations with Communist China   For some time both the President and his chief adviser, Henry Kissinger, believed that the war in Vietnam could be ended only by reducing tensions with the Soviet Union and the People's Republic of China. Even before becoming President, Nixon had written an article in *Foreign Affairs* magazine advocating normalization of relations with Red China. His anti-Communist credentials, dating back to his earliest political campaigns, made it possible for Nixon, probably alone of all American political leaders, to seek understandings with the two major Communist powers. No one could accuse him of being "soft on Communism." His hard line against recognition of Red China or admitting it to the United Nations and his vigorous attacks on those who had "lost China" had contributed to the isolation of the People's Republic of China. But more than two decades of turbulence and change had created a very different world. And Nixon prided himself on his pragmatism — flexibility in adapting to new situations. The assumption that monolithic Communism threatened to overrun the free world had been shattered by the clear split between Moscow and Peking (Beijing), a reality that made it tempting to American leaders to play off one against the other. To prepare the American people for the dramatic change a careful step by step procedure was designed.

Kissinger, a great admirer of the balance of power concept developed in the nineteenth century by European statesmen after the defeat of Napoleon, envisioned understandings with the two largest Communist powers as the essential ingredient of long-term international stability and security. Secret contacts with the Chinese beginning in Warsaw late in 1968 and continuing through Pakistani and Romanian contacts in 1969 and 1970 paved the way for Kissinger's secret trip to Peking in July 1971 and an invitation from Chairman Mao to President Nixon to visit China early in 1972. In a dramatic public announcement of his forthcoming visit, Nixon explained: "I have taken this action because of my profound conviction that all nations will gain from a reduction of tension and a better relationship between the United States and the People's Republic of China." The response of the American people was overwhelmingly enthusiastic, although the old China Lobby cried "betrayal" and "sell-out" of a reliable ally, Taiwan.

Détente With the Soviet Union   Simultaneously with its search for normalization of relations with Red China, Washington sought a better understanding or détente with the Soviet Union. Nixon and Kissinger assumed that the Russian desire for American technology and foodstuffs would encourage Kremlin leaders Brezhnev and Kosygin to agree to a general relaxation of tensions. After negotiating secretly for months with Anatoly Dobrynin, Soviet Ambassador to the United States, Kissinger secured an agreement in principle in May 1971 on strategic arms limitations. Initiated in Helsinki late in 1969, the first Strategic Arms Limitation Talks (SALT I) focused on establishing ceilings on the numbers of both defensive and offensive ballistic missiles. But not until the Moscow Summit meeting in May 1972 would a specific agreement be signed.

Détente advanced another step in September 1971 when the Soviets agreed to guarantee the free movement of traffic to and from West Berlin in exchange for an Allied agreement that West Berlin would not be treated as "a constituent part" of West Germany nor "be governed by it." A Nixon visit to the Soviet Union in May 1972, after the China trip, was also arranged.

The China Trip, February 1972   A carefully staged spectacle telecast throughout the Western world, Nixon's trip to China in mid-winter 1972 produced the Shanghai communique clarifying American and Chinese positions on a wide range of divisive issues concerning East Asia. The two nations agreed to broaden contacts in "people-to-people" exchanges and to improve trade relations. Although carefully avoiding any abandonment of the Republic of China (Taiwan), the United States terminated its ostracism of the People's Republic of China by agreeing to "concrete consultations to further the normalization of relations." Dire warnings by strong supporters of Taiwan attracted little sympathy in the general euphoria of the moment.

PEACE WITHOUT VICTORY

Continuation of Vietnamization and Bombing   The sensational developments in détente, however, failed to expedite a settlement of the Vietnam War. Renewed secret talks in Paris in late summer 1971 made no progress, as the issue of exchange of prisoners of war became a new, highly emotional obstacle. When the North Vietnamese stepped up infiltration into the South, Nixon in December resumed heavy bombardment of the North. But, having set in motion the "Vietnamization" of the war, the President found it politically necessary in an election year to maintain schedules of troop withdrawals. Early in January 1972 he announced that troop ceilings would be reduced to 69,000 men.

The failure of South Vietnam's army to contain heavy North Vietnamese attacks across the borders was met, not by American soldiers, but by massive bombing of the North by American B-52's. In mid-April 1972 Nixon ordered the bombing of Hanoi and its port of Haiphong for the first time. The announced intent was to pressure Hanoi to cease its military operations and to negotiate in good faith.

The apparent endless cycle of North Vietnamese infiltration, Viet Cong attacks, ineffective South Vietnamese resistance, and American bombing discouraged large numbers of Americans who longed for peace. Nixon's decision to mine Haiphong harbor, through which flowed supplies from Communist allies, triggered new anti-war demonstrations and protests. Senator Mansfield warned that: "We are courting danger here that could extend the war, increase the number of war prisoners, and make peace more difficult to achieve." Senator George McGovern, emerging as the front runner to capture the Democratic presidential nomination, charged that "the only purpose of this dangerous course is to keep General Thieu in power a little longer." But Jimmy Carter, Democratic Governor of Georgia, urged the nation to ". . . give President Nixon our backing and support — whether or not we agree with specific decisions."

The administration took comfort in a Harris poll showing that fifty-nine percent of those polled supported the mining of Haiphong. And the emergence of George McGovern, the favorite of the anti-war activists, as Nixon's likely opponent in November brought smiles of anticipation to Republican stalwarts who viewed McGovern as far to the Left of the average voter on many issues. Moreover, when the Soviet Union failed to call off the summit meeting, it appeared that Nixon's bold move was based on a sound analysis of the situation.

The Moscow Summit, May 1972   Less than two weeks before his departure for Moscow, Nixon in a televised address to the American people announced his terms for lifting what amounted to a blockade of North Vietnam. He said that ". . . all American prisoners of war must be returned" and "there must be an internationally supervised cease-fire throughout Indochina." In a significant departure from past statements, the President made no mention of a required withdrawal of North Vietnamese forces from the South. This subtle signal of omission was aimed at Moscow and Hanoi.

After prolonged and sometimes frenetic negotiations, the Moscow Summit Meeting in May produced a limited SALT agreement on the principles arrived at a year earlier. An anti-ballistic missile (ABM) agreement limited the number of sites, defensive missiles and tests of defensive weapons. Agreement was also reached setting a ceiling on the number of offensive ballistic missiles (ICBM) and launchers at existing levels. The two nations also agreed to establish a Standing Consultative Committee to monitor compliance.

In addition, President Nikolai Podgorny of the Soviet Union agreed to go to Hanoi to urge a negotiated settlement of the Vietnam War on the basis of secret American proposals. Washington would accept a tripartite electoral commission, that included the Viet Cong, to organize and administer the election of a government of South Vietnam. Détente had reached new heights. And Nixon visualized "peace with honor" before November's elections.

Difficulties with South Vietnam   Kissinger immediately followed up this new American initiative with energetic efforts to obtain a cease-fire. After much shuttling between capitals, he eventually obtained Hanoi's agreement to sign a truce by October 31 to be followed by the withdrawal of the remaining American troops and the establishment of the tripartite commission. But Kissinger failed to budge President Thieu of South Vietnam to accept the deal, so the United States could not sign the agreement without repudiating its ally. Nevertheless, both Kissinger and Nixon continued to indicate that ". . . a significant breakthrough in the negotiations" made peace imminent. By election day it was clear that "peace with honor" was not at hand, but it seemed to matter little to American voters who gave Nixon a landslide victory.

Buoyed by the magnitude of his re-election triumph, Nixon pushed for the settlement of the war. Having established "Operation Enhance" to build up South Vietnam's military strength before the expected truce, Washington used threats of reduction in this aid to pressure Thieu to accept the agreement. Nixon also advised Thieu in a secret letter that in return for his cooperation he had Nixon's assurance that the United States "will respond with full force should the settlement be violated by North Vietnam."

The Christmas Bombings   Post-election discussions with the North Vietnamese to obtain a new cease-fire agreement did not go well. When the chief North Vietnamese negotiator at Paris announced on December 14 that he was returning to Hanoi for several weeks to study the situation, Nixon felt betrayed by North Vietnam's "perfidy." Four days later the President ordered "Operation Linebacker II," a round-the-clock bombing of Hanoi, Haiphong and other targets in the North to force the Communists into "serious negotiations." In the next twelve days American planes dumped over 36,000 tons of explosives on North Vietnam — an amount equal to ten times the total tonnage between 1969 and 1971. The "Christmas bombings" aroused bitter international and domestic protests, especially after the destruction of the largest hospital in Hanoi. It appeared to some that Nixon was trying to "bomb North Vietnam back into the Stone Age," as Air Force General Curtis LeMay had once suggested.

A Peace Agreement, January 1973   When Hanoi on December 29, 1972 expressed a willingness to resume negotiations on the "highest level," Nixon called off the bombing. The way was now clear for discussions that produced on January 27, 1973 a cease-fire in Vietnam. The United States pledged to end all its military activities against North Vietnam and agreed not to continue "its military involvement or intervene in the internal affairs of South Vietnam. . . ." In addition, Washington promised to withdraw all its military forces within sixty days and close down its bases. Prisoners of war were to be released by both sides within the sixty day period. The agreement also provided that "the reunification of Vietnam shall be carried out step by step through peaceful means on the basis of discussion and agreement between North and South. . . ." Thus Nixon extricated the United States from the war without turning South Vietnam directly over to the Communists and without abandoning American prisoners of war. The truce terms satisfied his definition of "peace with honor."

But the ink was barely dry on the peace documents when the two sides began to maneuver for advantage. Thieu had no intention of cooperating with Hanoi as long as he could count on American economic aid, and as long as the Communists were intent on unifying Vietnam under their control. By late 1973 bloody fighting had broken out in South Vietnam.

Moreover, the January truce did not apply to Cambodia where the United States continued to bomb Communist bases and supply lines. After Nixon vetoed a Congressional bill that prohibited the use of funds for further war in Cambodia, a compromise was worked out that finally terminated the bombing in August 1973. Within two years the Communists toppled the pro-western Cambodian government.

As the Nixon administration became paralyzed by the Watergate investigations it became difficult to persuade Congress to furnish funds to South Vietnam. But American civilian advisers remained in Saigon, and Congress reluctantly voted economic aid to a beleaguered former ally. After Nixon's resignation in August 1974, the new President, Gerald Ford, tried to bolster the tottering South Vietnamese with more last minute aid. Congress and the American people, however, had had enough, and South Vietnam was left to go it alone. To many Americans the lesson was clear — never again get involved in the Vietnam quagmire nor in a civil war in Asia.

In March and April 1975, as South Vietnamese resistance collapsed, Americans remaining in Vietnam and thousands of Vietnamese fled in undignified haste by air and by sea. On April 29, 1975 the victorious Communists entered Saigon. The Vietnam War, the longest of all American wars had ended. The United States had expended human and material resources on a lavish scale (pp. 137-8) without achieving victory.

AFTER VIETNAM

The Dominoes Do Not Fall   In the aftermath of the tragedy in Vietnam the so-called "dominoes" in Southeast Asia (Thailand, Malaysia, Singapore, Indonesia, and the Philippines) that, according to a generation of America's leaders, would fall to Communism if the United States abandoned South Vietnam, not only remained stable but grew stronger. By 1977 each of these nations enjoyed a growth rate of better than six percent and a prosperous trade with the United States. That the domino theory never had applied to Southeast Asia appeared clear and logical to a new generation.

A Crumbled Monolith   Ironically, the Communist nations (China, Vietnam, and Cambodia), began to quarrel among themselves. Within five years of the American withdrawal from Vietnam, the latter's invasion of Cambodia shattered the illusion that commitment to an international ideology took precedence over national interest and advantage. The spectacle of Communist Vietnam, supported by the Soviet Union, invading Communist Cambodia, supported by the People's Republic of China, put to rest any lingering faith in the assumption that Moscow directed and totally controlled a unified international Communist conspiracy. During his February 1979 visit to the United States Vice Premier Teng Hsiao-ping (Deng Xiaoping) of Red China verified the deep antagonism between the two Communist powers by warning the American people of the threat of the Soviet Union's hegemony aspirations. When the People's Republic of China invaded Vietnam "to punish" her for the invasion of Cambodia, the free world watched in fascination and concern. The disintegration of monolithic Communism did not end international tension.

Removing The Bamboo Curtain   Teng's trip to the United States had followed President Carter's dramatic announcement in late December 1978 that the United States was recognizing as of January 1, 1979 the People's Republic of China and establishing full diplomatic relations. At the same time Carter notified the Republic of China (Taiwan) that, according to the provision of the Mutual Defense Treaty of 1954 between the United States and Taiwan, the United States was giving notice of the abrogation of that treaty effective January 1, 1980. The two Chinese parties were to resolve the eventual relationship between Taiwan and mainland China. Although Senator Barry Goldwater and China Lobby veterans denounced Carter's action as a betrayal of a faithful ally and as an unconstitutional usurpation of power by the President, public opinion in general supported the President. The business community found the appeal of trade with China irresistible, while others were attracted to the opportunity to "play China off against Russia."

Comparative Military Expenditures (in billions of current dollars)				
Year (ending June 30)	NATO countries	Warsaw Pact countries	United States only	U.S.% world total
1966	91	62	55.9	35%
1968	110	73	79.4	37%
1969	112	79	80.2	35%
1970	111	85	79.3	32%
1971	111	92	76.8	29%
1972	117	98	77.4	29%
1973	121	108	75.1	27%
1974	135	122	78.6	26%
1975	145	136	86.8	25%

SALT II   The United States and the Soviet Union in SALT I in 1972 curtailed an expensive competition in defensive nuclear missiles and in land-based and submarine offensive ICBM launchers. With each nation interested in further restraints on the weapons of terror without jeopardizing its own security, negotiations continued during the next six years for a new treaty. By the end of 1978 SALT II had taken shape as a basic agreement to remain in force through 1985, but the negotiations snagged over specific details of sublimits. Each nation initially would be limited to an equal total number of 2400 strategic delivery vehicles, a number that would be reduced to 2250 by 1985. In addition, SALT II would establish sublimits on launchers of land based and submarine based ICBM's equipped with multiple independently targetable warheads (MIRV's), and on airplanes equipped for long-range cruise missiles. As the year ended the Carter administration faced growing discomfort in many quarters that SALT II might be too advantageous to the Soviets. Critics pointed to the relative decline in military expenditures by the United States (see table above) as evidence of a dangerous trend. Détente seemed to have arrived at a crossroads, but the Cold War had long since ended.

Chapter Five

Prosperity and Its Limits

"Practical men, who believe themselves to be quite exempt from any intellectual influences, are usually the slaves of some defunct economist."

—John Maynard Keynes,
The General Theory of
Employment Interest
and Money

In the last months of 1945, first a trickle and then a flood of troop ships docked in American ports from New York and Baltimore to San Francisco and Seattle, depositing thousands of soldiers daily at discharge centers. The soldiers filled out forms, and suddenly changed back into civilians, they headed home on the first train they could find. These men and women —within a year after Hiroshima the size of the armed forces fell from 12 to 3 million— returned to the richest and most powerful economic state in the history of civilization.

This American horn of plenty contrasted dramatically with the rest of the world, including other advanced industrial countries whose economies had been crippled by wartime devastation. The war had cut the Soviet Union's productive capacity by 40 percent. Germany and Japan's steel industries had been reduced to rubble. Many Europeans lived on fewer than 1500 calories a day, and starvation was epidemic in Asia. Even in 1947, with European industrial reconstruction well under way, the United States produced 57 percent of the world's steel, 43 percent of its electricity, and 62 percent of its oil.

During the depression of the 1930's the Roosevelt administration's New Deal policies, such as social security payments, farm price supports, a minimum wage, and rural electrification, had supported the concept that the federal government had some responsibility for the material welfare of individuals. Federal attempts to stimulate private investment and consumption, from the ill-fated National Industrial Recovery Act to work-relief programs such as the Works Progress Administration, bolstered the morale of the unemployed and anticipated the role of government in economic growth after World War II. But the New Deal failed to bring general prosperity or get rid of high unemployment rates: in 1941, almost 10 percent of the labor force was still out of work.

Federal demand for military equipment and supplies and the contracts the government made with private corporations to obtain them, more than New Deal policies, ended the Great Depression. The steel industry, which produced an average of 22 million tons a year between 1931 and 1935, expanded its production to 90 million tons by 1944. The Kaiser shipyards in Oakland, California geared to turn out a fully-outfitted warship daily at the height of the war. The gross national product — the total dollar value of goods and services produced in a given year — climbed from $99.7 billion in 1940 to over $210 billion in 1945.

The cost of fighting the war forced sharp upward revisions of the income tax; but even with higher taxes government expenditures far exceeded tax income. Between 1938 and 1944 federal taxes rose from $7 to $40 billion — but during the same period federal expenses jumped from $8 to $101 billion. Consequently, the American government turned towards vigorous deficit financing after 1941, a policy that Franklin Roosevelt and his advisers had used most reluctantly as a means of stimulating the economy during the 1930's. The United States issued short- and long-term bonds on its credit, in other words, borrowed from individuals and businesses, to make up the difference between tax receipts and total expenses. Because of deficit financing, the country's national debt rose to about $280 billion by the end of the war, nearly six times what it had been at the time of Pearl Harbor. But instead of bankrupting or destabilizing the United States, deficit spending underwrote business and consumer prosperity.

As public and private demand for manufactured goods increased in the early 1940's, military service siphoned millions of workers out of the labor market. Suddenly, especially in occupations that required special skills or technical knowledge, the labor surplus of the Great Depression turned into a severe labor shortage. Many economists consider a low four to five percent unemployment rate a sign of a healthy and prosperous economy. In 1933, a quarter of the labor force was out of work. By 1943, however, the unemployment rate had dropped to just over one percent, proof of frantic wartime recruitment of labor that also helped to assist the widespread entry of women and blacks into industrial jobs. Wages and salaries increased; most workers could count on overtime pay if they wanted to work more than 40 hours a week. Businesses enjoyed rising profits. Because of pressure to produce larger quantities of goods more speedily, factories tried to introduce more efficient managerial methods, assembly techniques, and machinery.

In peacetime prosperity, businesses ordinarily direct their higher profits towards capital purchases — new and more equipment, offices, factories, and the like. Families take pay checks to buy consumer goods that they want and possibly could not earlier afford. During the 1930's businesses put off expansion or replacement of their plants and machinery because of declining sales and the precariousness of the future. In the same way, families with lower incomes "made do" with old appliances, automobiles, and housing. But in the early 1940's, American resources, as plentiful as they were, had limits; and until victory, production of military necessities came first. Businesses channeled resources towards tanks and artillery instead of goods such as refrigerators and houses. Civilians suddenly with the money to buy products they had foregone during the depression often ran up against shortages and rationing. Gasoline and meat became precious commodities; in 1943 and 1944 less than a thousand passenger cars were manufactured for domestic use. Nonetheless, the jobs and profits of World War II meant that more Americans ate better, wore finer clothing, and had more money for recreation than they had in the 1930's.

Since a large portion of the war income of businesses and families could not be spent on goods they needed, they increased their savings — in the form of bank accounts, payroll savings bonds, and other government securities. These savings created a reservoir of purchasing power while helping to pay for war costs. At the end of the war, these savings together with pent-up capital and consumer demand stimulated peacetime prosperity.

RECONVERSION AND INFLATION

Prosperity and Pessimism   In 1945, the United States enjoyed an abundance of resources — food, energy, industrial plant, and trained workers — unmatched in the world. The war had reactivated the American economy instead of leaving a trail of economic wreckage. Seemingly unlimited reserves of oil and coal made fuel for industry, transportation, and heating extremely cheap. Industries such as aviation and electronics were still in their infancy.

Nonetheless, most business and union leaders, government officials, and economists were pessimistic about the immediate economic future. Conventional wisdom held that the Great Depression would return in force as the federal government cancelled war contracts and millions of ex-soldiers looked for jobs at the same time workers in defense industries were laid off. In August 1945, the Office of War Mobilization and Reconversion forecast unemployment as high as eight million by the following spring. The fresh memory of the 1930's obscured the more serious problem of the post-war years — inflation that grew out of deregulation of prices and the pressure of private demand for goods in short supply.

The Employment Act Laissez-faire, the belief that government should not regulate, control, subsidize, or interfere with private enterprise, has been on the wane in the United States since the time of the Civil War, even though the ideal of "free enterprise" continues to attract many members of the business community, especially at moments when government intervention works against their interests. In 1945, the expansion of federal power and the multiplication of government controls over the previous 12 years made many Republican leaders anxious to reduce the economic "regimentation" of the New Deal and war years. President Truman and his advisers, on the other hand, sought legislation to use the government's fiscal powers (its ability to raise funds through taxation or borrowing and its ability to reallocate and redistribute wealth as it buys goods or makes welfare payments) and monetary powers (its ability to regulate the amount of currency and credit) to try to prevent economic downswings.

Even, "free enterprise" Republicans in Congress, worried at the prospect of post-war depression and conceding that federal operations had great impact on private investment and consumption, supported a compromise Employment Act. Passed in February 1946, this act extended the government's economic responsibility *in behalf of* the private sector. According to the act,

> The Congress hereby declares that it is the continuing policy and responsibility of the federal government to use all practicable means consistent with its needs and obligations. . . in a manner calculated to foster and promote free competitive enterprise and the general welfare, conditions under which there will be afforded useful employment opportunities. . . and to promote maximum employment, production, and purchasing power.

The Employment Act stated goals rather than policy. But it made explicit the proposition that the federal government should monitor economic conditions and foster economic growth to promote, if not guarantee, the welfare of citizens in a capitalistic society. The Employment Act made the President the chief economic manager of the nation, advised by a three-person Council of Economic Advisers, obliged to submit an annual Economic Report to Congress describing the current state of the economy and making appropriate recommendations for the future. Also, the act confirmed the economic activity of the New Deal and implied that the Keynesian economics developed at Cambridge University in the 1920's and 1930's was valid.

Keynesian Economics   John Maynard Keynes, a British economist, became a prominent economic voice in Great Britain after his brilliant and prophetic opposition to the harshness of the Treaty of Versailles. Keynes, turning laissez-faire upside down and setting up a framework for government-led capitalism, believed that the fiscal and monetary instruments that a government holds gives it the power to counteract sharp downward cycles in the private sector of the economy. This viewpoint attacked the prevailing assumption of Keynes' generation — that capitalism, because of competition and self-interest, had a natural tendency to correct market imbalances.

According to Keynes, capitalism was not self-regulating. Supply and demand, prices and wages, savings and investment, he said, did not all move towards levels that benefited the largest number of buyers and sellers, workers and consumers, families and businesses. Keynesian theory dealt with economic problems stemming from surpluses, deflation and high unemployment.

Keynes maintained that during depressions private investment might not take place even when capital funds could be borrowed at very low interest rates. Declining consumer demand could reduce profits or profit expectations to a point where investor ability and willingness to buy new or more equipment would virtually dry up. Thus, said Keynes, both private investment and business activity could fall towards zero and not be able to revive themselves.

Keynes believed that the level of consumer spending determined the inclination of private investors to finance new capital projects. Likewise, consumer spending depended on the employment rate and security of workers who used their incomes to purchase what investors produced. When workers were laid off or frightened of the future, Keynes went on, profits would decline, resulting in more lay-offs and possible consumer panic.

In such an economic climate the Keynesian solution was government expenditure to create jobs, to rekindle consumer demand and private production, and to stimulate greater private investment. However, since government tax revenues decreased in periods of rising unemployment and taxation tends to lower consumer purchasing power, Keynes advised tax cuts, borrowing and deficit spending to counteract depressions. Since the government had the legal right to tax and thus collect revenue to pay off these obligations at a later time, he felt this system of deficit spending did not endanger the well-being of the government.

President Roosevelt distrusted Keynesian economics; the first dramatic use of deficit spending came after Pearl Harbor. Although the Employment Act signaled a movement towards the Keynesian system, the "new economics" only entered the White House economic orthodoxy with the Kennedy administration in 1961. Before Kennedy, presidents used deficit finance skeptically for political and humanitarian reasons; by the 1960's presidents regarded it as an attractive economic policy.

The Problem of Inflation   In early 1946, the high unemployment rate that had worried President Harry Truman and Congress failed to materialize. Instead, prices began rising suddenly when accumulated savings and a backlog of private demand for goods pushed spending far past national production capacity. The wartime Office of Price Administration, with its ration coupons, rent controls, profit restrictions, and wage and price ceilings, had become unpopular among buyers and sellers alike — despite its effectiveness in stabilizing prices. Manufacturers and farmers, straitjacketed by price controls, wanted to exploit a seller's market. Consumers were ready to pay high prices for goods that had been restricted or unavailable during the war.

Congress extended the OPA for a year in June 1945. But after the defeat of Japan in August, influential Congressmen, with Republican Senator Robert Taft leading the attack, started pushing to dismantle all price controls. President Truman, on the other hand, worried by inflation, wanted Congress to extend the OPA to 1947, and in his January 1946 State of the Union message called inflation "our greatest immediate problem."

In June 1946, however, a politically sensitive Congress, worried by the upcoming mid-term elections, dropped most OPA controls. Truman, trying to force Congress to pass a stronger anti-inflation law, responded by vetoing the bill. Almost immediately, the relative price stability of the previous three years vanished.

In the season of the first post-war elections, meat prices skyrocketed, an automobile purchase meant a long waiting-list or commonly a bribe, and housing, often hastily and badly built, was expensive or inadequate. An average annual inflation rate of over 18 percent on top of public irritation over wartime regulation helped to give the Republicans control of both houses of Congress for the first time since 1930 in November 1946.

Labor Reacts   Post-war inflation, causing the rapid diminution of the wage earner's buying power, brought with it union discontent and spectacular strikes. In the last months of 1945, a wage dispute between the United Auto Workers and General Motors ended after workers received an 18 1/2 cent hourly wage increase, an agreement that set a pattern for the rest of American industry.

But in April 1946, John L. Lewis led 400,000 coal miners on strike, demanding not only 18 1/2 cents more an hour but also 10 cents on each ton of coal mined to go into a miners' pension fund. Since at that time coal was the country's principal source of energy, the strike had quick and harsh impact on the steel industry, transportation, and the production of electricity. Just as White House mediation settled this crisis in late May, a continental railroad strike loomed. The strike was the greatest threat to freight movements since the Pullman strike of 1894.

With the rail system near paralysis and anti-union pressure rising in Congress, the President went on radio on May 24. "Pearl Harbor," he said, "was the result of action by a foreign enemy. The crisis tonight is caused by a group of men within our own country who place their private interests above the interests of their country."

The next day, Truman addressed a special session of Congress and asked for what amounted to a conscription of railroad workers and a federal takeover of the industry. Railroad leaders surrendered. The threat of federal action ended the strike just three minutes before the President delivered his speech. The Democratic House of Representatives, however, supported the President's proposal 306-13.

The Taft-Hartley Act   Robert Taft, who blocked consideration of the railroad takeover and a draft of strikers in the Senate, saying that the proposal violated "every principle of American jurisprudence," was not a friend of labor. Son of President William Howard Taft, an articulate opponent of the New Deal and federal intervention in the economy, the Ohioan became Majority Leader of the Senate after the November elections. Joined by other Republicans when the new Congress met in January 1947, Taft set out to design a comprehensive labor bill that would modify the Wagner Act of 1935 to curb the power of organized labor and limit the government's role in labor-management relations. The final Taft-Hartley Act, passed by Congress on June 23 over presidential veto, placed limitations on the rights and conduct of the trade unions, none of them as injurious to the future of organized labor as those who called it a "slave-labor bill" maintained.

The Taft-Hartley Act outlawed the *closed shop* (in which employers could hire only union workers) but permitted the *union shop* (in which non-union employees had to join a union within 30 days if the majority of workers in a company voted for it). It forbade "unfair labor practices," including featherbedding (in which unions compelled employers to pay for jobs that had actually been eliminated by automation), jurisdictional strikes (arising from disputes between unions over which has the right to do a job), and union refusal to bargain with employers. The act allowed employers to sue unions for broken contracts, outlawed union contributions to political campaigns, and forbade strikes by federal employees.

Moreover, unions could not strike without giving 60-day notice of their desire to begin negotiations with employers. In 1932, the Norris-LaGuardia Act had virtually outlawed the use of the labor injunction by federal courts to prevent strikes. Now, the Taft-Hartley Act gave the National Labor Relations Board and the President the power to ask for federal court injunctions, the NLRB to prevent violations of the law and the President to restrain a union from striking for 80 days when a strike jeopardized national health or safety. In addition, Section 14(b) permitted states to outlaw union shops, resulting in a subsequent rash of state "right to work" laws.

Section 14(b) and the rebirth of the labor injunction were the most fearsome aspects of the act to unionists. Labor leaders said that the 1947 act would cancel the gains of organized labor during the New Deal. Truman's veto and subsequent Democratic efforts to repeal the law, however, reflected the increased power and political force of unions after the 1930's, even though the enactment of the Taft-Hartley Act demonstrated declining enthusiasm for the labor movement and the rising prestige of businessmen after World War II.

Rapid Growth   In the late 1940's, savings, private demand, and the export of American goods helped to prevent a post-war depression. The need to build and modernize factories, a shortage of office buildings and housing, the desire for appliances, automobiles and luxuries, a rising birthrate, and the growth of new industries created jobs and kept unemployment low. The deflation of the 1930's resulted chiefly from inadequate demand; the inflation of the late 1940's derived from private demand exceeding available goods as the United States moved from a military to civilian-oriented economy.

THE TRIUMPH OF WELFARE CAPITALISM

The Employment Act of 1946 gave Congressional sanction to active economic planning by the federal government but was only one significant step in a long trend towards *welfare capitalism* from the New Deal to the present. The movement towards a federally-managed economy has made the fiscal, monetary, and regulatory powers of the public sector the paramount forces in the economy. The government uses these powers to try to control market imbalances and economic self-interest of individuals and firms, to channel private consumption and investment toward economic growth, and to insure minimal standards of living and services for citizens. In *welfare capitalism*, government intervenes in private acquisition and production to create a more equitable climate of private ownership.

The Fair Deal   President Truman's surprising re-election in 1948, coupled with Democratic majorities again controlling both houses of Congress, seemed to provide an opportunity to extend New Deal programs when Congress met in January 1949. In his State of the Union address that year, Truman declared that "every individual has a right to expect from our government a fair deal," a phrase that he used as a clarion call for a federal re-orientation to the social programs of the 1930's. He called for change in the social security and farm programs, a higher minimum wage, repeal of the Taft-Hartley Act, the enactment of a national medical insurance plan, extension of public electrical power programs, federal aid to schools, and an increase in low-income housing.

The 1949 Congress enacted and enlarged more welfare programs than in any year since 1938. In 1949, Congress raised the minimum wage from 40 to 75 cents, and the Housing Act mandated the construction of 810,000 subsidized low-income housing units. In 1950, amendments to the Social Security Act extended coverage to more than 10 million new workers.

But Truman failed to secure repeal of the Taft-Hartley law. His administration's proposal to substitute direct farm payments for crop restrictions to protect farm income and lower food prices died because of Republican hostility to agricultural subsidies and opposition of large-scale growers who chafed at subsidy limitations. Furthermore, the American Medical Association mounted a campaign against national health insurance, and the Roman Catholic church refused to support federal aid to education unless parochial schools shared in the benefits.

Truman neither enjoyed nor generated the broad support for his programs that had buoyed Roosevelt's New Deal. Although

Congress raised the minimum wage and expanded social security coverage, his heavy-handed manner with Congress alienated many powerful lawmakers. But most of all, Truman's Fair Deal faced a rural-based coalition of anti-New Deal Republicans and southern Democrats, as well as a Congress preoccupied more with the international threat of Communist expansion and the possibility of internal subversion than with social reform.

"Creeping Socialism" In the 1950's both the Republican and Democratic parties faced considerable intra-party strain over the question of the proper degree of federal intervention in the private sector. The Republicans, badly divided between followers of Senator Taft who contended that their party had not offered a genuine alternative to Roosevelt's welfare capitalism, and moderates who cautiously endorsed the legacy of the New Deal, needed the popular General Eisenhower, Allied Commander during World War II, later head of Columbia University and NATO, to keep the "Old Guard" and progressive factions of the party on speaking terms.

Although President Eisenhower acquiesced in the idea that the federal government had some obligations to protect the economic well-being of citizens, he preferred that Washington advise and assist states, local communities, and individuals rather than expand the economic role of the federal government. Likewise, he deplored deficit financing and remained suspicious of Keynesian economics throughout his years in the White House. Along with his key economic advisers, George Humphrey, Secretary of the Treasury, and Arthur Burns, chairman of the Council of Economic Advisers, he sought to curb the expansion of the national debt by balancing the budget. He also tried to reduce the scale of federal taxes and expenditures.

Although businessmen, bankers, and corporate attorneys played critical roles in shaping economic policy during the Roosevelt and Truman administrations, the Eisenhower team supported and nourished corporate enterprise more actively than its predecessors. Secretary Humphrey, a Cleveland industrialist who kept a portrait of former Secretary of the Treasury Andrew Mellon in his office, believed that economic expansion should derive from business profits and private investment. Charles Wilson, former head of General Motors and Secretary of Defense, said, "what is good for our country is good for General Motors, and vice versa." Remarked the Democratic presidential candidate, Adlai Stevenson, in 1956, "While the New Dealers have all left Washington for the car dealers, I hasten to say that I, for one, do not believe the story that the general welfare has become a subsidiary of General Motors."

For the business leaders surrounding the President, achieving balanced budgets and reducing federal intervention in the economy remained an elusive goal. From 1933 to 1953 most Republicans had shaken their heads over expanding federal government as annual federal expenditures climbed in twenty years from about $5 to $74 billion, and as civilian employment in government grew from 600,000 to 2,400,000. But Republican unwillingness to reduce military expenditures as well as broad political pressure to retain social benefits, such as farm subsidies and social security made Republicans in power unable to lower spending or shrink basic welfare programs. The Eisenhower administration achieved a balanced budget in only three of its eight years. In 1961, the federal budget was over $81 billion.

Eisenhower found many ventures of welfare capitalism personally distasteful. In June 1953, speaking to Republican leaders in South Dakota, he said, "I believe for the past twenty years there has been a creeping socialism spreading in the United States." Asked what "creeping socialism" meant at a Washington press conference six days later, Eisenhower cited the continuing expansion of the Tennessee Valley Authority. Public criticism was sharp. Later that month, Gabriel Hauge, White House assistant for economic affairs, sent the President a memorandum urging him to drop "creeping socialism" in future speeches as too extreme a phrase. Said Hauge, the slogan had been a "hallmark of the Old Guard Republicans for years against Roosevelt."

The administration never really solved its own confusion over the degree to which the federal government should support the material welfare of its citizens. While the executive branch remained philosophically at odds with the expanded role of the government in private lives, it established the Department of Health, Education and Welfare in 1953. Yet HEW's first secretary, Oveta Culp Hobby, opposed free federal distribution of polio vaccine in 1955, calling it "socialized medicine. . . through the back door."

Unstable Economic Conditions   In 1949, the pent-up demand for consumer goods and the reservoir of savings that spurred postwar expansion began to dry up. The construction industry stagnated, and the unemployment rate rose abruptly to six percent. But this brief recession evaporated in the summer of 1950, when war broke out in Korea. Business and households, expecting war shortages, price increases, and new government controls, engaged in anticipatory buying — in other words, increased buying because of the fear of future inflation. More important, the federal government's purchases of military equipment, tripling between 1950 and

1953, began to stimulate economic growth.

But defense cutbacks in 1954, following the Korean War, curtailed demand temporarily and generated a second recession. In 1954, unemployment rose from 2.9 to 5.6 percent. Although long-term growth trends proved quite steady in the mid-1950's, a third and more severe recession hit in 1958. The unemployment rate jumped to 6.8 percent — the highest level in the United States between 1941 and 1974. Before both the 1954 and 1958 recessions, corporations geared their production to high levels of consumer spending. When buying leveled off, businessmen faced sudden increases in their inventories, forcing them to reduce production and to lay off workers. But two other things aggravated the 1958 downturn. First, the Federal Reserve, attempting to combat inflation, had raised the interest rate on short-term business loans to the highest point in 27 years — discouraging private investment and new corporate ventures. Second, the American automobile industry suddenly faced stiff competition from foreign manufacturers and imported cars.

New Directions in Industrial Production   Change in economic history usually takes place as a rising or ebbing tide rather than as a wave. Contradictory trends assert themselves simultaneously, with wide variations between single industries and the whole economy, between short-run and long-run time, and between geographic regions.

In 1960, John Kennedy, the Democratic candidate for president, could make political hay out of the aftershocks of the 1958 recession. But despite the astringent economic policies of the Eisenhower administration the gross national product — the sum total of goods and services produced in a single year — increased from $1810 per person in 1950 to $2780 per person in 1960. Total household consumption rose every year in the 1950's, with purchases of houses, automobiles, and recreational goods (from television sets to sporting equipment) expanding at an especially rapid rate. The booming advertising industry reflected a growing corporate need to manipulate and stimulate demand. In 1958, John Kenneth Galbraith, an eminent Harvard economist, categorized the United States as "the affluent society."

Corporate power and prestige grew in the 1950's. Manufacturing, retailing, and finance concentrated in fewer and larger companies. Capitalism grew less competitive. Small business operations, suffering from less efficient management and machinery, were burdened by higher per unit cost of production. Giant productive complexes — old corporations like General Motors, new corporations such as International Business Machines, financial networks such as Bank of America or Chase Manhattan, and retailing chains such as Sears or Safeway — exerted awesome power in markets. While a nostalgic sentiment for "free enterprise" remained, the limited competition of corporations, large enough so that each seller had great influence in setting prices of goods and services, made the old notion of freewheeling competition obsolete. This market structure, called *oligopoly,* differed from the days of unregulated monopoly markets. For example, General Motors competed — more through product differentiation and advertising than prices — with Ford, Chrysler, and American Motors; in the 1890's a *monopoly,* Standard Oil, had enough market power to determine singly the price of oil products throughout the nation.

Since World War II the United States has become increasingly an economy of corporations large enough to have the power to administer prices. But if the age of the small entrepreneur is dying, consumers have become more conscious of corporate responsibility for public well-being. Many concerned citizens have sought intricate government regulations over production and distribution to harness corporate titans. This consumer movement has led to the expansion of the power of old regulatory offices such as the Federal Trade Commission and has helped to create new offices such as the Environmental Protection Agency.

After World War II self-employment became less the norm than work on assembly lines or in offices within a corporate hierarchy. Workers and white-collar managers assumed more anonymous roles in gigantic companies that sometimes employed hundreds of thousands of persons. The ruthlessness and adventure of early industrialism largely vanished. These gigantic paternalistic corporations offered private pension funds, medical plans, group insurance, and adult education. But if corporate life became more benevolent, social critics, especially in the 1960's, labeled assembly line mechanical production and corporate organization as efficient at the expense of the individual's spirit.

Machines have played a progressively significant role in enterprise since the 18th century and the displacement of workers from industries because of technological improvements has been a serious labor problem for many generations. In the 1950's, however, industrial automation — the introduction of assembly systems regulated by electronic data-processing equipment (often called computers) — made it possible in many industries to convert raw materials into finished products from factory panels operated by a few technicians. New industries such as air transportation, plastics, and electronics, developed astonishing technologies with amazing speed, often stimulated by government expenditures for defense or for the space race. These new industries had lasting effects on consumer habits.

Bethlehem Steel Corporation's steel bar mill in Lackawanna, N.Y. is monitored from the mill pulpit (above), which is the mill's principal control center. Built in 1976, 10 computers guide the plant's operations. *(Photo Courtesy of Bethlehem Steel Corporation)*

The Revolution in Agriculture   After World War II, farming, the oldest enterprise of all, underwent rapid change in production and productivity because of capital development and automation. And like other small businesses, though it remained a mainstay of wishful Jeffersonian rhetoric, the family farm suffered. For more than a century agricultural technology has threatened small producers by (1) forcing farmers to buy expensive equipment to remain competitive, (2) driving farmers who could not buy equipment out of business, and (3) increasing productivity to a point where surpluses and resultant declining prices endangered small, indebted farmers with bankruptcy. After 1933, farmers became a specially protected minority with incomes supported by federal subsidies. The government calculated these subsidies from the average costs of farmers but allowed more efficient farms to receive government subsidies too. Highly mechanized farms on superior land had production costs far lower than the national average yet enjoyed benefits equal to marginal farmers. Thus, income supplements to economically secure farmers indirectly encouraged larger-scale farming.

Corporate farming expanded after 1950, organized by financial syndicates with large numbers of shareholders, highly-educated managers, and an enormous amount of specialized machines. The average size of a farm rose from 151 acres in 1930 to 374 acres in 1970. At the same time the farm population of the country declined from 25 to 5 percent. By 1972, 10 percent of the farms in the United States produced 61 percent of total output. Still, rural poverty festered — in 1972, 36 percent of farms earned less than $2500 and collectively produced 2 percent of the national food output.

The farm came to be a place of combines, corn and cotton pickers, milking machines, irrigation systems, hybrid seeds, soybeans and sorghum, hormonal feeds, selective breeding, genetic manipulation of livestock, and the widespread use of chemical fertilizers and insecticides. The research done by the Department of Agriculture, in state universities, and by private companies, such as Ralston Purina and International Harvester, has aided this more sophisticated agriculture. Agriculture in the United States has come to depend on complex processing, refrigerating, transporting, and distributing systems. It is, as well, linked to diplomatic ventures as the United States becomes ever more an exporter of commodities, especially cereal crops, to other countries.

Kennedy Keynesianism   In January 1961, the Kennedy administration came to Washington, bringing with it an impressive roll call of college professors, social scientists, and Keynesian economists. The Keynesians, of considerable force in many university departments, had smarted in the 1950's at the Eisenhower administration's chilly reception to their ideas of economic management. They now enjoyed a committed friend in the White House. Under the leadership of Walter Heller, head of the Council of Economic Advisers, the "new economics" that had troubled and angered "small government" traditionalists for more than a generation became fashionable in the federal government.

Kennedy's proposition, that federal taxes, spending, and borrowing should be managed in order to support economic growth, still startled many voters, newspaper editors, and Congressmen who were devoted, almost religiously, to maintaining balanced federal budgets and unregulated "free enterprise." After 1961, spearheaded by the research and the policy recommendations of economists such as Paul Samuelson, Alvin Hansen, and John Kenneth Galbraith, the Keynesian system developed into a new orthodoxy in Washington. Although many southern Democrats and Republicans continued to voice strong opposition to growing levels of federal spending, Congressional majorities supporting Keynesian economic management consistently outvoted them after 1963.

Anxious to "get the country moving again," Kennedy, in 1961, ten days after his inauguration, proposed heavy federal spending to lower unemployment from its 6.7 percent level and spur a stagnant gross national product. He made his Keynesian intentions clear at a Yale commencement address in June 1962, saying,

> Honest assessment plainly requires a more sophisticated view than the old and automatic cliche that deficits automatically bring inflation. . . . Borrowing can lead to overextension and collapse — but it can also lead to expansion and strength.

Kennedy led the way in trying to convince a skeptical Congress to lower taxes, allowing consumers and investors to keep more of their income. Since his administration wanted to keep federal expenditures steady through deficit financing, a tax reduction would stimulate private production and consumption.

In 1962, Congress approved higher rates of depreciation for industry, resulting in lower corporate taxes. Congress also tried to give incentives to private investment by allowing a seven percent tax credit on purchases of machinery. But it rejected an outright tax cut. In February 1964, while President Lyndon Johnson pushed for memorial passage of Kennedy's legislative proposals, Congress cut personal income taxes between 7 and 21 percent and corporate taxes by 4 percent, releasing during the next year more than $11 billion of private spending power. This helped to trigger rapid economic expansion in the middle 1960's. The greatest beneficiary of this new Keynesian policy was business. Said *Business Week*, "the lesson of 1964 is that fiscal policy needs to be used actively and steadily if balanced long-term growth is to be achieved."

The War on Poverty Between 1950 and 1960 the gross national product rose from $286 to $506 billion. By 1965, it stood at $688 billion. Even after adjustments are made for increasing prices, annual national output almost doubled in these fifteen years. But American academics, political leaders, and voters became more conscious of millions not sharing in "the affluent society." In 1960 Michael Harrington's *The Other America* riveted the attention of intellectuals and opinion makers on the conditions of life in the cellar of welfare capitalism — a world of rats, malnutrition, illiteracy and despair. According to Harrington, "the fundamental paradox of the welfare state" is that "it is built not for the desperate, but for those who are already capable of helping themselves. . . . The poor get less out of the welfare state than any group in America." While most direct income support went to the poor, others gained much more through lucrative public contracts and government jobs.

In 1964, the Johnson administration, concerned about poverty amidst plenty, attempted to reduce structural unemployment — a condition caused not by fluctuations in the business cycle but by the absence of marketable labor skills in certain individuals. The mainstay of this "war on poverty" was the Economic Opportunity Act, passed in August 1964. When he signed the bill, Lyndon Johnson said, "for the first time in all the history of the human race, a great nation is able to make and is willing to make a commitment to eradicate poverty among its people."

The Office of Economic Opportunity, under the direction of Sargent Shriver, who had been the director of the successful Peace Corps during the Kennedy Administration, oversaw a complex enterprise that included "community action" programs, training centers for unemployed youth, urban and rural poverty assistance teams, loans to acquire land for family farms, and loans to industries in poor areas for hiring and training the perennially unemployed.

Despite annual appropriations of up to $1.5 billion in the middle 1960's, the OEO experienced declining popularity among Congressmen and the public. OEO agencies were attacked for spending funds sloppily. Many whites thought too much money was being spent on blacks. Some believed that federal money was being used in black neighborhoods to organize anti-white groups and fight "city hall." After 1967, as the war in Vietnam absorbed a greater share of federal funds, OEO encountered considerable resistance in getting appropriations. In December 1971, President Richard Nixon vetoed a new $6 billion anti-poverty bill to extend OEO and set up a broad child development and day-care program. The Senate failed to override the veto, 51-36, seven votes short of the necessary two-thirds majority. Thus began the scrapping of OEO. By early 1973, the "war on poverty" had faded into oblivion.

Medicare   Johnson's health care legislation fared better. Back in 1945, Harry Truman had sought in vain a system of health insurance to pay for hospital and nursing costs. In 1960, Congress began making grants to states to help pay for the medical expenses of old people with low incomes. But in July 1965, Congress passed an act, popularly called Medicare, to provide compulsory health insurance under the Social Security program to allow the elderly to pay only a small fee for each period of hospitalization. The new law also created a low-cost voluntary insurance program to help pay for doctors' fees. Medicare was to be paid for out of social security taxes. When President Johnson flew to Independence, Missouri to sign the bill with former President Truman, who had urged such a bill twenty years earlier, the two old New Dealers beamed as they posed for the news cameras. The American Medical Association, which had predicted medical anarchy if the act passed, did not support a threatened doctors' boycott. Eventually 95 percent of the medical profession joined the program. By the middle 1960's the position that the federal government had no responsibility for the economic and physical well-being of its citizens had been driven to the outer fringes of American politics.

THE SOURCES OF ECONOMIC GROWTH

In 1954, David Potter, a Yale historian, wrote *People of Plenty,* a book pinpointing the abundance of resources as the chief shaping force of the American character. Because of plenty, Potter said, class conflict over the equitable division of scarce resources, though it had fueled socialist movements in other parts of the world, had little meaning in the American mind. According to Potter,

> the very meaning of the term 'equality' reflects this influence. ... A European, advocating equality, might very well mean that all men should occupy positions that are roughly on the same level in wealth, power or enviability. But the American, with his emphasis on equality of opportunity, has never conceived of it in this sense.

Potter, however, was not an uncritical enthusiast of material growth and equality of opportunity: he felt that the American emphasis on upward mobility and expanding wealth exacted a psychological price by alienating the individual from his community and his past. Four years later, in his widely read *The Affluent Society,* John Kenneth Galbraith added that the quest for private wealth resulted in the underallocation of resources for public goods and services, such as mass-transit systems and education.

Despite such academic warnings, most Americans after World War II were enchanted by the panorama of products that stretched before them in department stores, showrooms, and supermarkets. But this materialism that went hand-in-hand with the quick upward thrust of the economy at mid-century did not insure happiness. The Affluent Society was also called the era of The Rat Race and The Lonely Crowd.

Construction   In the ten years after World War I, most large cities became metropolitan, in other words, cities around which satellite towns and villages clustered; many formerly independent towns were absorbed into city centers and became neighborhoods. But after a construction boom from 1922 to 1928, the building industry stagnated for almost twenty years.

The impact of post-World War II construction was enormous. In densely settled areas cities merged into "corridors" or "chains" of urban centers, industrial complexes, and suburban towns that stretched over whole regions, such as from Portsmouth, New Hampshire to Richmond, Virginia, or from Santa Barbara to San Diego, California. New urban skylines appeared. Countryside and city blurred as developers and corporations bought open land for housing and commercial use; the center of gravity of cities and town shifted away from downtowns and main streets to suburban satellites.

After 1945 the marriage and birth rate rose rapidly, and between 1940 and 1960 the American population increased from about 130 to 180 million, in an era of negligible immigration. The cherished dream of millions of young families with rising incomes to live in single-family houses resulted in the rapid building of suburban developments and housing within commuting distance of downtown areas. Suburbia had once been the province of the wealthy; now, the movement from city centers turned into a mass migration. It is estimated that by 1960, 50 million citizens, or almost a third of the nation lived in suburbia. In 1971, 40 percent of the occupied housing in the United States had been built during the previous twenty years.

A whole literature has grown up around this culture of suburbia, much of it full of diatribes against its conformity and intellectual suffocation. However, it is clear that most white, upwardly mobile Americans found suburbia's tranquility, amenities, pleasing appearance, and superior schools — as well as its racial homogeneity — to their taste. But as middle class families, including blue-collar workers enjoying wages high enough to let them leave row houses and apartments, started moving towards urban peripheries, residential construction stagnated or declined in many central city neighborhoods. The unlikelihood of profits in urban residential building discouraged new investment, and much city housing fell into disrepair. Eight of the nation's ten largest cities had fewer people in 1960 than in 1950.

As the middle class left the city, southern blacks and Puerto Rican immigrants, lured to industrial cities by the promise of well-paying factory jobs, moved into these rundown neighborhoods. But the good jobs they anticipated were harder and harder to find: the trend toward automated, highly technical production and towards consumer service jobs demanded more advanced skills and education than these migrants to the city could offer.

Inner city property values declined, and city revenues, tied to taxes on property, were threatened. Meanwhile, because unemployment in most large cities rose, more residents depended on municipal services that cities had greater difficulty funding. The only urban construction that thrived was building for corporate and institutional offices, making many downtowns vibrant commercial centers by day and deserted "ghost towns" at night. Business construction boomed, as factories and plants replaced facilities that were technologically obsolete or too small to meet consumer demand. But as with housing, more enterprise moved toward the edges of cities. Many corporations built new facilities in the suburbs. In retailing, downtowns gradually lost the supremacy they had over surrounding areas; city satellites and suburbs grew more economically independent and self-sufficient.

While downtowns sported new steel-and-glass offices to complement older masonry "skyscrapers" of the 1920's and 1930's, retailers established more "branches" in new suburban areas. The city department store and the main street proprietor competed with the shopping centers, a complex of stores with parking lot for shoppers' automobiles. Retailers in shopping centers, often connected to regional and national chains, could undersell small proprietors while offering greater selections of products.

The new residents of suburban areas needed publicly-funded schools, sewer and water systems, and recreational facilities. But the most significant public building of the 1950's and 1960's was for roads and highways. Suburbia depended on the independent movement that automobiles allowed. In the absence of a "walking neighborhood" or convenient public transit, even buying a quart of milk or a visit to the local library required private transportation. Highways, acting as arteries of the metropolis, became the link between office buildings in the central city and houses in suburban towns.

TABLE I: Construction 1927-1977			
(figures adjusted for changes in dollar value to the level of purchasing power 1957-1959, in billions of dollars)			
Year	Total Construction	Private Construction	Public Contruction	Public Construction as a Percent of Total
1927	33.2	27.5	5.7	17.1
1937	19.1	11.5	7.6	39.8
1947	29.5	24.6	4.9	16.6
1957	49.9	35.8	14.1	28.3
1967	61.1	41.0	20.1	32.9
1977	81.7	63.8	17.9	21.9

Automobiles   In the 1950's railroads, fifty years earlier the most powerful industry in the nation, carried less than 50 percent of intercity freight traffic in the United States. Except for commuter lines, ever less able to support themselves without public assistance, railroads became insignificant in passenger travel. This victory of the automobile and highway began with Henry Ford's assembly line in 1909 and climaxed with the Federal Highway Act of 1956.

Congress financed federal highways as early as 1921. The WPA built over 650,000 miles of highways, roads, and streets. But in 1955, President Eisenhower, stressing defense advantages, proposed a federally-funded highway building program that amounted to an executive imprimatur on the future leadership of automobiles and trucks in American transportation. Super-highways, connecting all major cities of the country, would be financed by special taxes on gasoline and diesel fuel. The following year, in 1956, Congress approved the Federal Highway Act, the largest public works act ever passed, appropriating $32 billion for 41,000 miles of limited-access interstate highways to be built over the next 13 years.

In 1955, *Time* magazine named H. H. Curtice, head of General

Motors corporation, "man of the year." It had been a record year for the automobile industry — 7.9 million new passenger cars were sold — and more than half of them had been made by General Motors. GM, with 514,000 employees and 119 plants, was the largest manufacturing corporation in the world. *Time* called the automobile the "quintessential" American product.

Not surprising. Between 1945 and 1955 American automobile registrations jumped from 26 to 52 million. By 1976, the figure stood at 110 million. In post-war America more than 25 percent of jobs in the labor force stemmed directly or indirectly from automobile manufacture. Although many citizens winced at hearing the Secretary of Defense in 1953 link the well-being of General Motors and the nation, the economic health of the nation was bound to the industry then and now. A collapse of the automobile industry would generate a catastrophic depression.

The automotive corporations together determined the well-being of fields as separate as steel, rubber, radio, and plastics. No single industry, however, profited more from the car culture than petroleum. Household expenditures for gasoline rose from $5.4 billion in 1950 to $22.2 billion in 1970 — on account of increasing registrations and larger, more powerful engines. But for consumers, the price of gasoline remained remarkably low until the four-fold increase of imported oil prices and short-term energy shortages of 1973 and 1974. Although automobiles have been denounced in the last 15 years as a major cause of urban decay and environmental damage, their popularity remains undiminished on account of their convenience and their importance as status symbols.

New Technologies   Construction and transportation, significant in post-war economic expansion, were "old" industries. In the 1940's and 1950's a welter of "new" industries grew out of inventions and technological refinements. Business machines that stored, retrieved and processed information had a profound impact on managing industrial production and systemizing record-keeping. As with many new technologies, intense government research during World War II assisted computer development. In 1946, a computer was introduced for use in nuclear physics calculations a thousand times faster than its predecessors and able to do in two hours the estimated work of a hundred engineers for one year. In 1954, about 20 computers were shipped to commercial customers; ten years later, more than 4,500 were shipped, and some 25,000 were in use. International Business Machines, a small company before 1950, had grown into the fifth largest corporation in the country by 1970.

Great advances took place in aviation. In 1945, there were 421 planes in commercial use in the United States. In 1970, there were 2,437 in use. In the same twenty-five years airline revenues climbed from $214 million to $7.2 billion. After Boeing Aircraft's introduction of commercial jet transport in 1958, interregional and transatlantic travel times were halved. In 1971, more than 3 million Americans traveled to Europe on vacation — almost all of them in jet aircraft. The ocean liner, before 1939 the single mode of travel between the hemispheres, became an anachronism in transportation.

There was, as well, a boom in petrochemicals and plastics. Chemical companies such as Dupont, Monsanto, and Dow developed and synthesized organic chemicals to produce a family of materials of remarkable versatility and cheapness. The creation of these laboratory-made "synthetics" introduced scores of lightweight, durable, resilient fibers and substances, such as nylon and fiberglas, both introduced in 1938. In the 1940's and 1950's such materials replaced more expensive commodities in goods as different as clothing, containers, and furniture.

New electrical appliances, such as dishwashers, washing and drying machines, and air conditioners, came into widespread use, freeing families from the drudgery of much household labor and making living conditions more comfortable. Factory prepared foods, juices, vegetables, meats, and cereals alike, elaborately packaged and often frozen, made household cooking faster and easier. In 1955, frozen foods was a $2 billion industry with more than 2,000 brands on the market. By 1967, the value of processed food manufactures totaled $53 billion. More than half the products in a supermarket today did not exist before World War II.

But no single technology developed after 1945 had as much social and cultural impact as television. In 1946, 8,000 households owned television sets. In 1976, more than 69 million did — more than 97 percent of American households. In 1949, $58 million was spent on television advertising; by 1976, the figure had grown to over $6.7 billion. After World War II, television grew into the principal instrument of national communication, with transforming impact on American politics, consumption, entertainment, and use of leisure time. Television demonstrated its political power in the exposure of Senator Joseph McCarthy in 1954, the Kennedy-Nixon debates in 1960, and the televised war in Vietnam in the late 1960's. Without television Davey Crocket, Elvis Presley, the Beatles, and the Superbowl would not have become part of the pop culture of American life.

Public Spending   In 1950, total government expenditures added up to $70 billion. By 1970, the figure had risen to $333 billion. Since during the same twenty years the gross national product climbed from $212 to $982 billion, government expenditure remained a relatively constant fraction of total American output. But the impact of public spending on the expansion of private industry and consumption was great. Not only did government — federal, state, and local — purchase goods, such as school buildings, missiles, typewriters, and interstate highways. In 1977, it employed 15.4 million civilians out of a total labor force of 82 million as well as another 2 million on active military duty. The salaries and wages of diplomats, soybean inspectors, and policemen among other millions added up to a substantial share of total consumer buying power. Governments supplemented incomes through social security, unemployment, veterans', and farmers' benefits, further add to the ability of citizens to consume. Between 1948 and 1968, for example, social security benefits rose from $2.6 to $38.1 billion; by 1975, that figure had increased to $78.4 billion.

THE COUNTERCULTURAL ATTACK

The birth rate in the United States, about 19 per thousand in 1935 and 20 in 1945, rose sharply in the late 1940's and 1950's to about 25 per thousand before it returned to rates below 20 per thousand after 1965. By 1975, it had dropped to 14.8 per thousand. This "baby boom" from about 1945 to 1960 helped to stimulate consumer demand for articles from diapers to schools and created a post-war generation that grew up in suburbs that took prosperity and economic growth for granted.

These children, born into an era of unprecedented economic growth and sheltered from having to earn a living, never seriously questioned the future of material expansion. As they grew older, these middle-class youth, unable to comprehend or sympathize with the economic uncertainty their parents had known in the Great Depression, often reacted with contempt to their parents' materialism, quest for security, and extraverted conformity. The "baby boom," Tom Wolfe wrote, knew not depression and war but "only the emotional surge of the great payoff."

The victory over McCarthyism after 1954 enhanced the prestige of liberal dissent in the late 1950's. In the early 1960's, when the "baby boom" began to reach college age, students at some of the nation's most exclusive colleges worked at the registration of black voters in Southern states. These idealistic students, coming in direct contact with overt racial discrimination and bigotry for the first time, discovered a United States that contradicted their comfortable childhoods. There seemed to be another country, a land less just than the one they had read about in suburban schools. These young activists returned to campuses with grim tales of open racism, political corruption, and economic stratification beyond academia. By 1962, the year the radical Students for a Democratic Society was founded, politicized students felt that abused minorities and the working class should have much more political and economic power, and a few recommended violent revolution to achieve it.

Outright campus turmoil began at the University of California at Berkeley in the autumn of 1964. After the Oakland *Tribune* protested student picketing against its alleged racial discrimination, charging that the picketing had been organized on university property, the Berkeley administration forbade student organizations to use campus property to distribute leaflets and solicit members. The ensuing Free Speech Movement demonstrations electrified television audiences across the country, underscoring the political activism that was growing in colleges from Berkeley to Ann Arbor to Cambridge.

The escalation of the Vietnam war in 1965 galvanized much more widespread student dissent. At Vietnam Day demonstrations on campuses across the country that October, less radical students repelled by the war or frightened of military service joined the protests. Campus anti-war turmoil continued through the 1960's, reaching its most violent and convulsive point following the American invasion of Cambodia in 1970 and the National Guard's shooting of students at Kent State University in Ohio. But during the decade political protest deferred to a broader cultural attack from a more exotic radicalism spreading from the San Francisco Bay Area across the continent after 1966.

To describe this phenomenon, Theodore Roszak, a social historian, coined the term *counter culture*. For Roszak, youth were revolting against their parents' "frozen posture of befuddled docility" and the social "ideal men usually have in mind when they speak of modernizing, up-dating, rationalizing, planning." Said Roszak, "Drunken and incensed, the centaurs burst in upon the civilized festivities that are in progress."

The counter culture was fascinated by the mystical and the occult. Its vision of a future free of rules and social obligations gave it a false sense of moral superiority. Wide use of marijuana and hallucinogenic drugs discredited firm reality. As youth glorified the irrational, logic and order seemed to be enemies rather than tools of understanding. "Reason though dead," said the critic Leslie Fielder, "holds us with an embrace that looks like a lover's embrace but turns out to be rigor mortis."

The counter culture's freedom in sex, dress, and behavior ultimately had more profound impact on American society than campus uprisings over race, constitutional rights, or war. The youth rebels of the 1960's did not budge the Pentagon or IBM; instead, they initiated a revolution of manners. The consensus of the 1970's, that individuals generally have the right to do as they wish, was the counter culture's most potent legacy. Older social norms, such as what constituted pornography and obscenity, were fragmented, often leaving the judiciary to decide the limits of personal freedom by court decree.

Although many rebellious youth in the 1960's idealized a culture of poverty, they were almost exclusively the beneficiaries of middle-class prosperity. For them, affluence was a kind of birthright. Many rebels grew up so distant from the actualities of industrial production and the working class that providing for and distributing consumer goods seemed "irrelevant." The young, as much as their elders, valued their automobiles and stereo component systems — and too few bothered to ask where they came from. They were another generation of the "people of plenty," believing in an environment of limitless resources and automatic technological solutions to economic problems. Said author Joan Didion, writing sadly of social confusion in 1967,

> At some point between 1945 and 1967 we had somehow neglected to tell these children the rules of the game we happened to be playing. Maybe we had stopped believing in the rules ourselves, maybe we were having a failure of nerve about the game. Maybe there were just too few people around to do the telling. These were children. . . less in rebellion against the society than ignorant of it, able only to feed back certain of its most publicized self-doubts, *Vietnam, Saran-Wrap, diet pills,* the *bomb.*

The environmentalists foresaw a different future than the counter culture, a world of shortages, pollution, and material deprivation. Political rebels dismissed them as a smokescreen for capitalists and property holders, trying to rationalize the economic status quo; other youth, caught up in a romantic worship of nature, were sympathetic. But the counter culture, unlike the environmentalists, never pondered the limits of economic expansion. Political radicals and social drop-outs took issue with the *equity* and *quality* of material growth. The environmentalists challenged the *desirability* and even the *possibility* of continued economic development.

Environmentalism received wide public attention from the time

Rachel Carson published *Silent Spring* in 1962, a book that exposed the side-effects of pesticides. In 1970, shortly after an oil rig off the coast of Santa Barbara, California fouled miles of beaches, environmentalism reached the height of its political power. In September, Congress created the Environmental Protection Agency; and in May 1971, Congress, on environmental grounds, killed plans for supersonic air transport.

Some environmentalists were influenced deeply by the writing of Thomas Malthus, who had written in the 18th century, at the beginning of the Industrial Revolution, that population growth tended naturally to outdistance the growth of resources. Malthus had grossly underestimated the ability of technology to assist workers in trying to wrest produce from the land. The "neo-Malthusians," however, wondered if technological advancement could counteract the problem of resource shortages in the future, particularly at a time when the known supply of fossil fuels was declining at an alarming rate.

AN ERA OF DECLINING ECONOMIC SECURITY

Uninterrupted prosperity from 1962 to 1969 made Keynesian economic management seem capable of sustaining growth painlessly and indefinitely. Wrote economist Walter Heller, "the cost of fulfilling a people's aspirations can be met out of a growing horn of plenty — without robbing Peter to pay Paul." Between 1960 and 1970 the gross national product rose from $506 to $982 billion, an increase of almost $2000 per citizen in a period of relatively stable prices.

This economic optimism faded suddenly in the first years of the 1970's. Inflation, rising sharply after 1968, averaged levels higher than 6 percent through the 1970's — with high unemployment rates to boot. Severe recession between 1974 and 1976 increased awareness of growing dependence on imports of foreign oil, the inability of economic policy to counter high rates of inflation and unemployment, and the declining power of the dollar in international money markets helped create a crisis of confidence. Said economist Robert Heilbroner, writing in *The New Yorker* in 1978, the crisis was not only "of present realities but of expected developments, not of economics alone but of belief." By the end of the 1970's a cautious, conservative, even ominous mood disturbed many Americans.

Price-Wage Controls   The prosperity of the middle 1960's was tied to government expenditure, both for increased social services and for the war in Vietnam. Federal expenditures more than doubled between 1960 and 1970 from $97 to $208 billion, and national defense costs rose from $47 to $79 billion between 1965 and 1969. Because of domestic controversy over the war, Presidents Johnson and Nixon were both unwilling to finance the Vietnam war through tax increases and relied on government borrowing to pay for it. This had strong expansionary impact on consumer spending. The military, relatively indifferent to costs, put vast sums of income into the hands of consumers, while directing production toward articles, such as helicopters and artillery, that were neither capital investments nor goods that directly benefited consumers. This military spending contributed to an inflation rate rising to politically dangerous levels, from 1.7 percent in 1965 to 2.9 percent in 1967 to 5.9 percent in 1970.

Consequently, in the Economic Stabilization Act of 1970, Congress empowered the President to fix prices and wages to counteract the declining value of the dollar. On August 15, 1971 President Nixon announced a general freeze in prices and wages — with important exceptions in the case of agricultural commodities, profits, dividends, and interest rates. The President wanted to curb increases of prices and incomes without antagonizing business leaders whose investment affected the rate of American growth and whose satisfaction was the key to his continued political power.

To spur consumption and investment, Nixon asked Congress to remove the excise tax on automobiles and grant tax credits for new investment. The White House believed the deficits resulting from these decreases in taxes could be kept at a minimum through reduced government expenditures. The August 15 announcement initiated the most direct federal management of wages and prices since the time of the Korean War.

Price and wage controls remained in increasingly confusing and complicated "phases" until 1974. But at the urging of the Secretary of the Treasury, George Schultz, the tendency by the end of 1972 was towards "decontrol." In January 1973, controls were virtually abandoned. A year later, the inflation rate had risen to an 11 percent annual rate. Economists debated the degree to which "decontrol" fueled inflation in 1973. But most economists agreed that the Nixon remedies for inflation were an unequivocal failure, and that price control remained the most serious — and vexing — economic problem of the era.

The Wheat Deal In 1972, the Department of Agriculture acted as a liaison between the Soviet Union and four grain-exporting corporations to sell about $1 billion of American wheat to the Soviet Union. American farmers had large surpluses of grain, and the Russians promised to pay in gold bullion. The Wheat Deal seemed mutually beneficial and consistent with growing "detente" between the two nations.

By early 1973, however, the Wheat Deal had come under violent attack for its purported impact on increasing consumer prices. Since the 1972 harvest had been fixed by farmers at spring planting, and because the United States guaranteed large immediate deliveries in 1973, the pressure of buyers drove up grain prices and the cost of animal feed for meat producers. The Wheat Deal, occurring at the same time the Nixon administration "decontrolled" food prices in supermarkets, contributed to the especially fast rises in food prices. Between March 1972 and March 1973 meat prices for consumers leapt an average of 43 percent.

In spring 1973 Congress was alarmed by inflating food prices. Newspaper editorials blamed the Department of Agriculture for the sale of wheat to Russia at "bargain prices." The United Nations announced the global wheat reserves were at a 20-year low. Wholesale prices, an accurate indicator of consumer prices to come, spiraled that summer. In one month prices of grain soared by 70 percent; of poultry, by 42 percent; and of livestock, by 22 percent. By the end of summer, based on a 1967 index of 100, the wholesale price index stood at 142.7. In other words, $142.70 was needed on the average to buy wholesale goods that had cost $100 seven years earlier. George Meany, head of the AFL-CIO, termed the rate of inflation "beyond belief."

In 1970, food exports totaled $4.4 billion. Three years later, they increased suddenly to $11.9 billion — and continued to rise at mid-decade. Because of global demand, Congress moved in 1973 to revise the agricultural subsidy system it had created 40 years earlier in order to increase farm production and limit the subsidies individual growers could receive. The emphasis on full production and food exports signaled the increasing power of the United States as an agricultural nation in the late 20th century.

The Energy Crisis   In 1973, the American economy reeled from rising prices that followed "decontrol." From the end of the year to the spring of 1974, the country also faced a severe shortage of oil products, including gasoline, diesel fuel, and heating oil. This shortage had several causes. First, while demand for oil products increased in the early 1970's, the nation's refining capacity remained constant. Second, after the United States supported Israel in the Yom Kippur war of 1973, Arab nations embargoed the export of crude oil to the United States for several months. About the same time the Organization of Petroleum-Exporting Countries (OPEC), an international combine of oil-rich nations, quadrupled its prices of crude oil. The OPEC action, along with global food shortages, helped to trigger world-wide inflation in the middle 1970's.

The Energy Crisis underscored the extent to which American economic health depended on petroleum, the source of three-quarters of the nation's energy consumption by the late 1970's. The Arab embargo and OPEC's price increases also indicated the United States' need for imported oil. In 1960, the United States produced 2.6 trillion barrels of crude oil and imported 370 million barrels; in 1977, it produced almost 3 trillion barrels and imported 2.4 trillion barrels. In the same eighteen years, American production of oil fell from 33 to 14 percent of world production.

The Recession of 1974 In 1974, the United States, afflicted with an annual inflation rate of over 11 percent and an unemployment rate of over 9 percent, entered the deepest recession of the post-World War II period. In this downturn, both prices and unemployment rose, an especially unsettling economic condition because economists had thought that this was impossible. Economic theory had taught there was an inverse relationship between prices and unemployment.

Many factors contributed to this inflation, including the global demand for commodities, the power of corporations to set prices at a high level even when consumer demand dropped, the buying power that unemployed workers received from unemployment benefits and expanding consumer credit, and union insistence that incomes of workers rise at a time of declining production and productivity.

Despite the increase in prices, consumer demand dropped. The fear of unemployment increased household thriftiness and thus dampened production. Consumers cut back on "big purchases" such as houses, automobiles, and appliances. Housing starts, about 2 million in 1972, fell to 1.1 million in 1975. Automobile sales, 9.7 million in 1973, declined to 6.7 million in 1975. In the second quarter of 1976, two years after the beginning of the Energy Crisis, employment and consumer demand revived. Businesses, expecting further demand, increased their inventories for the first time in two years. The inflation rate, however, remained close to 6 percent.

Continuing Economic Problems Although economic growth returned in 1976, the inflation rate in the late 1970's remained high and, in early 1979, surpassed an annual rate of 12 percent. The increasing dependence on oil imports and foreign consumer goods meant that American trade deficits rose and that the dollar, once the bastion of international finance, became a less trusted currency than the German mark, Swiss franc, or Japanese yen among international bankers.

The United States, accustomed to its role as the prime mover of the global economy after World War II, suffered over its economic instability. Stagflation — inflation accompanied by unacceptably high levels of unemployment and low rates of economic growth — was troubling since Keynesian economics offered no remedies for it. Some economists wondered if impending shortages of natural resources, especially energy, required centrally planned allocation and state control of the economy. But it appeared that this kind of economic management was unlikely in the near future. American faith in private economic leadership, in other words, in an economy run by managers of private firms making decisions they think necessary to maximize profits, was too deeply rooted in the national folklore.

TABLE II: Economic Growth 1927-1975				
(figures unadjusted for changes in dollar value)				
Year	Gross National Product (billions)	Total Government Expenditures (billions)	Percent of GNP	National Debt (billions)	Percent of GNP
1927	94.9	11	11.8	18	19.5
1946	208.5	78	37.4	269	129.0
1950	286.2	70	24.4	257	89.8
1955	399.3	111	27.8	274	68.6
1960	506.0	151	29.8	283	55.9
1965	688.1	206	29.9	313	45.9
1970	982.4	333	33.9	369	37.6
1975	1528.8	557	36.4	532	34.8

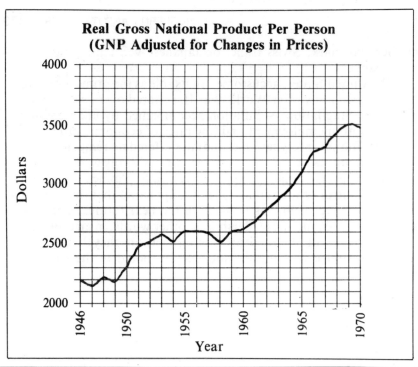

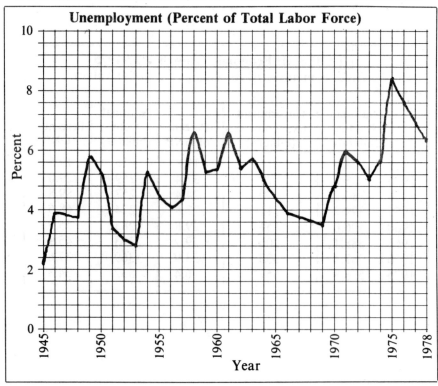

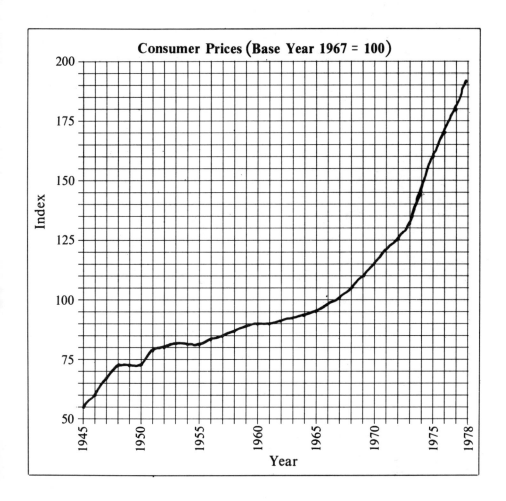

Consumer Prices (Base Year 1967 = 100)

Chapter Six

The Supreme Court, Individual Liberty, and Equality

Ever since Hammurabi published his code to "hold back the strong from oppressing the weak," the success of any legal system is measured by its fidelity to the universal ideal of justice. Theorists beset us with other definitions of law: that it is a mask of privilege, or the judge's private prejudice, or the will of the stronger. But the ideal of justice survives all such myopic views, for as Cicero said, "We are born to it."

— Earl Warren

Although May 17, 1954 was an historic day for race relations and the Supreme Court, the decision the Court made then originated three years earlier. Black, nine-year-old Linda Brown was being bused past the front door of the white Summer Elementary School, seven blocks from her Topeka, Kansas home, to the all-black Monroe School, about a mile away. Her parents objected and decided to contest an 1867 Kansas law, under which Topeka had racially segregated its elementary schools.

In 1954 the Supreme Court decided that Linda Brown had been denied her constitutional rights by the city of Topeka. The court in *Brown v. Board of Education of Topeka, Kansas* ruled that, "In the field of public education the doctrine of 'separate but equal' has no place. Separate educational facilities are inherently unequal. Therefore, we hold that the plaintiffs have been deprived of the equal protection of the laws guaranteed by the Fourteenth Amendment." The *Brown* decision ruled unconstitutional the school segregation laws of seventeen states and the District of Columbia which covered 40 percent of the nation's public school students. The Court's decision

on public education climaxed more than fifty years of legal efforts
to crack the walls of segregation and inaugurated the civil rights
revolution of the 1950's and 1960's.

THE ROLE OF THE SUPREME COURT

Following the "court-packing" fight of 1937, the role of the
Supreme Court in the American constitutional process had by 1945
undergone great change. Basic policy decisions are usually made by
the elected or "political" branches of government. The Congress
enacts laws and the President executes them. The Court's function is
to interpret the law. But what does "interpret" mean?

From the 1880's to the 1930's the Supreme Court often protected corporate and other property interests by ruling that federal
and state legislative efforts at economic and social regulation were
unconstitutional. The Court by exercising judicial review acted as a
restraint on the legislative and executive branches, but the only restraint of significance on the Court had to be self-imposed. As the
Court overturned legislation, a potentially dangerous tension
existed between popular rule by the people's elected representatives
and rule by life-time appointed, non-elected judges.

Many defenders of the New Deal's social and economic legislation believed the Court exceeded its proper function as the interpreter of the Constitution. They charged the Court was becoming a
policy-making body and usurping the legislature's role. They held
the Court was too "activist"; that it should exercise more "self-
restraint." The Court seemed to stretch too far Chief Justice Charles
Evans Hughes's maxim, "We are under a Constitution, but the Constitution is what the Supreme Court says it is."

After the court-packing fight, in which the Court narrowly
emerged unchanged, the justices exercised more "self-restraint" vis-
a-vis the political branches of government and upheld New Deal
social and economic legislation. One might say, "The Court followed the election returns"; certainly the justices were influenced
not only by Roosevelt's proposal, but also by the overwhelming
popular majorities that the New Deal ran up at the polls.

By 1945, the Court rejected its earlier role as a frequent
defender of property adversely affected by government regulation.
The judges limited their function and gave the political branches
more freedom to govern. The Court, however, declared in 1938 that
it would jealously guard, through its power of judicial review, certain "preferred freedoms" of the Bill of Rights against legislative or

executive encroachments even if it meant taking an "activist" role. This distinction took on great significance in the Court's "judicial activism" of the 1950's and 1960's as the justices moved strongly to protect individual liberties from government acts.

THE VINSON COURT

Under Chief Justice Frederick M. Vinson, the Court from 1946 to 1953 decided important cases involving such First Amendment questions as free speech and the rights of the Communist Party; church-state relations; use of Presidential power; and the civil rights of black Americans. But the Court rarely cast the issues in clear focus or ruled with unanimity or persuasiveness.

Free Speech   In the decision, *Dennis v. United States* (1951) the Supreme Court restricted freedom of speech. In 1940, on the eve of World War II, the Congress enacted the Smith Act, or Alien Registration Act, to guard against the violent overthrow of the United States government by totalitarian political movements. The law made it unlawful to "advocate. . . overthrowing any government of the United States by force or violence," to publish printed matter "advising or teaching" such overthrow, to organize groups to so teach or advocate, and to conspire to commit any of the foregoing acts. The so-called "membership clause" forbade "knowing" membership in any such group. Civil libertarians thought the law violated the First Amendment provisions on freedom of speech, press, and assembly.

In 1949, at the height of the Cold War, when a Gallup poll showed that 7 out of 10 Americans believed that membership in the Communist Party should be forbidden by law, the eleven leaders of the United States Communist Party were convicted in a federal district court for violation of the Smith Act. The federal prosecutor's indictment did not charge an actual conspiracy to overthrow the government, but rather charged that the Communist leaders had conspired to organize groups that advocated such violent overthrow. In 1919 a unanimous Court had ruled that only speech which threatened a "clear and present danger" to legitimate government activity could be repressed by the government. Rigorous application of that precedent would have challenged the constitutionality of the Communists' conviction. But the United States Supreme Court in *Dennis v. United States* (1951) treated the indictments as charges of direct conspiracy — action not simple association and speech — to overthrow the government.

The Supreme Court upheld the constitutionality of the "advocacy" section of the Smith Act. The "clear and present danger" doctrine was modified in effect to read "clear and present or future danger." Chief Justice Vinson wrote for a badly divided Court, "Obviously, (the clear and present danger doctrine) cannot mean that before the government may act, it must wait until the rebellion is about to be executed, the plans have been laid, and the signal is awaited." Vinson claimed that it was the very existence of the Communist conspiracy that was the danger. Justices Douglas and Black dissented vigorously and called the Smith Act a "virulent form of prior censorship of speech and press." They did not see the United States Communist Party as an imminent threat to the United States government. The result was that henceforth, though no Communists held elected office in the United States, and there were only an estimated 55,000 party members in America, the Communist Party became legally a criminal conspiracy beyond the protection of the Constitution. More prosecutions and anti-Communist legislation followed at the federal and state levels.

Church and State   Between 1947 and 1952 the Supreme Court ruled in three cases on the First Amendment's words — "Congress shall make no law respecting an establishment of religion. . . ." The main question was, what is an unconstitutional "establishment of religion?" The Court and the public divided. Many, often Roman Catholics and evangelical and fundamentalist Protestants, wanted public support for religious education. Others, Jews, the main stream of American Protestantism as represented by the National Council of Churches, and secularists, feared the entry of organized religions into public areas and urged a strict separation of church and state. In 1947 a divided Court upheld the use of New Jersey tax monies to bus children to parochial schools as a reasonable use of the state's power to support the general welfare of children. The next year a religious education program, privately run by religious groups, carried on in the public schools during the school day was declared to "fall squarely under the ban of the First Amendment."

In 1949 a troubled Court declared "we are a religious people whose institutions presuppose a Supreme Being" and upheld a "released time" religious education program which allowed children with parental permission to leave school, usually for one period per week, to attend churches for religious instruction. Ironically in our secular age issues of Church and State have dogged the Court and divided Americans. Flag salute cases in the early 1940's and school prayer, birth control, and abortion decisions of the 1960's and 1970's have kept the issue of separation of church and state at a fighting level.

Truman's Seizure of the Steel Industry   In 1952 the Court in a 6-3 decision, *Youngstown Sheet and Tube Co. v. Sawyer,* ruled that President Truman could not seize the steel industry to stop a strike and to force resumption of steel production during the Korean War. In his action Truman claimed very broad powers as Chief Executive and Commander-in-Chief under the Constitution. In a memorable confrontation between the executive and the judiciary, the Court ruled against the President. Truman returned the steel industry to its private owners.

Civil Rights   In the twentieth century the Supreme Court and lower federal courts have been the major protectors of civil rights. The lawyers of the National Association for the Advancement of Colored People (NAACP) consistently attempted through the judicial process to guarantee blacks the right of due process, equal protection of the laws, and the vote as set forth by the Fourteenth and Fifteenth Amendments.

The NAACP worked from 1910 on to end grandfather clauses, poll taxes, literacy tests, all-white Democratic primaries, and other measures that kept the Negro from voting. In 1915 the NAACP won its first major legal victory when the Court ruled the grandfather clause, which eliminated from the vote individuals whose grandfathers had not voted, unconstitutional as a blatant violation of the Fifteenth Amendment. The Court nullified the all-white primary in five decisions ranging over a period from 1927 to 1953, a noteworthy example of the gradualism of the judicial process.

In 1927 the Supreme Court ruled that restrictive housing covenants, those agreements by a buyer not to sell his home to a Negro or some other specified person, were private contracts and not forbidden by the Fourteenth Amendment's equal protection clause. But in 1948 the Court, though it continued to rule that restrictive covenants are private matters, ruled that such covenants could not be enforced by state courts, for such action would constitute a state denial of equal protection of the law. The restrictive covenant, the bulwark of housing segregation, was thus made unenforcible by legal means.

After 1946 the Interstate Commerce Commission and the Supreme Court ruled against discrimination in interstate transportation. The rulings were based on the equal protection clause of the Fourteenth Amendment and the Interstate Commerce Act of 1887 which made it unlawful for any interstate carrier "to subject any particular person. . . to any undue or unreasonable prejudice or disadvantage in any respect whatsoever."

In three cases between 1938 and 1950 involving graduate education, the Court chipped away at the South's segregated educational system. First, the Court ruled in 1938 that Missouri could not send a qualified black law-school applicant to an out-of-state law school merely because Missouri had no public black law school. The Court ruled that the applicant had a right to go to a public law school in Missouri that was "substantially equal to those which the state afforded there for persons of the white race." Second, in 1950 the Court ruled in a case involving Texas that a hastily built black law school constructed to comply with the Missouri precedent was not the equivalent of the University of Texas Law School. The new school was not equal in physical facilities or in the "intangibles" that make for greatness in a law school, such as "reputation of the faculty, experience in the administration, position and influence of the alumni, standing in the community, tradition and prestige." The Court decided, "We cannot find substantial equality in the education offered white and Negro students by the state."

In another 1950 decision, the Court ruled against a series of state laws governing the University of Oklahoma that required that blacks sit in separate rooms adjoining the main classroom and at special desks in the library, and eat at a separate time in the cafeteria. The Court ruled such restrictions impaired and inhibited the plaintiff's "ability to study, engage in discussions and exchange views with other students, and in general to learn his profession."

THE WARREN COURT

In September, 1953, President Eisenhower appointed California's Governor Earl Warren to replace the heart attack victim, Vinson, as Chief Justice. The President later called the appointment "the biggest damned-fool mistake I ever made." Nevertheless, the Warren Court from 1953 to 1969 left a mark on American constitutional development and the daily lives of the American people unequaled by any court since the Marshall Court.

In 1953 Earl Warren was a popular sixty-two-year-old California politician who had been in public office since 1919. He had been a racket-busting district attorney, a tough attorney-general, and an unprecedented three-term governor. In 1938 and 1946 he won the Democratic, Republican and Progressive Party nominations for attorney-general and governor. He supported progressive social and economic legislation. In light of his later rulings as Chief Justice in favor of racial equality, of due process for the criminally accused and of legislative reapportionment, there is irony in his early support for the evacuation and detention of 110,000 Japanese-

Chief Justice Earl Warren   *(Credit: photo no. 200S-ADA-3295L in the National Archives)*

Americans in World War II, his tough law enforcement record as a prosecutor and his opposition to legislative reapportionment in California in 1948.

Preferred Freedoms   The Court in the Warren years became noted as an activist Court, but not in the tradition of the pro-property activism of the Supreme Court of the 1880's to 1930's. The Warren Court exercised judicial review to protect "preferred freedoms" from federal and state legislative and executive abuses or from the repressive forces of private groups or organizations. Justice Hugo Black believed the clause in the Fourteenth Amendment, "nor shall any state deprive any person of life, liberty, or property, without due process of law," made the first eight amendments to the United States Constitution secure against state as well as federal actions. Traditionally the Bill of Rights had limited only the federal government. In 1925 the Court ruled that the First Amendment provisions on freedom of speech and press protect citizens from state actions that violate the due process clause of the Fourteenth Amendment. In the 1950's and 1960's the Court declared most of the first eight amendments to the United States Constitution restrain actions by the states, though Justice Black's hope to see them all so interpreted was not achieved.

The Warren Court's decisions under the "due process" and "equal protection" clauses of the Fourteenth Amendment expanded individual rights under law and established new assurances of legal equality. The Court nullified local, state and federal government actions which violated citizens' constitutional rights, and, to right old wrongs, went on to order affirmative action — such as legislative reapportionment and school busing. Often the oppressed and the poor believed they could not achieve their "rights" or legal equality through the political process. As minorities, often unpopular and persecuted, they saw little chance to win at the polls and elect legislative majorities to enact laws in their interests. Such groups felt wronged and lacked political clout. They believed they had solid constitutional arguments for their claims so they turned to the Court for a judicial remedy to their grievances.

The Court responded by a vigorous exercise of judicial review and orders of affirmative action, and in the process reversed an unprecedented forty-five previous Supreme Court decisions between 1953 and 1960! The Court's supporters applauded this shaping of basic law through Court initiatives. To many the Warren Court was the most important and innovative branch of the federal government in domestic affairs. But its critics charged it was becoming a policy making branch, traditionally the function of the people's elected representatives in the legislatures. Some critics said it was becoming a "super-legislature." Justice Harlan, in 1964, expressed reservations on the Court's initiatives when he wrote,

> . . . These decisions give support to a current mistaken view of the Constitution and the constitutional function of this Court. This view, in a nutshell, is that every major social ill in this country can find its cure in some constitutional 'principle,' and that this Court should 'take the lead' in promoting reform when other branches of government fail to act. The Constitution is not a panacea for every blot upon the public welfare, nor should this Court, ordained as a judicial body, be thought of as a general haven for reform movements.

Some feared that the Court's rulings might cause a severe loss of popular support. Widespread acceptance of the Court's moral and intellectual reasoning for its rulings is vital. For unlike the Congress, which has the "power of the purse," or the President, who has the "power of the sword," the Court, unless strongly supported by the legislature and/or executive, has only the "power of its opinion."

The most significant decisions of the Warren Court centered on race relations, legislative reapportionment, and criminal due process. But the Court ruled on important cases with often controversial results in matters of church and state and freedom of speech, press, and assembly. The Court set limits on the enforcement of the Smith Act and legislative investigations and ended the "separate but equal" interpretation of individual rights.

Church and State Relations   In 1962 the Court ruled the New York's Board of Regents's prayer for public schools, "Almighty God, we acknowledge our dependence upon Thee, and we beg Thy blessings upon us, our parents, our teachers and our Country," "wholly inconsistent with the establishment clause." The Roman Catholic hierarchy, led by New York's Francis Cardinal Spellman, and Protestant fundamentalists, such as Billy Graham, were "shocked" and denounced the "shame" of the decision. Most Jews, many Protestant liberals, and secularists applauded the Court. The public division was deep and the feelings strong. The following year the Court on the same grounds ruled 8-1 against a Pennsylvania law requiring a daily reading of ten Bible verses and a Maryland law requiring a daily Bible reading and recitation of the Lord's Prayer. The 1963 decision outlawed such practices that existed in 41 percent of the nation's school districts and in 37 states and the District of Columbia. The public reaction in 1963 was less heated than a year before and there was increased acceptance.

In 1965 in a 7-2 decision the Court in *Griswold v. Connecticut* ruled unconstitutional an 1879 Connecticut law which made it a crime for any person to use or advise the use of any birth control means. Justice Douglas ruled,

> We do not sit as a super-legislature to determine the wisdom, needs, and propriety of laws that touch economic problems, business affairs, or social conditions. . . . The present case. . . concerns a relationship lying within the zone of privacy created by several fundamental constitutional guarantees. . . . It concerns a law which, in forbidding the *use* of contraceptives rather than regulating their manufacture or sale, seeks to achieve its goals by means having a maximum destructive impact upon that relationship. Such a law cannot stand. . . . Would we allow the police to search the sacred precincts of marital bedrooms for telltale signs of the use of contraceptives? The very idea is repulsive to the notions of privacy surrounding the marriage relationship. We deal with a right of privacy older than the Bill of Rights. . . .

In this case the Court went beyond any specific guarantee or principle of constitutional law to develop a specific "right of privacy." The dissenters charged the Court had exceeded its role as interpreter of the law and that it was involved in "judicial lawmaking." The decision had strong public support, for 81 percent of the public, according to a Gallup poll in November, 1964, believed birth control information should be available to anyone who wanted it.

Freedom of Speech and Press The Warren Court ruled in several cases to expand the First Amendment guarantees of free speech, press, and rights of association. The Court in 1964 stated, "Speech concerning public affairs is more than self-expression; it is the essence of self-government." There should be forceful, uninhibited debate. The Warren Court believed that only by a lusty exchange in the marketplace of ideas could truth be uncovered and progress made.

In 1964 in *New York Times v. Sullivan*, the Supreme Court overruled a conviction in an Alabama state court in which the *Times* was found guilty of libel when it carried an ad by some civil rights leaders which the jury found false and defamatory to the police chief of Birmingham and awarded the chief $500,000 in damages. A unanimous Court ruled the newspapers libel only if they publish material they know to be false or with reckless disregard of whether it is true or false. This rule was extended in 1966-67 to include comment on most public figures as well as government officials. The ruling outlawed seditious libel and provided a strong preferred position to free expression in our system of self-government.

The Warren Court and the Smith Act   In 1957 and 1961 decisions, the Court limited the reach of the Smith Act. The Court held that the Justice Department must prove that the defendants advocated actual violent overthrow of the United States government now or in the future, not merely that they held a belief in the overthrow. The justices did not restore the "clear and present danger" doctrine, but they did make prosecution more difficult. In the 1961 *Scales* decision, the Court also limited the prosecutors' ability to gain convictions under the "membership" clause. The justices in a 5-4 decision ruled that to gain a conviction for "knowing membership" the prosecution must prove that the defendant understood the organization's revolutionary purpose and participated vigorously to that end. The majority did not strike down the Smith Act as a violation of the First Amendment, as dissenters Black and Douglas urged, but it made successful prosecutions more difficult than under the earlier *Dennis* decision.

Curbing the Abuses of Legislative Committees   By 1957 the Supreme Court moved to curb the abuses of Congressional and state legislative investigations into "un-American" activities. Legislative committee investigations are a necessary part of the legislative process, but their purpose is to educate the legislators and the public to the problem, define the issues, get the facts, and aid the legislators in drafting corrective legislation. Committees are not criminal courts. The techniques and methods of Senator Joseph McCarthy in the early 1950's led to charges that he damaged the reputations and violated the rights of many witnesses.

Witnesses at such anti-Communist investigations were compelled to appear before legislative committees to testify in public under oath, but the witnesses did not have the rights of a defendant in a courtroom. They did not have the right to be informed in advance of the possible charges against them. Nor did they have the right to confront and cross-examine witnesses who testified against them; to subpoena witnesses on their behalf; to have a lawyer; or to testify then and there in their own behalf. The hearings often took the tone of a criminal prosecution, but the witnesses did not have the legal rights of due process. Sensational public hearings occurred in which witnesses suffered such penalties as loss of reputation, dismissal from their jobs, and loss of pension payments. Witnesses who were uncooperative with investigating committees were liable to criminal contempt proceedings and possible jail sentences.

John Watkins, a labor union organizer, appeared in April, 1954, before a subcommittee of the House Un American Activities Committee (HUAC). He did not invoke the Fifth Amendment and answered questions about his own activities in the Communist Party. He refused, however, on the basis of the First Amendment's free speech clause, to answer "certain questions that I believe are outside the proper scope of your committee's activity." Watkins was found guilty in federal court of contempt of Congress.

In June, 1957, Earl Warren for the Supreme Court ruled, "The Bill of Rights is applicable to investigations as to all forms of governmental action. . . . (A legislative investigation) is justified solely as an adjunct to the legislative process." Warren labeled the House of Representatives' resolution creating HUAC so vague that the witness could not be assured of an adequate "standard of specificity" with respect to the pertinency of the questions asked him. Warren asked, "Who can define the meaning of un-American?" The Court declared the investigative body must tell a witness the subject of the inquiry, and how the committee's questions relate to it. There should not be exposure simply for the sake of exposure. Watkins' conviction was overturned for the indictment suffered from the "vice of vagueness" and so violated his rights of "due process" under the Fifth Amendment.

THE WARREN COURT AND SCHOOL DESEGREGATION

The May 17, 1954 *Brown v. Board of Education* decision broke new constitutional ground for the Supreme Court and ushered in the Civil Rights Revolution of the next fifteen years. In the arguments before the high Court, the states' lawyers had maintained that the Tenth Amendment — "the powers not delegated to the United States by the Constitution, nor prohibited by it to the states, are reserved to the states" — made education the exclusive concern of the states. The NAACP's lawyers supporting Linda Brown claimed the Fourteenth Amendment — "no state shall. . . deny to any person within its jurisdiction the equal protection of the laws" — forbade state segregation laws.

Debates in Congress and the ratifying state legislatures in 1866-1868 had not discussed in detail the Fourteenth Amendment and public education. In 1896 in *Plessy v. Ferguson* the Supreme Court ruled that an 1890 Louisiana intrastate train segregation law was not in conflict with the Fourteenth Amendment as long as the separate facilities were equal. That segregation precedent, the "separate but equal" doctrine, became the guiding rule for numerous state and federal court decisions from 1896 to 1954.

In the three graduate school cases between 1938 and 1950 (see

p. 188) the Court attempted to enforce the equality of separate facilities. On May 17, 1954, the Supreme Court squarely faced the segregation issue — can any separate educational facilities or practices be truly "equal?"

In Linda Brown's case the question was: could a state under the Tenth Amendment legislate school segregation, or do such laws violate the Fourteenth Amendment? Chief Justice Warren wanted the Court to speak with one clear voice. He feared that concurring opinions and dissents would make public compliance difficult to obtain. Warren wanted a brief decision in ordinary language, an opinion that every weekly newspaper could reprint in full and which all citizens could read and understand. He won all he wanted, an achievement of extraordinary judicial statesmanship. *Brown v. Board of Education of Topeka, Kansas* was Warren's first major opinion. It was brief, clear and unequivocal.

> Today, . . . it is doubtful that any child may reasonably be expected to succeed in life if he is denied the opportunity of an education. . . it is a right which must be made available to all on equal terms.
>
> . . . Does segregation of children in public schools solely on the basis of race, . . . deprive the children of the minority group of equal educational opportunities? We believe that it does.
>
> To separate (Negroes) . . . solely because of their race generates a feeling of inferiority. . . in a way unlikely ever to be undone. . . .
>
> We conclude that in the field of public education the doctrine of "separate but equal" has no place. Separate educational facilities are inherently unequal. . . . We hold that the plaintiffs . . . (are) deprived of equal protection of the laws guaranteed by the Fourteenth Amendment.

In the 1954 decision, the Supreme Court simply ruled on the constitutional issue. The Court requested further argument to decide what method would be most effective to remedy the situation. On May 31, 1955, in the second *Brown* decision, *Brown II,* the Court ruled that primary responsibility for desegregation rested with local school authorities under the supervision of the local United States District Courts. The Court recognized that local conditions required different solutions. It called for "transition to a racially nondiscriminatory school system," and ordered that progress be made "with all deliberate speed."

Public Reaction   The immediate reaction to the Supreme

Court's desegregation ruling was mixed. *The New Orleans Times-Picayune* editorialized ". . . The decision will do no service either to education or racial accommodation. . . . The public school systems face the prospect of considerable turmoil. . . . The revolutionary overturn of practice and usage cannot immediately result in the improvement of race relations." *The New York Herald Tribune* wrote, ". . . The Supreme Court of the United States squared the country's basic law with its conscience. . . ." The country's leading black newspaper, *The Amsterdam News,* of New York City claimed, "The Supreme Court decision is the greatest victory for the Negro people since the Emancipation Proclamation." With the significant exception of some in the Deep South, there was little adamant opposition.

Political Reaction   President Dwight D. Eisenhower (1953 to 1961) did not provide sufficient leadership to persuade the public to accept the *Brown* decisions. He refused even to say he agreed with the *Brown* decision. "I think it makes no difference whether I endorse it or not," he said in 1956. "The Constitution is as the Supreme Court interprets it; and I must conform to that and do my very best to see that it is carried out in this country." In 1956 he privately told a speechwriter, "I am convinced that the Supreme Court decision *set back* progress in the South *at least fifteen years. . . .* It's all very well to talk about school integration — if you remember you may be also talking about social *dis*integration." During the Presidential campaigns of 1956 and 1960, however, both major political parties gave support in their platforms to the desegregation decisions.

The initial public reaction, as related by a Gallup poll in late May, 1954, was that 54 percent of Americans approved "that all children, no matter what their race, must be allowed to go to the same schools." In the South only 24 percent approved and 71 percent disapproved. There was a grudging belief among many Southerners that desegregation was inevitable, but there existed a lack of effective pro-Court leadership at the national and local levels. This vacuum was soon filled by anti-Court forces led by individuals such as James Byrnes, former Supreme Court Justice, Secretary of State, and then Governor of South Carolina, and Senator James Eastland of Mississippi, chairman of the Senate Judiciary Committee. In 1956 Byrnes claimed the Court had not interpreted the Constitution, it had amended it. He held the decision set back progress in race relations. He raised the fear of racial intermarriage and miscegenation and suggested that the states end public education to block integration.

Senator Eastland asked rhetorically, "Who is obligated morally or legally to obey a decision whose authorities rest not upon the law but upon the writings and teachings of pro-Communist agitators... who are part and parcel of the Communist conspiracy to destroy our country?" Thus began the assaults on the Warren Court as a radical, Communist front. By the 1960's occasional billboards called for the impeachment of Earl Warren as segregationists, the John Birch Society, and militant "law and order" advocates blasted the Court.

The white Citizens' Councils in the South organized popular opposition to the *Brown* decisions as early as 1956. Most southern politicians dusted off old nullification doctrines, which called for states to interpose their power between the federal courts and local school boards in schemes of "massive resistance." These politicians promised to aid private schools with state subsidies and tuition grants. They also used pupil placement acts, local control laws, complicated legal steps for Negro parents, multiple forms to fill out for transfer to all-white schools, redistricting, interposition and nullification of federal court orders to thwart desegregation. By 1964 the southern states had passed 471 laws to evade or avoid compliance with desegregation. An atmosphere of intimidation and fear went hand in hand with the increasingly heated rhetoric by some politicians. Moderate Southerners of 1954-55 became silent as they saw a few outspoken colleagues and neighbors dismissed from their pulpits, their classrooms, or their jobs. By 1956 the spirit and practices of resistance had swept across the South.

In 1956, 101 southern Congressmen and Senators signed a "Southern Manifesto." This document denounced the Supreme Court and called for resistance to school desegregation by "any lawful means."

> We regard the decision of the Supreme Court in the school cases as a clear abuse of judicial power. It climaxes a trend in the federal judiciary undertaking to legislate, in derogation of the authority of Congress, and to encroach upon the reserved rights of the states and the people. . . .
> . . . The Supreme Court of the United States. . . undertook to exercise their naked judicial power and substituted their personal, political and social ideas for the established law of the land.

Little Rock   In September 1957 national and world attention focused on Little Rock, Arkansas when the court-ordered desegregation of Little Rock's Central High School was the first great test of federal power versus state interposition, court-ordered desegregation versus white supremacy, and Presidential authority versus a defiant southern governor. The Little Rock case set important precedents, and the pattern of actions was later repeated.

As early as May 20, 1954, the school board of Little Rock, Arkansas, voted to drop its segregated practices and voluntarily accept the desegregation ruling of the *Brown* decision. The first step was desegregation of the high school in September, 1957. Local leadership for peaceful integration appeared to have overcome attempts in the state legislature to pass constitutional amendments and laws to block desegregation.

But on the night of September 2, 1957, Governor Orval E. Faubus ordered the Arkansas National Guard to Central High School in Little Rock "to maintain order," but in reality to block desegregation. On the next day President Eisenhower in a press conference said in regard to the desegregation of Central High School and the action of Governor Faubus that "You cannot change people's hearts merely by laws." He added that there are people who "see a picture of mongrelization of the race. . . ." On the same day the federal district court ordered desegregation at Central High School to proceed "immediately."

From September 4 to September 20, the Arkansas National Guard, under orders of Governor Faubus, defied the federal court's order to admit the nine Negro students to Central High School. On September 21 the federal judge enjoined Governor Faubus and the Arkansas National Guard from blocking desegregation in Little Rock.

On Monday, September 23, desegregation began, and an angry white mob rioted. *The New York Times* described the situation, "A mob of belligerent, shrieking, and hysterical demonstrators forced the withdrawal today of nine Negro students from Central High School. . . ." About 1,000 white supremacists — screaming "niggers," "nigger-lovers," and "lynch" — forced the Little Rock authorities to persuade the Negro students to leave the building by noon after three hours and thirteen minutes of integration. On September 24 President Eisenhower, carrying out his constitutional responsibility to "execute the law," ordered federal troops into Little Rock. He also ordered 10,000 Arkansas National Guardsmen into federal service to join with the United States Army to end mob chaos and to enforce the federal court's orders.

The troops stayed at Central High for the rest of the school year. The Little Rock school authorities declared the situation at Central High School "intolerable" — one of "chaos, bedlam, and turmoil" and asked the federal district court for a two-and-a-half-year suspension of school desegregation. Chief Justice Warren ruled for the Supreme Court in September, 1958, in *Cooper v. Aaron,* "Constitutional rights. . . are not to be sacrificed or yielded to the violence and disorder which have followed upon the actions of the Governor and Legislature (in Little Rock). . . . Law and order are not here to be preserved by depriving the Negro children of their constitutional rights." There was to be no delay or retreat.

Governor Faubus then ordered all the high schools of Little Rock closed to prevent "violence and disorder." They remained closed throughout the 1958-59 school year. The Court next struck down the school closing laws, and the city's high schools opened in September, 1959, with token desegregation.

The Slow Pace of Desegregation   Despite all the litigation, in 1964 only 9.3 percent of black children in the formerly segregated states attended desegregated classes. Most of the desegregation was in the border states and of a limited nature, except in Texas. In the eleven states of the Old Confederacy only 1 percent of black children were in desegregated schools. Until 1964, a few courageous black children and parents, civil rights organizations, and some lonely and isolated federal judges carried the burdens of school desegregation. They received no Presidential or Congressional aid.

The Presidency and Congress Act   In 1963 and 1964, ten years after the Supreme Court's *Brown* decision, Presidents John F. Kennedy and Lyndon B. Johnson finally gave vigorous support to school desegregation and the active civil rights movement. They pressured the Congress to enact a Civil Rights Law which aided in the school desegregation process. The 1964 act allowed the United States Attorney General to initiate school desegregation suits — a morale boost and a financial relief to hard-pressed black parents and civil rights organizations.

Title VI of the act required the United States government to end funding to all federally assisted programs with racial discrimination. This stipulation was a major tool for school desegregation, especially after Congress enacted a law in 1965 granting massive sums of federal money for elementary and secondary education. The Office of Education, equipped with clear guidelines and an adequate administrative staff, carried out effective day-by-day legal enforcement. From 1964 to 1969, Title VI of the 1964 Civil Rights law became the major vehicle of change, replacing the slower, case-by-case court litigation process of the previous decade. The legislative and executive branches finally caught up with the judiciary.

The Warren Court and School Desegregation in the 1960's   Typical of the court struggles in the 1960's was the case of *Griffin v. School Board of Prince Edward County* (1964). Following the 1954 ruling, the Virginia legislature enacted fifty-six laws to resist desegregation.

In 1956 the Virginia legislature passed laws to close integrated public schools, end state funds to such schools, and provide state and county monies for tuition grants to private schools. This was a thinly veiled plan to avoid court-ordered public school desegregation and yet make public monies available to "private" schools which would be segregated. In 1959 the Virginia Supreme Court struck down these laws. The Virginia legislature repealed the state compulsory attendance law and left attendance to county option. When the federal courts ordered Prince Edward County to desegregate its schools in 1959, the county closed its public schools until 1964. Whites established a whites-only private school, and the state and county made tuition grants and tax credits available for "private schools." Blacks refused such grants and credits and worked through the courts to reopen the public schools on a desegregated basis.

In the *Griffin* decision, a unanimous Supreme Court ruled that the closing of the public schools and the tuition grants and tax credits to private schools "denied ... Negro students... the equal protection of the law." In reference to *Brown II* the Court held "there has been entirely too much deliberation and not enough speed" in desegregation. The Court ordered the county's schools reopened and authorized the lower federal court to order county officials to levy taxes to run a desegregated public school system.

This decision defined what state and local governments could not do to segregate students. It also ordered local government to take affirmative action to right old wrongs. This court demand for affirmative action raised judicial activism another degree.

In *Green v. School Board of New Kent County* in 1968, Justice Brennan spoke for a unanimous Supreme Court that the Virginia County's racial freedom-of-choice plan was unconstitutional. In 1965 rural New Kent County adopted a freedom-of-choice plan which allowed students to choose the school they wanted to attend. Civil rights advocates argued the plan was a means to keep intimidated blacks in segregated schools. Justice Brennan ruled that *"Brown II* was a call for the dismantling of well-entrenched dual systems" and that the school board had "the affirmative duty to take whatever steps might be necessary to convert to a unitary system in which racial discrimination would be eliminated root and branch...." New Kent County's eleven-year delay and its "freedom-of-choice" plan failed to meet the standards of *Brown II.*

Several lower court federal judges in the 1960's went further towards judicial activism to desegregate the schools. They rebuked arguments based on residential patterns to maintain "neighborhood schools." These judges rejected the use of "inaccurate and misleading" aptitude tests in pupil placement, unequal per pupil educational expenditures, and class assignments by "tracks" which led to racial segregation. They ordered various methods of pupil assignment to bring "maximum effective integration," including busing; ordered teacher integration; and some judges ruled "the track system must be abolished."

The Warren Court and Legislative Reapportionment   Chief Justice Earl Warren referred to the state legislative reapportionment decisions of the 1960's as the most important decisions of his tenure on the Supreme Court. The decisions dealt with the fundamental issue of who is represented and with what impact in the state legislature. Prior to the landmark case, *Baker v. Carr,* decided on March 26, 1962, the Supreme Court had avoided ruling on the apportionment of state legislatures. In *Colegrove v. Green* in 1946, Justice Felix Frankfurter urged the Court to exercise judicial restraint and warned that the judiciary "ought not to enter the political thicket" of Court-directed legislative reapportionment. In the reapportionment decisions of 1962 and 1964, the Court rejected this approach. The unanimity of the school desegregation decisions ended and there were strongly worded dissenting opinions.

Background — Arguments on Legislative Apportionment   For decades, and in some cases since the eighteenth century, many states had legislative representation plans which apportioned representatives on grounds other than equal population districts, at least in *one house* of the legislature. The arguments for such plans were many and varied. Some people argued for representation on the basis of political subdivisions such as townships or counties; some for recognition of different geographic regions; others advocated plans to secure representation for economic or ethnic groups — at least for one house of a bicameral legislature. This last group often made an analogy to the national Congress with the House of Representatives and its representation by population and the Senate and its two Senators per state. They also held that each state had a constitutional right to establish its own apportionment plan. The defenders of the existing order claimed the issue was essentially a political one that should be resolved by the political branches of government. They held that legislative apportionment was not a dispute resolvable by the judicial processes of the courts. The proponents of judicial intervention claimed that the federal courts had jurisdiction because citizens' "equal protection of the laws" was being denied by state action in violation of the Fourteenth Amendment. Should one man's vote be the equal of another's? Such people believed the Court could fashion an effective judicial remedy.

In the years since the drafting of state constitutions and the enactment of apportionment statutes, the population had increased and moved from farms to cities and their surrounding suburbs. The majority of state legislatures were not apportioned according to this new distribution of population. There was a rural stranglehold on most state legislatures. Rural legislators were not about to vote themselves out of office or their constituents out of favored positions. Reformers believed the federal courts were the only hope to achieve proportional representation. People in metropolitan areas believed legislatures ignored urban needs — housing, transportataion, and social services — in favor of farm and other special interests. There was much complaint about "rotten boroughs," "minority rule," and "unresponsiveness."

The advocates of reapportionment rejected the "federal analogy" to the United States Congress. They pointed out that the House of Representatives' apportionment according to population and the Senate's according to states had been a political compromise to break the stalemate in the Constitutional Convention of 1787. Reapportionment supporters explained that they were arguing about state legislatures, which must comply with the Fourteenth Amendment, and that Congress is not affected by the Amendment's equal protection clause.

Fundamental to the dispute was the question of political power. Who was to control the state legislatures? Slogans such as "one man, one vote" and "states' rights" often discouraged serious analysis and thoughtful discussion of questions such as: What is representative democracy? How is the majority to be protected against the tyranny of a minority entrenched in power by unfair methods of representation?

Baker v. Carr, 1962   In 1962 in *Baker v. Carr*, the Supreme Court in a 6-2 decision ruled that it had jurisdiction in a Tennessee legislative reapportionment controversy. The Court entered the "political thicket." The Tennessee constitution established a bicameral legislature that was to be apportioned according to population and reapportioned every ten years in accord with the federal census. To the distress of the great number of city voters this rule was not being followed. They sought legal redress in the federal courts under the Fourteenth Amendment. The Supreme Court ordered the federal district court to apply the equal protection clause to the voters' complaints and to enforce reapportionment. Justice Frankfurter, in dissent, feared the Court had plunged into a hopeless quagmire of endless and fruitless litigation.

Public opinion strongly supported reapportionment as a reaffirmation of equality and majority rule. Rural and small town conservatives, farm organizations, certain lobbyists who liked their cozy relationships with entrenched state legislators — and many legislators — denounced the Court's ruling. A study of the 1960 census disclosed that in forty-four states legislative apportionments permitted less than 40 percent of the population to elect majorities in the legislatures; in thirteen states, one third or less could elect a majority of both houses in the legislature. Vermont's House of Representatives had one representative from each town. Thus one town with a population of thirty-eight cast the same vote in the state legislature as another with a population of 33,155. Vermont had not redistricted its House of Representatives since 1793. In California 10.7 percent of the population could elect a majority in the state Senate.

Under the threat of court action, many state legislatures moved quickly in 1963 to reapportion voluntarily. Cases came before federal courts in thirty-one states, before state courts in nineteen states, and before both federal and state courts in eleven states. In twenty-four states the courts held the legislatures unconstitutional or suspect.

Reynolds v. Sims, 1964   The Alabama constitution of 1901 directed that both houses of the state legislature be apportioned according to population and be reapportioned after each census. But the legislature had not been reapportioned since 1900. On June 15, 1964, in *Reynolds v. Sims,* Chief Justice Warren ruled for a majority of eight to uphold a lower federal court order to the Alabama legislature to reapportion. Warren wrote,

> Legislators represent people, not trees or acres. Legislators are elected by voters, not farms or cities or economic interests. As long as ours is a representative form of government elected directly by and directly representative of the people. . . it would seem reasonable that a majority of the people of a state could elect a majority of that State's legislators. . . . The Equal Protection Clause demands no less than substantially equal state legislative representation for citizens. . . an honest and good faith effort to construct districts, in both houses of its legislature, as nearly of equal population as is practicable.

The Success of Court Ordered Reapportionment   The political interests opposed to the reapportionment decision of 1964 quickly mobilized in Congress. Senator Everett M. Dirksen (R., Ill.) the minority leader, proposed a constitutional amendment to allow state legislatures to continue to have one house represented on a basis other than population. In August, 1965, after vigorous debate the Dirksen amendment, though it gained a majority vote in the Senate, 57-39, failed by seven votes to gain the two-thirds vote needed.

By 1966 almost four-fifths of the state legislatures had been reapportioned according to population. *The New York Times* reported on March 18, 1967, that a little noticed campaign to call a federal constitutional convention by majority vote in two-thirds of the state legislatures had succeeded in thirty-two of the needed thirty-four states. An anti-Court, political coalition consisting of Senator Dirksen, the American Farm Bureau Federation, segregationists, anti-reapportionment groups, and law and order advocates was on the verge of convening the first constitutional convention since 1787. Such a convention would not be limited to one subject. It could be a "wide-open, unpredictable dabbling with our historic charter. . . ." Twenty-six of the thirty-two legislatures were malapportioned when they passed pro-convention resolutions. Publicity checked the movement, and no more states passed such resolutions.

By 1967 within three years of the *Reynolds* decision, all fifty state legislatures had complied with the Court's reapportionment ruling. The specter of the "political thicket" raised by Justice Frankfurter, the Dirksen Amendment, and the drive for a constitutional convention proved ineffective opponents to the "one man one vote" movement. These developments represented a victory for the supporters of judicial activism over judicial restraint.

THE WARREN COURT AND CRIMINAL DUE PROCESS

Due Process   Americans historically have prided themselves on their allegiance to "fair play" and the "rules of the game," concepts called "due process of law" in criminal law and justice. The Warren Court took major and controversial steps to extend due process to those accused of crimes.

The constitutional provisions of greatest importance in criminal cases are the Fourth, Fifth, and Sixth Amendments. The most relevant points are the following (emphases added):

4th Amendment

The right of the people to be secure in their persons, houses, papers and effects against *unreasonable* searches and seizures, shall not be violated, no warrant shall issue, but upon *probable cause,* supported by oath or affirmation, and particularly describing the place to be searched, and the persons or things to be seized.

5th Amendment

No person. . . shall be *compelled* in any criminal case to be a *witness against himself.* . . .

6th Amendment

In all criminal prosecutions, the *accused* shall enjoy the *right.* . . to have *assistance* of *counsel* for his defense.

Such limitations on government police actions and safeguards for individuals had long been recognized in the federal courts. The Warren Court redefined these rights and extended their protection to individuals in state criminal proceedings under the Fourteenth Amendment — "nor shall any state deprive any person of life, liberty, or property, without *due process of law.*" The unanimity of the Warren Court in the school desegregation cases and the strong majority in the legislative reapportionment decisions gave way to deep and often bitter division in the Court on these issues of due process.

In the 1960's crimes of violence increased dramatically. The public was scared and demanded "law and order." Many accused the Court of "coddling criminals," and the moves to "impeach Earl Warren" and "curb the Court" spread.

Gideon v. Wainwright, 1963   On March 18, 1963, the Court in *Gideon v. Wainwright* ruled the Fourteenth Amendment's due process clause guaranteed all poor defendants free legal counsel in state felony prosecutions (crimes that are more serious and carry heavier punishments than those classified as misdemeanors). Clarence Earl Gideon, "a fifty-one-year-old white man who had been in and out of prisons much of his life," was charged with robbing the Bay Harbor Pool Room in 1961 in Panama City, Florida. Gideon was a drifter, not a professional criminal, nor a violent man. A prematurely aged man with trembling hands and voice, he was among "the most wretched of men." At his trial in the state court his request for a court-appointed free lawyer was denied. Gideon defended himself, lost, and was sentenced to five years in jail. He sent a hand-written appeal to the United States Supreme Court. Although in 1942 in *Betts v. Brady,* the Supreme Court had denied free legal counsel to indigents in state courts, the Supreme Court took Gideon's case and appointed Abe Fortas, a later justice of the Supreme Court, to argue Gideon's claim. Fortas argued that counsel in a criminal trial is a fundamental right of due process enforced on the states by the Fourteenth Amendment. In the Court's unanimous decision overturning the *Betts* precedent, Justice Black wrote,

> ". . . Any person hailed into court, who is too poor to hire a lawyer, cannot be assured a fair trial unless counsel is provided for him. This seems to us an obvious truth."

Gideon was retried in 1963 with counsel in the same courtroom and by the same judge as in the initial trial. He was acquitted — after two years in jail!

The Warren Court also ruled in 1956 that an indigent prisoner has the right to a free trial transcript in preparation of an appeal, and in 1963 that a poor prisoner has the right of free counsel in preparing an appeal. In 1967 the Court held that indicted persons have the right to free counsel at a police line-up and that police line-up identification in the absence of counsel must be excluded from later trial proceedings.

The Escobedo and Miranda Decisions   Two 5-4 decisions in the mid-1960's expanded the rights of suspects in state criminal cases and embroiled the Court in prolonged controversy. At issue were the Fifth Amendment's right against self-incrimination and the Sixth Amendment's right to counsel. The cases of *Escobedo v. Illinois* (1964) and *Miranda v. Arizona* (1966) raised the questions whether criminal suspects had the right to counsel before trial, such as in police interrogations; and whether, if the right of counsel is denied, the prosecution can use "voluntary" confessions obtained in the absence of counsel at the trial or must the judge exclude such evidence on the grounds of the Fifth Amendment.

On January 19, 1960, in Chicago, Illinois, Danny Escobedo's brother-in-law was fatally shot. On January 30 a man in police custody accused Escobedo of the shooting. Danny was brought to the police station, handcuffed, kept standing and told that "his accomplice" accused him of the shooting. Escobedo asked for his lawyer. The police told Escobedo that his lawyer "didn't want to see him." The interrogation continued, and through a tricky line of questioning Escobedo was led to sign a confession of guilt. At no time was Escobedo advised of his constitutional rights. Escobedo's lawyer had gone to the police station and made repeated requests to see Danny. The lawyer was told to wait until the interrogation was over. After the conviction Escobedo appealed. The questions posed to the Supreme Court were: (1) once the police focused on Danny Escobedo as a suspect and the proceedings ceased to be a general investigation, did the refusal of the police to honor Escobedo's request to consult with his attorney constitute a violation of the

Sixth and Fourteenth Amendments and (2) should Escobedo's confession have been excluded from his trial in accord with the Fifth Amendment?

Justice Arthur Goldberg ruled for the Court,

> We hold... that where... the investigation is no longer a general inquiry into an unsolved crime but has begun to focus on a particular suspect, the suspect has been taken into police custody, the police carry out a process of interrogations that lends itself to eliciting incriminating statements, the suspect has requested and been denied an opportunity to consult with his lawyer, and the police have not effectively warned him of his absolute constitutional right to remain silent, the accused has been denied 'the Assistance of Counsel' in violation of the Sixth Amendment to the Constitution as 'made obligatory upon the States by the Fourteenth Amendment,'... and that no statement elicited by the police during the interrogation may be used against him at a criminal trial. . . .

The dissenting justices said the ruling would end voluntary confessions and claimed "it reflects a deep-seated distrust of law enforcement officers. . . ."

The *Escobedo* decision led to a call for clearer guidelines as to the constitutional procedures for police interrogation of criminal suspects. Left undecided were such questions as: Must the police warn a suspect of his right of counsel? Does the right of counsel include the right of an indigent to court-appointed counsel during an interrogation? Under what circumstances can the right to counsel be waived?

The Court delivered its answer on June 13, 1966, in *Miranda v. Arizona,* when it spelled out the "Miranda warning" as the rules for police to follow. On March 13, 1963, police arrested twenty-three-year old indigent Ernesto A. Miranda, a ninth-grade dropout and schizophrenic, for kidnapping and raping an eighteen-year-old girl in Phoenix, Arizona. The girl identified Miranda in a police line-up. He was then questioned by police. He did not request, nor was he advised of his right to counsel. Two hours later he confessed and signed a written confession. At his trial Miranda's lawyer moved the confession be excluded as evidence on the grounds that it was drawn from Miranda in violation of his Sixth Amendment right to counsel. The judge allowed the confession to stand as evidence, and Miranda was convicted. Miranda's lawyers appealed to the United States Supreme Court. An old prosecutor, former California district attorney and attorney general, Earl Warren wrote the decision. Warren ruled,

> The prosecution may not use statements. . . stemming from
> custodial interrogation of the defendant unless it demonstrates
> the use of procedural safeguards effective to secure the privi-
> lege against self-incrimination. . . . As for the procedural safe-
> guards. . . . Prior to any questioning, the person must be
> warned that he has a right to remain silent, that any statement
> he does make may be used as evidence against him, and that he
> has a right to the presence of an attorney, either retained or
> appointed. The defendant may waive. . . these rights, provided
> the waiver is made voluntarily, knowingly, and intelligently.

Even if a defendant waived these rights, he could call for an
attorney at any time during the interrogation. Warren went on, "the
constitutional foundation underlying the privilege is the respect a
government — state or federal — must accord to the dignity and
integrity of its citizens. . . ."

Four justices dissented with often bitter words. Police officials
claimed "their hands were tied." Many politicians charged the
Warren Court with "coddling criminals."

In 1967 in *In re Gault,* the Court extended the right of counsel
to juveniles and held that in the pre-trial interrogation the juvenile
must be told of his right of silence and that what he says can be used
against him in juvenile court proceedings.

The Fourth Amendment — Mapp v. Ohio, 1961   In 1961 the
Court in *Mapp v. Ohio* ruled to exclude all evidence from state criminal trials obtained by police in violation of the Fourth Amendment's restraints "against unreasonable searches and seizures."

At 1:30 p.m. on May 23, 1957, three Cleveland police officers
rang the doorbell of Dollree Mapp. The police said they wanted to
question her — they didn't say on what subject. The police suspected
"Dolly" Mapp was hiding a person wanted for questioning in a
recent bombing and that she had illegal gambling materials. Miss
Mapp called her lawyer who advised her not to let the police in without a search warrant. She opened the second-floor window and
asked if they had a warrant. They didn't, and she refused admit-
tance. They placed the Mapp house under surveillance.

Three hours later seven policemen broke into Dolly Mapp's
home. She demanded to see a warrant. A policeman held up a piece
of paper, she grabbed it, and "placed it in her bosom." A struggle
ensued. The officers recovered the piece of paper. The police did not
find what they were looking for, but they did find "obscene materials" — four pamphlets, a couple of photographs, and "a little pencil doodle" — the possession of which violated Ohio law. Dolly
Mapp was arrested, tried, and convicted for "knowingly having

(possessed). . . lewd and lascivious books, pictures, and photographs."

In the state trial no warrant was produced. The police entry, search and seizure were illegal. The Supreme Court faced the question, should it reinterpret the Fourteenth Amendment's provision that a state must not deny a person liberty without due process of law to exclude from state criminal trials evidence gained in violation of the Fourth Amendment?

Justice Tom Clark, Attorney General under President Truman, wrote a majority opinion that material seized in violation of the Fourth Amendment is "inadmissable in a state court. . . . We can no longer permit (the Fourth Amendment) to remain an empty promise."

"Wiretaps" and "Bugs" — Berger v. New York, 1967   The Warren Court also took a strong stand against the abuses of the Fourth Amendment by the new electronic technology of "wiretapping" and "bugging." In *Berger v. New York* (1967) the Court ruled unconstitutional a 1938 New York law that permitted police use of wiretapping and bugging. This decision overturned a Court ruling in 1928 which upheld wiretapping. Justice Oliver Wendell Holmes had then called wiretapping a "dirty business." Many law enforcement officials, however, maintained tapping and bugging were essential police tools against organized and white-collar crime.

Eavesdropping is an old practice, indulged in by nosy neighbors, private sleuths, law enforcement officials — and some politicians — throughout the centuries. British common law condemned eavesdropping — listening by the naked ear under eaves of houses — as a "nuisance." Electronic technology changed the practice. By 1967 the federal government and most states forbade indiscriminate wiretapping, but most allowed court-authorized wiretaps by police. Only seven states had any laws to forbid official or private bugging, and six of those allowed court-ordered bugs.

The 1938 New York law allowed electronic surveillance if the police could prove to a judge that there was "reasonable ground" that evidence of a crime might be obtained, and if the police named the particular person, conversations, and telephone to be tapped. The order would last for two months, but could be extended by the judge.

The New York police obtained information by a court-authorized "bug" and convicted Ralph Berger in 1964 as a "go-between" in a bribe of the New York State Liquor Authority to get a license for a Playboy night club.

Justice Clark ruled for the Court that the New York law violated the Fourth Amendment as applied to the states by the Fourteenth. Clark wrote, "'The proceeding by search warrant is a drastic one'... and must be carefully circumscribed so as to prevent unauthorized invasions of 'the sanctity of a man's house and the privacies of life'.... New York's broadside authorization rather than being 'carefully circumscribed' . . . permits general searches by electronic devices. . . ."

Four of the justices defended the New York law. Justice Black held that the Fourth Amendment forbids only *unreasonable* searches and seizures," and does not erect walls of impenetrable "privacy."

The Warren Court did allow police to "stop and frisk" a suspect on the street without a warrant. In *Terry v. Ohio* in 1968, Warren ruled that police can stop "suspicious-looking persons" and "frisk them *for weapons*" when that is reasonably necessary for the safety of police and others. Any weapons or other evidence of crime produced in the frisk are admissable evidence in court.

Crime and the 1968 Presidential Campaign   From 1960 to 1967 the nation's population increased 10 percent, but crime rose 89 percent. Murders rose 40 percent; rape, 22 percent; assault, 55 percent; car theft, 52 percent, and robbery, 151 percent. Many Americans were scared. The demand for safe streets and the call for "law and order" and an end to the Court's "coddling of criminals" grew.

In 1968, a Presidential election year, Americans were bitterly divided over the Vietnam War, race relations, and campus turmoil. A Gallup poll showed that 63 percent of Americans believed the courts were too lenient on criminals. A Harris poll showed 81 percent of the American people felt "law and order had broken down." The Republican Presidential nominee, Richard Nixon, called for a strengthening of the "peace forces over the criminal forces." He denounced the *Escobedo* and *Miranda* decisions, called for court-authorized police use of wiretapping and bugging, and pledged to appoint "strict constructionists" to the Supreme Court. The Congress in June, 1968, enacted a comprehensive "Safe Streets and Crime Control Act." It greatly increased federal aid to local police departments and authorized wiretaps and bugs by federal, state and local law enforcement officers under court authorization and strict supervision. However, efforts in Congress to overturn *Miranda* and other Warren Court decisions on due process failed.

THE BURGER COURT

President Nixon appointed four strict constructionist justices in his first term in office. When Chief Justice Earl Warren retired, in June, 1969, Nixon named Circuit Court Judge Warren E. Burger to be Chief Justice. Burger was more conservative than Warren on the question of "judicial activism" versus "judicial self-restraint" and on the rights of the criminally accused. The Senate rejected the nominations of two conservative southern federal judges, Clement F. Haynsworth in November, 1969, by a vote of 55-45 and G. Harrold Carswell in April, 1970, 51-45. Haynsworth was accused of conflict of interest and Carswell of racism and mediocrity. Nixon finally succeeded in gaining the appointments of two federal judges, Harry A. Blackmun of Minnesota and Lewis F. Powell, Jr., of Virginia, and William H. Rehnquist, of Arizona, a former aide to Barry Goldwater and John Mitchell, to the Supreme Court.

The Burger court from 1969 to 1979 has often been divided. From 1972 to 1977 the "Nixon four" voted together in over 65 percent of all decisions, but in 1977-78 this bloc lost its cohesiveness and agreed on only 36 percent of the Court's decisions. Burger and Rehnquist have been consistently on the conservative side; and the old Warren Court justices, Brennan and Marshall, on the liberal side. There have been many split — 6-3, 5-4 — decisions, about 40 percent of all rulings since 1972. The Burger court has shown increased respect for states' rights and a preference that social issues be resolved by the political branches of government, not the judiciary.

The inconsistency of the Burger Court is possibly best seen in its rulings in two sensitive social controversies: the death penalty and abortion.

The Burger Court broke new ground in 1972 when it ruled all existing death penalty laws to be unconstitutional violations of the Fifth Amendment's "due process" clause and the Eighth Amendment's "cruel and unusual punishment" clause. In 1973 the Court in *Roe v. Wade* overturned all state laws making it a criminal offense for a doctor to perform voluntary abortions during a patient's first three months of pregnancy. Later, however, the Court pulled back. In 1976 the Court upheld new capital punishment laws in Florida, Georgia, and Texas. And in 1977 the Court ruled states need not finance elective abortions under Medicaid. The Court held that such financing was a state matter to be decided by the political branches of government, not the judiciary — a clear example of judicial restraint.

School Desegregation   Much of the business of the Court, however, has, as before 1969, often revolved around issues of school desegregation and criminal due process. The Court in *Alexander v.*

Holmes County Board of Education in October, 1969, rebuked the Nixon administration's attempts to delay school desegregation in Mississippi and ordered "every school district to terminate dual school systems at once and to operate. . . only unitary schools." In one year the percentage of Negroes attending formerly all-white schools in the South jumped from 18.4 percent to 38.1 percent. In *Swann v. Charlotte-Mecklenburg Board of Education* in April, 1971, the Burger Court unanimously upheld a lower federal court which ordered busing, among other remedial measures, to desegregate the Charlotte schools. The Court said busing was a legitimate tool to "dismantle the dual school systems." "Busing" and "neighborhood schools" were issues throughout the 1970's as federal courts rendered desegregation orders, including busing, in many large northern cities, notably Boston.

On July 25, 1974, in *Milliken v. Bradley,* the twenty years of unanimous, 9-0, Court rulings in school desegregation cases ended when the Supreme Court overruled a federal judge's order that Detroit and fifty-three surrounding suburbs must join in one metropolitan school district of almost 800,000 school children with massive busing to end school segregation. The Court split 5-4. The federal district trial judge had found that segregation existed by acts of city and state officials. The city's schools were 67 percent black; the suburban schools were 95 percent white. The trial judge ruled a metropolitan plan with large-scale busing was the only way to end dual educational facilities and create a unitary system.

Chief Justice Burger, ruling for the majority of five, including all four Nixon appointees, held that "disparate treatment of white and Negro students occurred within the Detroit school system and not elsewhere, and. . . the remedy must be limited to that system. . . . The constitutional right of the Negro. . . in Detroit is to attend a unitary school system in that district." He found no discriminatory action by the suburbs and thus ruled they could not be included in the desegregation order. the majority ruling barred any busing across district lines for integration, except where both districts are discriminating.

Justice Thurgood Marshall, the former chief counsel of the NAACP in the famous school desegregation cases of the 1950's and the first black Supreme Court justice, wrote an impassioned opinion for the four dissenters. He charged the majority with "emasculation of our constitutional guarantee of equal protection" and called the ruling "a giant step backward." Marshall held that the Court's order that Detroit eliminate segregation in its schools and its ruling that the metropolitan plan was illegal resulted in a contradiction impossible to resolve. Marshall bitterly held that a system 67 percent black could not be desegregated effectively.

In June, 1978, in *Regents of the University of California v. Bakke,* a divided Court ruled on the question of affirmative action as exercised at the University of California Medical School at Davis. The Medical School had set aside sixteen of one hundred admissions places exclusively for minority applicants, and some of those admitted had lower test scores than Allan P. Bakke, a thirty-two-year-old white engineer. Bakke argued that the special quota reserved for Blacks, Asians, and Chicanos denied him equal protection under the law in violation of the Fourteenth Amendment. Proponents of affirmative action called the quota not exclusionary, but a reasonable attempt to overcome the legacy of two centuries of slavery and years of segregation. The justices wrote six opinions and 153 pages of text — a far cry from the simple clarity of *Brown I.* Justice Powell ruled with four justices against the explicit reservation of sixteen admissions places for minorities and ordered Bakke's admission; but Powell joined the four dissenters to form a majority that upheld affirmative action programs in which race may be a "plus," but not the sole factor in admission. The long-awaited decision was inconclusive. The Court in *United Steel Workers of America v, Weber* in a 5-2, 1979 decision rejected a Louisiana white steelworker's claim of "reverse discrimination" and ruled "permissible" a voluntary affirmative action hiring program, including quotas, resulting from collective bargaining between private parties, a union and a company.

Criminal Due Process   The Burger Court's interpretation of criminal due process is mixed. The Warren Court's landmark decisions have not been fundamentally changed, but have been extended or curtailed by degrees. In 1972 in *Argersinger v. Hamlin* a unanimous Court extended the right to counsel to indigents in federal and state courts in all misdemeanor as well as felony cases. This was a logical extension of the *Gideon* ruling. In an Illinois case, however, decided in 1972, the Court ruled that a suspect did not have a right to counsel in a preindictment police line-up. The Court approved six-member juries in noncapital punishment cases in 1970, a year later denied juveniles the right to jury trials, and in a 5-4, 1972 decision ruled that juries need not be unanimous to reach a verdict. Justice Marshall claimed the Court had cut the heart out of the right to trial by jury.

The *Miranda* decision stood, but the Burger court in three decisions from 1971-1976 whittled away at that ruling. The Court allowed police to use a suspect's statements made without the "Miranda warning" as leads to find witnesses; it allowed prosecutors to use such statements to impeach the credibility of a defendant if he took the witness stand in his own defense and gave testimony contrary to his statement. The Court also refused to require "Miranda warnings" to grand jury witnesses.

In the area of search and seizure the Burger court both supported and limited the police. In regard to "stop and frisk," Justice Rehnquist for the Court in *Adams v. Williams* in 1972 ruled that a police officer can act on the basis of an anonymous tip and need not be suspicious from personal observation that the person carried a dangerous weapon.

In 1973 the Burger Court further enlarged the police power in search and seizure by eliminating the exclusionary rule first established by the Supreme Court in 1914. That rule established that an accused could request the court to exclude evidence from his trial if it was illegally obtained. Willie Robinson was arrested in April, 1968, by police in Washington, D.C., for a traffic violation, taken to the police station, and a police "body search" found heroin. Robinson's lawyer moved to exclude the evidence. The rule at that time was that police could only search for dangerous weapons or for evidence directly related to the arrest. The judge admitted the evidence, and Robinson was convicted and jailed. The Supreme Court upheld the conviction. Justice Rehnquist, for the majority, held that the police could use evidence found in the search of a suspect without a warrant if the suspect is in custody on an unrelated minor charge.

Wiretaps   The federal government in 1940 began to wiretap in "national security" cases. In 1946 Attorney General Tom C. Clark persuaded President Truman to let the FBI use wiretaps against domestic subversives and major criminals as well (see p. 270-1). The 1968 Crime Act, in accord with the *Berger* decision, supposedly restricted electronic surveillance by setting specific procedures. These required that a judge issue a warrant after a probable cause hearing. Attorney General John Mitchell and President Nixon in 1969 initiated wiretaps without court warrants and claimed the President had authority to tap or bug foreign agents or domestic groups or individuals without warrants if there was a threat "to attack or subvert the government by unlawful means." In 1970 *The New York Times* reported the federal government was using ninety-seven wiretaps and sixteen bugs in "national security" cases. In 1972 a unanimous Court through Justice Powell rebuked the President's action to tap or bug individuals or groups within the United States without a warrant as a violation of the Fourth Amendment.

First Amendment Decisions   On First Amendment issues the Court ruled in the 1971 "Pentagon Papers" case, *New York Times v.*

United States, that the government could not exercise restraint prior to publication of information. Justice Brennan, for the majority, wrote ". . . The First amendment tolerates absolutely no prior judicial restraints of the press predicated upon. . . conjecture that untoward consequences may result." In 1972 in a 5-4 decision, *Branzburg v. Hayes,* the Court ruled that the First Amendment does not grant newsmen the privilege to refuse information subpoenaed by grand juries investigating criminal acts. The Court held reporters who failed to comply could be jailed for contempt. Reporters claimed that if they could not keep their sources confidential, then sources would "dry up" and investigative reporting and an "informed citizenry" would be hurt. In 1978 in *Zurcher v. Stanford Daily,* the Burger court ruled the police armed with a court search warrant may enter a newspaper office and search for information regarding crimes. The press claimed its privileged position under the First Amendment and the confidentiality of its sources were seriously compromised.

In April, 1979, Justice White ruled for the Court in a 6 to 3 decision, *Herbert v. Lando* that CBS newsmen must disclose individual opinions held and editorial conference discussions prior to the presentation of an allegedly libelous television program, "60 Minutes," in 1973. Army Colonel Anthony B. Herbert claimed the television program libelled him when it cast doubt on his statements that he reported atrocities in Vietnam to his superiors. Herbert sued Lando, CBS and others for $44 million. Herbert's counsel claimed that the colonel had a right to know the beliefs and opinions and conversations of CBS producer Barry Lando and others to establish if Lando's television production had violated the standard for libel set in the 1964 *Times* decision (see p. 192). Justice White ruled that the Court could not require a libel plaintiff to prove malice and then "erect an impenetrable barrier" to the acquisition of the vital evidence. "Inevitably," White wrote, "unless liability is to be competely foreclosed, the thought and editorial processes of the alleged defamer would be open to examination." In dissent Justice Stewart wrote, "inquiry into the broad 'editorial process' is simply not relevant in a libel suit. . . it is not permissible. . . a lawsuit concerns that which was in fact published. What was not published has nothing to do with the case." Herbert said the case did not involve freedom of the press, but abuse of press privilege; but the president of CBS News said the decision represented "another invasion into the nation's newsrooms." Some feared the ruling would have a "chilling" effect on a free press.

The Court maintained high the "wall of separation between

Church and State" in decisions between 1973 and 1975. They disallowed state grants to nonpublic schools for building maintenance, state reimbursement of tuition to parents with children in nonpublic schools, state tax credits for other parents with children in nonpublic schools, and direct loans of instructional material, staff and services to nonpublic schools. The Court held these practices violated the "establishment" clause.

U.S. v. Nixon, 1974   On July 24, 1974, the Burger Court rendered a most important decision. In *U.S. v. Nixon,* "Nixon's appointee," Chief Justice Burger, ruled for a unanimous Court that President Nixon must deliver tapes and other materials subpoenaed by the Special Prosecutor in the Watergate investigations (see p. 285-7). The Court brushed aside Nixon's claim of absolute executive privilege based on the confidentiality of Presidential conversations, the constitutional separation of powers, and national security. The Court in effect said that no one is above the law, even a President, and that all must obey subpoenas to produce evidence in criminal proceedings. President Nixon obeyed the Supreme Court's ruling, handed over the incriminating tapes, and resigned in two weeks.

The Burger court did not overrule the landmark Warren Court decisions in *Brown v. Board of Education, Reynold v. Sims,* or *Miranda v. Arizona.* It broke new ground in the abortion and capital punishment decisions. The Burger Court demonstrated, as the Court has repeatedly in American history, its independence and it fulfilled its role as an impartial judicial arbiter when it rebuked excessive claims of Presidential power by the Nixon administration in the wiretapping and Watergate tapes cases. On the other hand, the Court appeared to go slow on desegregation, to retreat on individual rights claimed under the First Amendment, and to side with law enforcement officials in criminal due process cases.

Chapter Seven

The Struggle for Racial Justice

*We'll walk hand in hand, we'll walk hand in hand, we'll walk
  hand in hand someday*
*Oh, Deep in my heart, I do believe, We Shall Overcome
  Someday*
— Civil Rights Song

The place was Montgomery, Alabama, the capital of the
Confederacy, a black belt ante-bellum city. The date was December
1, 1955. Mrs. Rosa Parks, a seamstress in a downtown department
store, refused a bus driver's order to give her seat to a white man. She
was arrested for breaking the city segregation ordinance, found
guilty, and fined $14. The angry black community announced a one-
day boycott of the buses. It was almost 100 percent successful, and a
group of black ministers organized the Montgomery Improvement
Association (MIA) to lead a subsequent 382-day boycott struggle
to desegregate the buses.

The black people of Montgomery pushed their leaders into a
test of strength with the segregationist power structure of the city. A
twenty-seven-year-old Baptist minister, Martin Luther King, Jr.,
was chosen to lead the MIA. A newcomer to Montgomery, he united
the factions that divided the black community, brought the once
apathetic middle-class Negro minority into the movement, persuaded the Negro churches to become socially active, and sustained
the black masses in their vigorous and courageous boycott. His leadership and oratory, as well, inspired the black community.

The next month, unknown terrorists bombed King's home. The
bomb shattered the front porch and damaged the living room, and
his wife and child narrowly escaped injury. A crowd of blacks

quickly gathered in front of the bombed house and nervous city officials and police watched. King quieted the angry blacks and yet rallied their spirits. The young minister shaped a powerful social movement with such words as,

> We must meet violence with nonviolence. . . . We must love our white brothers no matter what they do to us. . . . Remember. . . God is with the movement.

Through the Montgomery boycott, courageous black people found a way to take direct action. They need not wait on others — lawyers, politicians, or judges — for their deliverance. Many blacks hoped massive, nonviolent direct action would lead them beyond tokenism to real intergration. The struggle for racial justice in America took new form.

RACE RELATIONS IN THE 1940's

The Balance Sheet, 1940   Some events of the thirties gave hope to black America, but the old problems of legal segregation, disfranchisement, and systematic discrimination remained. The New Deal liberals could not even muster the votes to enact a federal anti-lynching law. The balance sheet of black progress in 1940 might have listed on the negative side: in the South, disfranchisement, *de jure* segregation, lynching, economic subordination, and discrimination; and in the North, the growth of ghettos and their many problems. On the positive side would be the consolidation in the 1930's of the tradition of racial solidarity, self-help, and economic development bequeathed by Booker T. Washington; the existence of civil rights protest organizations such as the NAACP; the growth of black institutions: press, churches, fraternal organizations, and businesses; the impact since 1914 of the great migration of blacks from southern farms to northern cities and urban-industrial developments which broke down the traditional social relationships of rural life; the growth of a unique black culture such as the Harlem Renaissance; the black's newly won political leverage in key northern electoral states and in the Democratic Party; and the hopeful interracial unionism of the CIO.

The Legacy of World War Two   As World War II ended in 1945, black Americans returned to the battle of fighting racism on one front — at home. Americans had won the war against Hitler and his Aryan racial myth. The world was beginning to learn the horrors of racism with the opening of the Nazi torture chambers of Buchenwald, Dachau and Auschwitz and with the numbing revelations at the Nuremburg trials. The United States government had made ringing declarations for human rights in the Atlantic Charter of 1941 and in Roosevelt's Four Freedoms speech. Hopeful, yet skeptical, blacks demanded deeds as well as words.

Life, or at least the vision of what life might be, changed for some blacks dramatically during World War II. Young black men committed to the United States went to war and saw the world, but chafed at the humiliations of a completely segregated life in the military. Things had changed on the home front during the war. A. Philip Randolph, president of the Brotherhood of Sleeping Car Porters and Maids, had threatened an all black march on Washington to gain jobs for blacks. He had gained a presidential order in 1941 from Franklin D. Roosevelt to forbid discrimination in defense industries and to establish a Committee on Fair Employment Practices (FEPC) to oversee the order. The Negro press had become more militant. The National Association for the Advancement of Colored People (NAACP) had increased its membership from 50,556 to 450,000 during the war years. The Supreme Court in 1944 had ruled against discrimination in Pullman cars and the denial of black voting in southern primaries.

Post-War Developments   International events of the late 1940's were important for the American civil rights movement. The Afro-Asian peoples were breaking the hold of Western imperialism and moving to national independence. The new status of black African nations would increasingly inspire American blacks in the 1950's and 1960's. In 1948 the United Nations Commission on Human Rights, headed by Eleanor Roosevelt, drafted a charter, the Universal Declaration of Human Rights, which encouraged the disinherited everywhere. The ideological Cold War between the West and the Communist bloc was fought in terms of "freedom" versus "totalitarianism." The gap between America's racial practices and rhetoric became a significant issue in the international propaganda contest. At home the migrations of blacks to the cities continued, industrialism relentlessly eroded the old social order, and ghetto blacks exercised increased political power. Such were the international and domestic pressures for change in American racial patterns.

PRESIDENT TRUMAN, THE NAACP, AND THE COURT

Truman and Civil Rights   Harry S. Truman was the first President sympathetic to the broad expansion of civil rights for blacks. In 1946 in response to some particularly brutal racial violence, such as the clubbing and blinding by policemen in Aiken, South Carolina of Sergeant Isaac Woodward three hours after he was discharged from the Army, Truman created by executive order the President's Committee on Civil Rights. In 1947 the committee issued a report, *To Secure These Rights,* recommending "the elimination of segregation. . . from American life." The report was a blueprint for civil rights reformers for the next two decades. Truman commented, "We must make the Federal government a friendly, vigilant defender of the rights and equalities of all Americans." The President sent a package bill to Congress in February 1948, in which he urged the creation of a permanent civil rights commission, a joint Congressional committee on civil rights, and a civil rights division in the Justice Department; a strengthening of existing civil rights laws and passage of a federal anti-lynching law; guarantees of voting rights and, specifically, the abolition of the poll tax; a fair employment practices commission; an end to discrimination in all interstate transportation facilities; and home rule and voting rights in Presidential elections for citizens of the District of Columbia.

Congress, however, controlled by a coalition of Republicans and conservative southern Democrats, did nothing. In June, 1948, the President issued another executive order to end segregation in the Armed Forces, finally implemented during the Korean War. It is ironic that the military, a basically authoritarian organization built on a chain of command, took the lead in democratic employment and promotion practices. Truman also issued an order for fair employment in the federal government in 1948.

In the election of 1948, Truman pushed civil rights to the point where many Southerners walked out of the Democratic Party and formed the Dixiecrat Party, which carried four southern states for its Presidential candidate, Strom Thurmond, Governor of South Carolina. But Truman's actions earned him the mass of black votes in the big electoral states of the North — votes that proved decisive in his upset victory over the Republican candidate, Thomas Dewey.

Truman's successes in civil rights came through executive actions. Congress, with its rural bias, its cumbersome rules of procedure, its seniority system which favored the entrenched southern Democrats, and its Senate filibusters, passed no civil rights legislation from 1875 to 1957. Later, President Kennedy, too, relied on executive orders to combat discrimination in housing and employment until public opinion, mobilized by the Birmingham crisis of 1963, finally stirred Congressional action on a significant scale.

The NAACP and the Supreme Court Major initiatives for change in American race relations were made by the NAACP Legal and Educational Defense Fund lawyers, headed by Thurgood Marshall. The branch of government in the forefront of change was the United States Supreme Court. Constitutional amendments, the Fourteenth and the Fifteenth, were the instruments used by the lawyers and judges.

Since its founding in 1910 by W. E. B. DuBois, the NAACP had emphasized the value of political lobbying, public information, and court litigation to advance black rights. The NAACP realized that a despised minority had less chance of progress through the political process under majority rule than through court litigation under the constitutional guarantees that no state may deny "due process" or "equal protection of the law" or the right to vote "on account of race." From 1938 to 1954 the Court in many decisions (see p. 187-8) chipped away at discrimination and at the South's segregated educational systems. The climactic moment for the NAACP lawyers came on May 17, 1954. In *Brown v. Board of Education of Topeka, Kansas,* a unanimous Court, speaking through Chief Justice Earl Warren, ruled that "in the field of public education the doctrine of 'separate but equal' has no place. Separate educational facilities are inherently unequal." The decision knocked down the school segregation laws of seventeen states and the District of Columbia.

For the next ten years, in the face of growing white southern resistance, and in the absence of effective Presidential leadership and without any Congressional support, black children and parents, civil rights lawyers and the courts led the way toward integration. Change was slow. There was token compliance in part of the Upper South and a defiant "never" in the Deep South and Virginia.

THE MONTGOMERY BUS BOYCOTT AND MARTIN LUTHER KING

The Montgomery bus boycott of 1955-56 began a new era in American race relations. Massive, nonviolent, direct action campaigns presented a new strategy and set of tactics. The Baptist minister, Martin Luther King, Jr., served as philosopher, spokesman and leader of a black revolution. He and the civil rights movement inspired not only black Americans, but also others who had been discriminated against or excluded from the mainstream of American society, such as Hispanics, Indians, the poor, and women.

Martin Luther King, Jr.   Martin Luther King, Jr., was born in Atlanta, Georgia, on January 15, 1929, the son of a successful minister, the grandson of a sharecropper. Though a member of Atlanta's comfortable black middle class and from a closely knit religious family, young King learned of discrimination and racial injustice early, for in the 1930's Atlanta was a "Jim Crow" city. He had the advantage of an excellent education, Morehouse College, Crozer Theological Seminary and a doctorate at Boston University in 1954. After that he and his wife of one year, Alabama-born Coretta Scott, decided to "go South," and he accepted a pastorate in Montgomery.

King's Movement Towards Nonviolence   King's personal philosophy and strategy for social change had many roots. He made the words and deeds of Jesus Christ his lifelong guide. As a student at Morehouse, he read Thoreau's *Essay on Civil Disobedience*. He agreed that an individual should remain true to his conscience, even to the point of breaking unjust laws, and yet he should show his respect for law by accepting the penalty of imprisonment. In seminary King made a commitment that the Church must be as concerned with the improvement of conditions in this world as with the salvation of souls. While at Crozer, King was moved by a lecture on Mahatma Gandhi. An Indian leader of massive nonviolent civil-disobedience campaigns against British imperialism, Gandhi met hate, violence, and material power with love and suffering. King came to see the redemptive power of love and unearned suffering as powerful forces of social change. He also accepted a nineteenth century German philosopher Hegel's view that history is a dialectical process in which all progress comes through struggle and that "historical figures" move history in accord with the world spirit.

Primary to King was the goal of a Christian community of love gained by Gandhian means of nonviolent resistance. One should use nonviolence directly to resist evil. There should be no passive acceptance of evil. One should direct protest against the evil actions of people, not against the people themselves. King held that there should be no hate for nor humiliation of an oppressor, for the goal of nonviolent resistance is to awaken the moral conscience of the oppressor and to promote reconciliation. One seeks victory for justice, not a defeat of individuals. The nonviolent resister believes that suffering inflicted on innocent people by oppressors can be redemptive both for the sufferer and the oppressor who can be converted by the victim's courage and righteous cause. Not only should one abstain from physical violence, but also from violence of the spirit. At the center of nonviolence is love. To King love meant understanding, acceptance, a recognition of the humanity of all persons. All life is interrelated; all men are brothers. To do violence to one's brother is to do violence to oneself. The nonviolent practitioner must go to any length to heal the divisions in the human community. In King's eyes love was the only force that could bring this reconciliation. He believed that there is a "creative force in this universe that works to bring the disconnected aspects of this reality into a harmonious whole." This faith gave him hope in the ultimate triumph of justice in this world. Such was King's intellectual "pilgrimage to nonviolence." He added that the experience in the Montgomery bus boycott of 1955-56 "did more to clarify my thinking on the question of nonviolence than all the books that I have read."

Negro Churches   The Negro Protestant churches had long been important in the cultural and social as well as the religious life of black Americans. An all-black institution, the Negro church gave blacks opportunities to develop social programs, gain "political" and leadership experience, and supervise the churches' various property holdings. The Negro church was both a sanctuary in a hostile white world and a vehicle for salvation in the next world. In the 1950's it produced a new generation of young, politically conscious and socially active ministers.

The Montgomery Bus Boycott   In the Montgomery bus boycott blacks refrained from using the buses for over a year. The black masses urged on their leaders, and their leaders sustained the people. Initial negotiations with the bus company, private citizens and the city council proved fruitless. The police arrested and jailed King for "speeding." His home was bombed. Blacks were harassed, arrested and jailed on all sorts of minor charges. A grand jury indicted 115 blacks for breaking an old 1921 Alabama anti-labor law against boycotts. The blacks organized a car pool to get to work, and the city government requested a local court injunction against the car pool as a "public nuisance" and an illegal "private enterprise." Each repressive step by the whites solidified the blacks in their cause. The NAACP, claiming the Montgomery segregation ordinance violated the Fourteenth Amendment's "equal protection" clause, added a legal suit to the boycotters' direct action campaign. On November 15, 1956, the United States Supreme Court provided a major victory for the blacks and King's nonviolent approaches by striking down the Montgomery bus segregation ordinance as a violation of the Fourteenth Amendment. In 1957 King and his associates in the black ministry organized the Southern Christian Leadership Conference (SCLC) to coordinate and spread the new tactics throughout the South.

The Student Nonviolent Coordinating Committee (SNCC) On February 1, 1960, black students staged a sit-in at a "whites only" lunch counter in Greensboro, North Carolina. By the end of March student sit-ins, stand-ins, kneel-ins, wade-ins, and lie-ins had spread throughout the South. So began the civil rights revolution. The young black students went beyond gradualism and the tactics of the older leaders. Inspired by King and the Montgomery bus boycott, they adopted the tactics of direct nonviolent confrontation with southern segregation. In April, 1960, at Shaw University in Raleigh, North Carolina, they organized the Student Nonviolent Coordinating Committee (SNCC).

The SNCC workers, living among the black masses of the South, became the shock troops of the revolution. Most accepted nonviolence only as a tactic of social change rather than as a philosophy of life. They thought more in terms of political conflict, and they talked of "power structures." SNCC hoped to build a black-white "populist" coalition to alter radically American society and values in order to bring not only increased equality of opportunity but also more equality of results. They hoped to empower the powerless, to redistribute wealth more equitably, to make all people political participants, and to make those on the "outside" into "insiders" in a new society. Students worked in the racist black belt counties in voter registration, freedom schools, organization of sharecroppers, and the building of economic cooperatives and political-action groups. SNCC led the effort to crack the segregationist bastion, Mississippi. The task culminated in the voter registration and community action projects of the Mississippi Summer Project of 1964.

In 1961 black and white, northern and southern "freedom riders" rode buses through the South to force compliance in Alabama and Mississippi with earlier federal rulings nullifying segregation in interstate travel. Violent mobs met the riders in Alabama, burned a bus, and beat riders. The police provided little or no protection. The Kennedy administration sent in hundreds of federal marshalls to protect the riders and their rights. Attorney General Robert Kennedy persuaded the Interstate Commerce Commission to implement the Supreme Court's ruling to ban segregation in interstate carriers and terminals.

The philosophy and strategy of massive, nonviolent resistance and civil disobedience as practiced by the civil rights workers of the South had an effect that went far beyond race relations and the South. The 1950's had been an era of apparent social stability; years of economic growth — the "affluent society"; and years in which material acquisitions, the "move to suburbia," and conformity to middle class values seemed the norm in white America. The 1950's also began with the Red Scare of McCarthyism in which many dissenters and reformers were labeled as un-American or subversive. In that atmosphere the Montgomery Bus Boycott, SCLC, and SNCC defied the status quo.

White students returning from the southern civil rights protests began the Free Speech Movement at the University of California at Berkeley in 1964, and the student movement dominated higher education for almost a decade. The anti-Vietnam War movement later adopted many of the civil rights movement's tactics. Welfare recipients, Indians, Chicanos, Puerto Ricans, feminists, homosexuals — those who felt oppressed or excluded adopted the "liberation" spirit of the civil rights movement and practiced its direct action methods. Some, disillusioned with the pace of social change, gave up on social activism and dropped out of society to experiment with a variety of individual and communal lifestyles. The southern civil rights movement helped create a new society, an open, freer, more tolerant, some would say more permissive society.

THE BIRMINGHAM DEMONSTRATION

Birmingham, Alabama, was the big 1963 story. The South's leading industrial city, Birmingham was a center of racial oppression. City Commissioner and Police Chief, Eugene "Bull" Connor, was a symbol of police brutality towards blacks. In the state capital in Montgomery, sat the defiant segregationist governor, George C. Wallace, who in his inaugural address earlier in 1963 declared

I draw the line in the dust. . . segregation now. . . segregation tomorrow. . . segregation forever. . . .

King said that if "Birmingham could be cracked, the direction of the entire nonviolent movement in the South could take a significant turn. It was our faith that as 'Birmingham goes, so goes the South.'" His Southern Christian Leadership Conference planned its attack on Birmingham for months. Their plans were so detailed they even counted the number of lunch-counter stools in each diner. Bypassing the politicians, in the spring of 1963 King made three specific demands of Birmingham's "power structure," the business leaders. The demands were: (1) desegregation of lunch counters, restrooms, fitting rooms, and drinking fountains in variety and department stores; (2) the upgrading and hiring of blacks on a nondiscriminatory basis throughout the business and industrial community of Birmingham; and (3) the creation of a biracial committee to work out a timetable for desegregation in other areas in Birmingham. The negotiations with business leaders failed. On April 3 the demonstrators made a few "probing sit-ins," and arrests for marching without a permit began.

On April 10 Connor acquired a local court order enjoining all demonstrations until the right to demonstrate had been established in court. On Good Friday, April 12, King and others defied the court order and marched on City Hall. King was arrested and for two days had no communication with the movement, his lawyers or his family. In response to a public statement by eight white clergymen in Birmingham that King was an outside agitator and a dangerous extremist, King wrote "A Letter from a Birmingham Jail," a powerful reaffirmation of King's nonviolent direct action philosophy. To the request that he wait for a more appropriate time, King replied, "justice too long delayed is justice denied." He added,

> I submit that an individual who breaks a law that conscience tells him is unjust, and who willingly accepts the penalty of imprisonment in order to arouse the conscience of the community over its injustice is in reality expressing the highest respect for law.

He renounced "the silence of the good people." He was released after eight days in jail.

The demonstrations continued. On May 2 a new tactic broke the stalemate. King sent a thousand black children into the demonstration. Bull Connor met them at the barricades with firehoses, electric cattle prods, police dogs, and clubs. King sent students in wave after wave; soon more than 2,500 filled the jails. Black Birmingham was united and defiant. The nation and the world were shocked daily by the scenes of police brutality on the front pages of newspapers and on television newscasts. As CBS commentator Eric Sevareid wrote, "A newspaper or television picture of a snarling police dog set upon a human being is recorded in the permanent photo-electric file of every human brain." Television made racial confrontations, exposes of poverty, social activism, and war part of the nightly television fare of most Americans. Birmingham could not be ignored. Gallup polls in May and June 1963 showed strong support outside the South for President Kennedy's position on civil rights, for school and housing desegregation, and for an end to discrimination in public accommodations and employment; but those polls also showed strong opposition to all such proposals in the South. A June poll, however, showed 83 percent of southern whites believed desegregation of public accommodations and schools was inevitable, and 49 percent believed such desegregation would come within five years.

On May 10, King and the city's business leaders signed an agreement that accepted the blacks' limited demands on lunch counters, jobs and formation of a biracial committee. The Birmingham story included more than this limited agreement. King became the

The Birmingham Demonstrations, 1963 *(WIDE WORLD PHOTOS)*

nation's number one black leader. His tactics worked. A new militancy was evident as the civil rights movement became a mass protest under black leadership. In 1963, 930 protest demonstrations took place in 115 cities in eleven southern states. There were more than 20,000 arrests, ten deaths, and thirty-five known bombings.

On June 11, 1963, President John F. Kennedy on national television threw the full moral force of his office behind civil rights. Kennedy responded to a growing tide of public opinion that clearly urged forceful federal action, saying

> We face. . . a moral crisis. . . . It cannot be met by repressive police action. . . . It is time to act in the Congress, in your state and local legislative body, and above all, in all of our daily lives. . . . This nation will not be fully free until all its citizens are free. . . .

Kennedy asked Congress for the most far-reaching civil rights legislation since Reconstruction.

March on Washington   On August 28, 1963, 250,000 blacks and whites marched on Washington to urge Congress to enact the civil rights bill. The major civil rights organizations, churches, students, some trade unions, and various liberal groups formed a civil rights coalition. Blacks called for "freedom now." They demanded the vote and equal access to public accommodations, jobs, education, and housing. Martin Luther King, Jr., captured the mood of the day with a moving statement of black aspirations in his "I have a dream" speech.

> I have a dream that one day this nation will rise up and live out the true meaning of its creed: "We hold these truths to be self-evident that all men are created equal."

The fall of 1963 was marked by violence and tragedy. On a September Sunday morning, a bomb exploded at the Sixteenth Street Baptist Church in Birmingham, killing four black girls and injuring twenty-one. In November a sniper shot down the President of the United States in Dallas, Texas. The ugliness in American life surfaced in acts of violence. The new President, Lyndon B. Johnson, called for quick passage of the civil rights bill as a memorial to the slain President. An aroused public opinion, the legislative skills of President Johnson, the memory of the martyred President, the lobbying of churches, labor unions, and civil rights groups — all worked to break a southern filibuster in the Senate and to pass the omnibus Civil Rights Act in July, 1964. Finally the Congress joined the Supreme Court and the Presidency to assert federal guarantees of civil rights.

The Civil Rights Act of 1964   Congress went beyond the Kennedy-Johnson recommendations in the ten-point law. The act outlawed discrimination in most public accommodations and in all government facilities. It established a federal Equal Employment Opportunities Commission, a fulfillment of the FEPC movement of the 1940's. The act provided federal assistance for communities trying to desegregate schools. In Title VI the act gave the federal government the power to end all federal financial assistance to state and local programs that did not meet federal desegregation guidelines. This provisión made it possible to bring desegregation by administrative decisions and to avoid much of the court litigation that had previously slowed desegregation to a snail's pace. The Attorney General was empowered to initiate federal court suits against discrimination in public accommodations, public facilities, education and employment cases. This grant of power to the Attorney General was intended to release the poor blacks and the civil rights organizations from the financial and legal burdens arising from continual litigation. The 1964 Civil Rights Law placed the federal government clearly on the side of the civil rights activists. Although the act attempted to strengthen the voting rights acts of 1957 and 1960, additional legislation would be needed to secure the right to vote for all black Americans.

THE NEW EQUALITY

The summer of 1964 saw the Mississippi Summer Project; increased civil rights agitation in the North against job and housing discrimination and *de facto* school segregation; riots against ghetto conditions in New York, Rochester, and Philadelphia; and passage of the Economic Opportunity Act — the beginning of the War on Poverty. These events all indicated clearly that the civil rights problem was more than a question of due process and equality before the law. Americans also began to see the problem as national in scope involving great social and economic needs. Blacks called for an end to segregated slum housing, inferior and ghettoized schools, high unemployment, poor police-community relations, and inadequate health care. Actions to end black individual and group powerlessness and despair seemed imperative if there were to be real black advancement and social stability. Americans saw not only poverty, but also a culture of poverty that imprisons the poor from generation to generation. The black revolt pushed these issues onto the national agenda and created a new black consciousness that challenged the traditional Americal social, political, and economic systems.

The War on Poverty and the Great Society   On January 8, 1964, President Lyndon B. Johnson told the nation and Congress, "This administration, today. . . declares unconditional war on poverty in America. . . ." In August Congress established the Office of Economic Opportunity (OEO), and Johnson named R. Sargent

Shriver, Jr., its head. America's economy and technology made possible the production of enough goods and services for all. Books such as John Kenneth Galbraith's *Affluent Society* and Michael Harrington's *The Other America* had made many Americans conscious of the impoverished minority in the midst of plenty. In 1959, over 39,000,000 Americans, or 22.4 percent of the population, lived in poverty (defined by the government in 1959 as an annual income for an urban family of four of less than $3,022). And more than 11,000,000 of the poor were of minority groups. That meant 56.2 percent of all minority persons were poor.

The war on poverty was that happy combination of good politics and good morality. Even conservatives such as Democratic representative Phil M. Landrum of Georgia backed Johnson's program. Johnson's program, hopefully, would get people "off welfare rolls and on the tax rolls." Some conservatives supported programs such as Head Start, the Job Corps, the Neighborhood Youth Corps and other OEO programs, for they feared aggrieved minorities were "social dynamite." The black revolution forced the federal government to face up to questions of economic want as well as civil rights, for Lyndon Johnson understood that if his administration were to push civil rights, then it should also combat poverty. He believed poor and lower middle class blacks and whites would move forward together or fight each other for limited jobs, housing, medical care, education and other social services. This old New Dealer hoped the war on poverty would be the major mark of his Presidency. Poverty must be fought, he said, "because it is right that we should." On May 22, 1964, President Johnson told a University of Michigan audience, ". . . We have the opportunity to move not only toward the rich society and the powerful society, but upward to the Great Society. The Great Society rests on abundance and liberty for all. It demands an end to poverty and injustice. . . ." The Tax Reform, the Civil Rights and the Economic Opportunity Acts of 1964 would soon be followed in the Eighty-ninth Congress by a flood of Great Society social legislation, unequalled since 1935.

LBJ's Howard University Speech and the "New Equality"   In President Johnson's most impassioned, and possibly most perceptive statement on race relations in America, he told a Howard University audience on June 4, 1965,

> . . . It is not enough just to open the gates of opportunity. All of our citizens must have the ability to walk through those gates. This is the next and most profound stage in the battle for civil rights. We seek not just freedom but opportunity — not just legal equity but human ability — not just equality as a right and

a theory, but equality as a fact and as a result. . . . Equal opportunity is. . . not enough.

Once legal segregation ended, many Americans believed that black Americans could and should make it on their own. Although whites thought that blacks would follow the pattern of earlier white immigrant groups, the situation of black Americans was different. White migrants came to America willingly and full of hope; the black man came in chains and despair. White immigrants brought established cultures and family ties which sustained them as strangers in a new land. The masters systematically destroyed the black slaves' former cultures — languages, religions and folk ways. The slave family had no legal standing, and the auction block was a constant threat to family life. White owners denied the black man the father's role as provider and authority. Two and a half centuries of slavery and a hundred years of segregation, disfranchisement, economic discrimination and subordination and "judge lynch" represented unparalleled disadvantages. This mark of color added to the crippling heritage of slavery.

The European immigrants flooded into America, and especially the cities, from the 1840's to World War I when unskilled labor was in great demand and a strong back and firm will made economic progress likely. But blacks moved to the cities in the mid-twentieth century to find few unskilled jobs available in the age of industrial technology. A black peasantry shifted from the harsh life of the plantations and share-cropping after emancipation to the despairing life of the city ghettos.

Johnson's Howard University speech called for a "new equality." In the period of transition from racial oppression to racial justice, it appeared that "special treatment," "affirmative action," what some would call "reverse discrimination," would be necessary to provide black Americans an equal chance. It was not enough to end the Jim Crow laws. One could not expect black Americans to compete equally in the economic race with those who had such a head start. There would be a need for special job training, intensive recruitment efforts by employers and educators, and a variety of such affirmative action programs, enforced by governments, if true equality were to come. The black revolution provided the primary initiative for change, but there was need and cause for special efforts by the whole society. Lyndon Johnson called for bold action, but in 1965 he was in a small minority of whites.

SELMA AND THE VOTING RIGHTS ACT OF 1965

Martin Luther King, Jr., took his crusade and his newly won Nobel Peace Prize to Selma, Alabama, in 1965. The issue there was voter registration. Many held that the blacks' right to vote, especially for local officials who directly and immediately affect one's life, such as sheriffs, school board members, and tax assessors, was essential to progress. Those who worked for black advancement long argued over which was more important, the vote or equality of economic opportunity. Local civil rights organizations had tried to register blacks using the cumbersome voting rights provisions of the 1957, 1960, and 1964 civil rights acts. In Alabama in 1947 there were 6,000 registered blacks and, in 1964, 110,000; but there were 370,000 of voting age, which meant that 70 percent were not registered. In the black belt almost no progress had been made. In Dallas County, Selma being its county seat, blacks made up 57 percent of the population, and yet only 335 blacks were among the 9,878 registered voters. In neighboring Lowndes and Wilcox Counties, where blacks outnumbered whites four to one, not a single black was registered. Intimidation, economic coercion, unfair administration of literacy tests, black fears and apathy, and uncooperative local registrars who seldom held office hours (the Selma Registrar's office was open two days a month) accounted for low black registration.

The Selma Demonstrations   Local activists and SNCC began work on voter registration in Selma in 1962. In January, 1965, King joined them. That winter 3,300 demonstrators were jailed in Selma. Sheriff James G. Clark arrested demonstrators daily as they marched to the courthouse to register. The demonstrators responded with prayers and songs. King called for a march to Montgomery to present demands to the state government. Governor Wallace refused permission for such a march, but, in keeping with the nonviolent defiance so characteristic of the movement, the march began. On March 7, under Wallace's orders to stop the march, one hundred sheriff's deputies and fifty state troopers met the marchers at the bridge on Route 80 in Selma. An observer, Benjamin Muse, wrote, ". . . The police moved in with tear-gas bombs and night sticks — the horsemen mounting what resembled a cossack charge — and drove them back to Selma." After this "Bloody Sunday," much of the nation was outraged. Clergy, labor leaders, students, and many political leaders rallied to the cause of Selma blacks. According to a Gallup poll taken at the height of the Selma demonstration , 76 percent of Americans favored strong federal legislation to guarantee the right to vote for all Americans.

President Johnson on March 15, 1965 addressed a special session of Congress and called for new voting rights legislation to guarantee "every American citizen. . . the right to vote. . . (we) must overcome the crippling legacy of bigotry and injustice." As he concluded, the President raised his head, paused for emphasis, and spoke the words of the anthem of the black revolution, "And we *shall* overcome."

But white violence and police brutality continued in Selma. On March 17 a federal court approved King's Selma-to-Montgomery march and ordered the state to provide police protection. President Johnson nationalized the Alabama National Guard and the federal government provided security for the five-day march. On March 25 Martin Luther King spoke from the Capitol steps where Jefferson Davis took the oath of office as President of the Confederate States of America in 1861. He spoke in triumph and called for more marches — on segregated schools, on poverty, and on "ballot boxes until race baiters disappear from the political arena."

The Voting Rights Act of 1965   The civil rights movement reached a peak of moral influence and political power when Congress passed the Voting Rights Act of August 4, 1965. This act substituted faster administrative procedures for lengthy court litigation to secure the vote for all. All literacy tests and other voter qualifying tests used to disfranchise blacks were ended in all states and counties where they existed on November 1, 1964, and where fewer than 50 percent of the people of voting age voted or were registered to vote in the Presidential election of 1964. This provision banned such tests in Louisiana, Mississippi, Alabama, Georgia, South Carolina, Virginia, Alaska, twenty-six counties in North Carolina, and one county in Arizona. The Attorney General was empowered on his own initiative or upon receiving twenty complaints to send federal registrars to replace local officials and to register voters. He was also authorized to send poll watchers to observe the fairness of elections. The Twenty-fourth Amendment to the constitution ratified in February, 1964 abolished poll taxes as a qualification for voting in federal elections. But the poll tax remained as a restriction for voting in state and local elections in Virginia, Alabama, Mississippi, and Texas. The 1965 Civil Rights Act expressed Congress' opinion that such taxes were unconstitutional and requested that the Attorney General test them in the courts. In 1966 the Supreme Court ruled that such use of the poll tax in these four states did violate the Fifteenth Amendment.

THE GHETTO AND RACIAL VIOLENCE IN THE NORTH

Watts   From August 11 to 17, 1965, a week after the passage of the Voting Rights Act, the Watts ghetto of Los Angeles exploded in rioting. The riot signalled the end of one phase of the civil rights movement; at least it challenged the nonviolent direction King had given the movement from the Montgomery bus boycott of 1955 to the Selma-to-Montgomery march of 1965. Watts in 1965, Newark and Detroit in 1967, Washington, D.C., in the hours after King's assassination in 1968, and scores of other American cities were torn by violence. These were spontaneous upheavals. The rioters' targets were primarily white businesses and the police. Time, exhaustion, and overwhelming police and military forces finally ended each riot. The riots were expressions of black hostility against the existing order. The rioters forced the nation to take notice, but few benefits or substantive changes came in the ghettos.

The Enduring Ghetto During the 1950's and early 1960's blacks in northern cities gave money and support to the southern civil rights activists. They rejoiced and suffered with the victories and defeats of the southern blacks. They welcomed the court decisions, the civil rights acts, the Presidential orders and speeches, and the war on poverty. City blacks, however, came to realize that the civil rights victories, mainly southern, had changed little in the lives of urban ghetto blacks.

More northern blacks attended segregated schools in 1965 than in 1954. In 1965 relative unemployment, blacks to whites, was higher than in 1950. The gap between the wages of black and white workers had widened. More blacks lived in all-black neighborhoods in 1967 than at the time of the school desegregation decision of 1954, and almost 30 percent of all blacks in 1967 lived in slum housing. The average black received about half the income of the average white. Blacks suffered an infant mortality rate twice as high as whites (see pp. 244 to 247).

The Black Muslims In the early 1960's a variety of black nationalist groups, particularly the Black Muslims under Elijah Muhammad, offered a black separatist alternative to the biracial, integrationist civil rights movement. Muhammad preached that the white man's rule was ending and that the blacks would soon rule. The Black Muslims glorified blackness, using the slogan "black is beautiful." They pointed to the blacks' African heritage with pride. They also preached hate for whites and Christianity. They did not advocate violence, nor did they carry weapons. They obeyed the law. But they supported all action necessary for self-defense.

All Muslims were expected to accept a rigid moral code and dietary restrictions, to avoid liquor, gambling, and smoking, to practice thrift, and to accept the religious practices and authority of Muhammad. They had great success with the rehabilitation of narcotic addicts, criminals, prostitutes, and other "failures" in American society. The Muslims stressed good work habits; unemployment was almost unknown among them. They strongly supported the patriarchal family. They waged a war against the social disorganization of black ghetto life. Their puritanical morality mirrored that of traditional white middle-class America, and their rules rebuked the stereotype of the black American.

Elijah Muhammad held out a vague promise of a future separate black territory in America. The Muslims avoided all political activity. They supported a separate black economy and denounced all black-white relations. "Why integrate with a dying world?" The Muslims, their ministers and their temples located in the heart of the ghetto, appealed to the young, to males, to the lower class — to those most alienated in black America:

> Its program offered them four things: an explanation of their plight (white devils); a sense of pride and self-esteem (black superiority); a vision of a glorious future (black ascendancy); and a practical, immediate program of uplift (working hard and uniting to create Negro enterprise and prosperity).

Muhammad's religion offered a rebirth. They offered a new name in place of the slave name — an X; a new religion — Islam; a new language — Arabic; a new homeland; and new black cultural and moral values. The movement grew from a few hundred in World War II to between 100,000 and 250,000 in the early 1960's.

Malcolm Little, a former street hoodlum, thief, dope pedlar and addict, pimp, and convict, known as Big Red, converted to the Nation of Islam while in prison. As Malcolm X he became the minister of Temple 7 in New York. A great organizer and powerful street-corner speaker, this product of northern ghetto life became the leading and most powerful voice of black urban America.

In 1964 Malcolm X broke with Muhammad and founded the Organization of Afro-American Unity. A black nationalist, unlike Muhammad he emphasized political action and social revolution, and he held out the possibility of coalition with radicals of all colors. He was developing his new position when black men assassinated him on February 25, 1965. Malcolm's split with the Muslims weakened that movement. Nonetheless, the Muslims and the appeal of Malcolm X reflected the frustration and "black rage" that smouldered in the ghettos.

After 1965 blacks watched the Vietnam War escalate and the war on poverty deescalate. Funds, manpower, and the attention of government leaders came to focus on Southeast Asia. Blacks also deplored the lack of vigorous enforcement of civil rights laws at home. The defiance of southern politicians, the violence of segregationists against nonviolent demonstrators, and the mockery of justice practiced in certain southern courts led many ghetto blacks to a cynical view of democratic procedures, the law, and due process. Some blacks believed there was no effective alternative to violence as a way to redress grievances or "move the system."

The Kerner Commission   After the 1967 riots, President Johnson appointed the "Kerner Commission," headed by Illinois Governor Otto Kerner. The president charged the commission with the study of three vital questions in the civil disorders. They were: What happened? Why did it happen?. What can be done to prevent it from happening again? The Commission's report stated,

> Race prejudice has shaped our history decisively; it now threatens to affect our future. White racism is essentially responsible for the explosive nature (of). . . our cities. . . . What white Americans have never fully understood — but what Negroes can never forget — is that white society is deeply implicated in the ghetto. White institutions created it, white institutions maintain it, and white society condones it. . . . This is our basic conclusion: our nation is moving toward two societies, one black, one white — separate and unequal.

King in Chicago in 1966 and "White Backlash"   Martin Luther King wrote shortly before his death:

> The decade of 1955 to 1965 — with its constructive elements — misled us. Everyone underestimated the amount of violence and rage Negroes were suppressing and the amount of bigotry the white majority was disguising.

King moved into Chicago in January, 1966, to begin a nonviolent, direct-action campaign against segregated slum housing, job discrimination and unemployment, and *de facto* segregated schools. This was the first test for his nonviolent techniques in a big northern ghetto. In the South King's targets had been clear and well defined — legalized segregation, disfranchisement, and brutality. The movement had the air of a morality play with good guys and bad guys. The nation's conscience could be aroused. But northern *de facto* segregation, economic and political exploitation, subtle discrimination, and institutional racism were more difficult targets to dramatize. Many black youths in the northern ghettos were alienated from and angry at society. King wrote, "Black nationalism is more fitted to their angry mood. . . . The critical task will be to convince Negroes driven to cynicism that nonviolence can win."

On July 10, 1966, at a mass rally King announced his demands on education, housing, jobs, transportation, public services, health care, and a guaranteed annual income. Chicago's ghetto erupted in riots on July 13. When King led marches that summer into white neighborhoods throughout Chicago — the response was negative. Many lower-middle-class and working-class whites of recent immigrant backgrounds saw King's demands as a threat to their jobs, neighborhood schools, and property values and rallied to defend themselves. They had recently climbed out of ghetto poverty themselves. They bitterly resented a coalition of poor blacks and upperclass whites that appeared to threaten their newly gained and marginal status as homeowners and secure jobholders.

Chicago's Mayor Richard Daley did not make the clumsy mistakes of the Bull Connors and Jim Clarks of Alabama. Daley had the Chicago police protect King and his demonstrators. On August 5 a mob of 4,000 whites in Chicago attacked King and 600 demonstrators, despite the protection by 960 police. King, hit in the head by a stone and knocked down, had met the northern white backlash. "I've never seen anything like it in my life," he said.

Three weeks later, King, Daley, and the religious, real estate, and banking interests of Chicago reached a ten-point agreement to open housing opportunities to blacks. But what appeared in August to be a great victory soon faded. Little actually happened. The agreements turned out to be paper promises which Chicago's leadership did not fulfill. King's nonviolent tactics and his influence were set back.

The Vietnam War and Civil Rights   Shifting his attention, to the war in Vietnam, King called the United States government "the greatest purveyor of violence in the world today." In his opinion the continuation of the war diverted the money, energy and national leadership needed to resolve the twin problems of race and poverty. The war, he claimed, siphoned off resources and attention from the war on poverty and the struggle for civil rights at home. Not only did the ghettos suffer from a lack of attention at home, but blacks fought and died on the front lines of Vietnam in disproportionate numbers. Some civil rights leaders criticized King for joining the peace movement and claimed his activities would dilute the civil rights movement's energies, alienate the Johnson administration, and arouse public hostility. King replied that as a Christian apostle of nonviolence he could not condone violence at home or abroad.

"Black Power"   King's leadership was challenged in the South at Greenwood, Mississippi, on June 16,1966. Stokely Carmichael, a leader of SNCC, yelled to a crowd of blacks, "We want black power!" The response came in a chant, "Black power! Black power!" Some disillusioned civil rights veterans questioned nonviolence and biracialism in the movement. King responded that he opposed violence in principle, and he added that in practice blacks would be slaughtered in a violent encounter. He reaffirmed his goal of a biracial movement on moral and practical grounds. It would be unjust to exclude whites who had suffered alongside blacks. He noted that blacks made up only 10 percent of the American population and that white allies were necessary to form a coalition to alter the character of American society.

What did Black Power mean? Black separatism? Riots and rebellions? Guerrilla warfare? To most whites, Black Power was an anti-white cry. It certainly reflected black disillusionment with the unfilled expectations of the early 1960's. To many blacks, it was a call for racial solidarity and pride, organization of black cooperatives and credit unions, and creation of black political-action groups.

Black Power advocates called upon blacks to define their own goals and means to gain control over their own communities. Most did not support violence, but justified its use in self-defense. Deploring the dependency and powerlessness of most blacks, they called for a restructuring of America's values and institutions. Whites who wanted to work in civil rights were told go into the white communities to combat racism there. Black Power advocates who still supported integration as a final goal insisted that it be the integration of a new black man into a radically different American society. Independence and power would provide blacks the capability to bargain on a more equal basis with white America. Blacks must act as a group. Integration as practiced simply took token individuals away from the black community, claimed the Black Power leaders, and did nothing for the black community, while soothing the consciences of upper-class whites.

Black Power shifted from rhetoric to programs after 1967. The election of black mayors, city councilors, and the creation of private all-black experimental schools; the winning of black community control, or at least influence, over public schools; the growth of black cooperatives and businesses; and the articulation of a black community voice in urban renewal and the decentralization of city governments are such expressions.

The Assassination of Martin Luther King, Jr.   In King's last year of life he continued to strive to resolve the problems of race and poverty. Working to rebuild the civil rights coalition, he attempted to unite the poor of both races. Drafting far-reaching proposals on education, jobs, housing, welfare, social services, and community participation, in the spring of 1968 King planned a Poor People's March on Washington. Blacks, Chicanos, Appalachian whites, Indians, the disinherited of all groups prepared to march. In early April he went to Memphis, Tennessee, to help win union recognition and a living wage for striking municipal garbage workers. On April 4, 1968, as King stood on the balcony of his motel, he was shot and killed by a white man. His career ended as it had begun — in 1955 he stood up for a department-store seamstress and her right to remain seated on a bus, and in 1968 he died in a struggle to assure garbage workers of a decent life. Many wondered, did his violent death mean that nonviolent approaches to racial change are impossible in American society?

Many blacks and whites mourned the loss of America's leading spokesman for interracial understanding and nonviolent change. But moments after the assassination the black communities in 125 cities erupted in violence. These outbreaks contradicted all King had preached. But blacks were angry, hurt and bitter. Stokely Carmichael told blacks to "get your guns." Police, 21,000 specially trained federal troops and 34,000 National Guardsmen — a record number of men for any American civil disturbance — eventually ended the riots. The 1968 riots resulted in forty-six killed (all but five, blacks); 2,600 wounded; 21,270 arrested; and thousands homeless. Within a week property damage estimates reached $45 million. Federal troops were sent into Washington, Baltimore, and Chicago. Over 15,000 troops sealed off the District of Columbia. Helmeted soldiers manned machine guns on the Capitol steps! Unlike their response in 1965 and 1967, however, the police and troops exercised discipline and restraint. In 1968 police and troops did not shoot in panic, and life was valued over property. In contrast forty-nine died in the 1967 Detroit riot. In riots between 1965 and 1967, 225 were killed, 4,000 wounded, and $122 billion was lost in property damage. But these facts offered no comfort. King was dead. And as the ghettos burned, the gulf between black and white seemed wider than ever.

The riots of April 1968, concluded the mass racial violence of the 1960's. A realization that mainly blacks were killed, wounded or arrested and black neighborhoods burned and the demonstrated overwhelming force of the white-controlled government may have been the reason the cycle of violence ended. The road of violence seemed to end in black futility. Energies in the black community were now turned inward to build local institutions, to work for economic development, and to construct political organizations.

The Civil Rights Act of 1968   On April 11, 1968, Congress passed, partly in tribute to King, another major civil rights act. The law outlawed discrimination in the sale or rental of 80 percent of all housing by January 1, 1970. To gain Congressional passage of the law, two exceptions were made. Owner-occupied apartment buildings of four or fewer apartments, dubbed "Mrs. Murphy's," and the private sale of a single-family home without a broker were not included in the anti-discrimination rule. The Attorney General was empowered to initiate suits if there is a "pattern" of housing discrimination. The law also made it a federal crime to intimidate, injure or kill a civil rights worker — a goal of southern civil rights activists for years. The Senate tacked on the so-called 'Rap' Brown Amendment that made crossing a state line with intent to incite to riot a federal crime. This reflected the fear of "outside agitators" and "incendiaries." Rap Brown, a SNCC leader, had said "Violence is as American as cherry pie" and had allegedly incited riot and arson in 1968 in Cambridge, Maryland. The Rap Brown Amendment would first be applied in the prosecution of the "Chicago Seven" — all white — for inciting a riot at the Democratic National Convention of 1968.

The Supreme Court and Equal Housing   After Congress' two-year struggle to pass the fair housing law, the Warren Court in a 7-2 decision, *Jones v. Mayer,* on June 17, 1968, ruled *all* discrimination in the sale or rental of housing illegal. The case arose when Joseph Lee Jones, a black, and his wife Barbara Jo, a white, were discriminated against in the purchase of a home in suburban St. Louis. They went to federal court. They argued that the 1866 Civil Rights Act which ruled that all citizens have the same right "to inherit, purchase, lease, sell, hold and convey real and personal property" forbade all discrimination in housing. The question before the Court was —could and did Congress, under the Thirteenth Amendment which forbade slavery and allowed Congress to enact appropriate legislation to enforce emancipation, enact the 1866 Civil Rights Act so as to forbid discrimination in the sale and rental of real estate? The Court answered yes. The majority ruled that housing discrimination was a "relic of slavery" and that Congress had the power to pass all laws "necessary and proper. . . for abolishing all badges and incidents of slavery." The 1968 Congressional and Court actions on housing were the last two major steps by those branches of government in the post World War II civil rights movement.

The "Poor People's March"   The "Poor People's March" planned by King was led by his successor at SCLC, the Reverend Ralph D. Abernathy. Thousands arrived in Washington in April, 1968, not to demonstrate and leave, but to camp on the mall near the Lincoln Memorial. They built Resurrection City out of tents and plywood. The spring rain soon turned "Tent City" into a sea of mud. King had talked about massive demonstrations and civil disobedience to shut down the government until effective action was taken to make the war on poverty more than a failing slogan. Without the inspirational leader and specific goals, the demonstration fizzled. Abernathy kept his followers in Washington for two months, but then police quietly and efficiently evacuated the few remaining demonstrators without serious incident. The "dream" was dead, the leader gone, and SCLC was soon more memory than reality.

THE "BACKLASH"

The Election of 1968 In November, 1968, Richard Nixon won the Presidency and called a retreat, that one of his aides called "benign neglect," in the struggle for civil rights. In the campaign Nixon sensed the popular demand of most whites for social order — the fears of racial riots, anti-war demonstrations, campus turmoil, street crime, and the unease with the lifestyles of the counterculture and the young. The great majority of voters were "unyoung, unpoor, and unblack; they were middle-aged, middle-class, and middle-minded." Nixon ran against Johnson's Vice-President, Hubert H. Humphrey, an old civil rights advocate. Nixon played on the fears of the white backlash and spoke against "forced busing." He competed with George C. Wallace, running on a third party ticket, for "blue-collar, working-class, ethnic" voters. They both believed the "ethnics" were becoming openly racist as the civil rights movement moved into northern cities. The Republican candidate supported "law and order" and "neighborhood schools," code words with clear racial appeals. Adopting a "Southern Strategy," Nixon successfully courted South Carolina Senator Strom Thurmond, the Dixiecrat Presidential candidate in 1948; named Spiro Agnew, Governor of Maryland, who was an outspoken opponent of black militants, as his running mate; pledged to replace Attorney General Ramsey Clark, whom he labeled "soft on crime" and an advocate of "forced busing," with a "law and order" Attorney General; promised to name "strict constructionist, states' rights conservatives" to the Supreme Court; and campaigned successfully in the South. Nixon won 43.4 percent of the popular vote to Humphrey's 42.7 percent, but when Wallace's 14 percent was added to Nixon's, there was a clear 57 percent for a slowdown in civil rights. Humphrey lost all the southern states except LBJ's Texas — but won 85 percent of the black vote.

Nixon and the Retreat on Civil Rights   To implement the retreat, President Nixon named John Mitchell to be Attorney General. He named "strict constructionists" to the Supreme Court.

On July 3, 1969, the Nixon administration announced that it would minimize the use of Title VI of the 1964 Civil Rights Act to cut off federal funds to compel school desegregation and would rely on the slower method of case-by-case court suits. In August, 1969, the Nixon administration asked a federal court to delay desegregation in thirty-one Mississippi school districts. For the first time since *Brown I*, the United States Justice Department sided with a southern state to thwart desegregation. The Supreme Court quickly rebuked this action and ordered desegregation "at once."

In 1970-71 Nixon continued to speak for "neighborhood schools" and against "busing." Nixon's position seemed good "backlash" politics since a Gallup poll in August, 1971 showed that 82 percent of Americans opposed the busing of black and white school children from one school district to another. The United States Civil Rights Commission declared the administration was "undermining the desegregation effort." In March, 1972, Nixon proposed that Congress pass anti-busing legislation and criticized the "contradictory court orders." But Congress did not enact Nixon's bill.

The Nixon administration awarded many contracts to southern businesses and increased federal spending in the South. But benign neglect was the word to blacks. The Office of Economic Opportunity was dismantled in 1973, and the unconditional war on poverty ended. The Court upheld the precedent of *Brown* but as the Detroit (see p. 214) and *Bakke* decisions (see p. 213) demonstrated, it broke no new ground. Many of the Great Society programs of the 1960's, such as federal aid to education, Medicare-Medicaid, and job training, continued on a reduced scale, but the experimentation, the commitment, and the cutting edge of federal reform were gone.

A Southern President   In 1976 Jimmy Carter, a Georgian black-belt white "peanut farmer," was elected President with strong support from the black community. Carter represented a "New South." No race-baiter, he supported civil rights, and as Georgia's Governor and as a candidate for President, pledged himself to racial justice. Black voter registration had grown dramatically since 1960, especially in the eleven states of the old Confederacy, where there were 1,463,000 registered black voters or 29.1 percent of the eligible black voting population in 1960, and 4,149,999 or 63.1 percent in 1976. Jimmy Carter won back the "Solid South," with the crucial aid of black voters. Carter appointed two blacks to major positions, Patricia R. Harris as his Secretary of Housing and Urban Development and Andrew Young as Ambassador to the United Nations. He vigorously recruited blacks for lower level federal offices. Yet many black Americans believed he was moving too slowly on civil rights, urban issues, and social legislation.

THE CIVIL RIGHTS MOVEMENT: AN EVALUATION

The civil rights movement had obvious achievements. Court decisions and legislative actions swept away legal segregation and voter disfranchisement and blatant denials of due process. America went far to assure blacks legal equality of opportunity. Blacks took control of the civil rights movement in the 1960's. Black Americans had a new pride and hopefulness. The movement changed American racial relations and attitudes as barriers fell, stereotypes collapsed and a greater tolerance developed. There was violence, backlash, hate; but new social relations did grow. One question remained in the 1970's. Did the civil rights struggle and the war on poverty bring substantial economic and social progress for black Americans?

A good reporter could give a common sense judgment by walking the streets, talking to people, and looking around. A more scientific judgment might be reached by analyzing numbers from sources such as the Bureaus of the Census and Labor Statistics. One can wander endlessly and aimlessly in a web of numbers. One can also ridicule or even be angered at an historian's attempts to generalize about human hopes, fears, achievements and defeats through a stream of numbers. But such an analytical effort, despite its traps and its impersonality, provides a factual basis for judgment as to whether blacks made progress, held their own or fell back.

Wattenberg and Scammon   Two experienced statisticians and social commentators, Ben J. Wattenberg and Richard M. Scammon, in an article in *Commentary* magazine in April, 1973, made such a controversial judgment.

> . . . Large and growing numbers of American blacks have been moving into the middle class, so that by now these numbers can reasonably be said to add up to a *majority* of black Americans.
> . .

They claimed that such an achievement was "nothing short of revolutionary. . . ," but they admitted "that the economic and social gap separating blacks and whites is still a national disgrace." They claimed that 52 percent of blacks had "safely put poverty behind them. . . ." Wattenberg and Scammon demonstrated that though blacks had not reached parity with whites, blacks had made substantial progress in income, employment, types of jobs and education. They admitted serious setbacks in black family breakdown and a frightening picture of the ravages of crime.

Scammon and Wattenberg urged Americans to recognize that progress had been made. They claimed that the civil rights movement, the war on poverty, a full employment economy, the Great Society programs, and particularly the efforts of blacks — especially in the years 1963 to 1967 — had made a difference. They urged civil rights activists to stop saying that all had failed, for such comment "give(s) further currency to the old stereotypes of black poverty — slums, rat-infested dwellings, a self-perpetuating welfare culture — and thereby help(s) to confer legitimacy on the policies of those who would shirk the hard task of social and economic integration." They held the narrowing of the economic class gaps was the fundamental step needed to bring the "only realistic solution to the race problem, integration."

Some Statistics   The following tables of more recent figures are for the reader to interpret. The reader may wish to update, expand or interpret data by consulting a variety of government publications.

STATISTICS ON BLACK AND WHITE AMERICANS*

1. **Population**				
	1960	1965	1970	1976
Total	179,232,000	194,303,000	203,235,000	214,649,000
White	158,832,000	171,205,000	178,098,000	186,225,000
Black	18,872,000	21,064,000	22,581,000	24,763,000
Black as % of white	10.5%	10.8%	11.1%	11.5%

2. Income in 1966 constant dollars

Family Median Income for	1950	1955	1960	1965	1970	1974	1976
Blacks and Other Races	$4,419	$5,408	$ 6,209	$ 7,205	$ 9,553	$ 9,902	$ 9,821
Whites	$8,146	$9,806	$11,216	$13,083	$15,006	$15,478	$15,537
Index – 1947=100							
Whites	101	122	139	163	187	192	193
Blacks	107	132	151	175	232	241	239

3. Persons below the poverty level

Poverty (non-farm family of 4 in 1977 — poverty level was $6,191)

	% of all persons	% of all whites	% of blacks
1959	22.4%	18.1%	55.1%
1960	22.2	17.8	41.8 *
1965	17.3	13.3	*1966
1970	12.6	9.9	33.5
1975	12.3	9.7	31.3
1977	11.6	8.9	31.3

4. Female-headed households

	1960	1965	1970	1976
White	3,557,000	3,882,000	4,185,000	5,380,000
% of White	8.7%	9.0%	9.1%	10.8%
Black and Other Races	950,000	1,125,000	1,395,000	2,102,000
% of Black and Other Races	22.4%	23.7%	26.7%	33.0%

5. Percentage of persons in families with a female head living in poverty

	All Families	Whites	Blacks
1959	49.4%	40.2%	70.6%
1960	48.9	39.0	*1966
1965	46.0	35.4	65.3 *
1970	38.1	28.4	58.7
1975	37.5	29.4	54.3
1977	36.2	26.8	55.3

6. Aid to Families with Dependent Children (AFDC)

	1960	1971
Total	3,073,000	10,600,000
Blacks	1,300,000	4,800,000
% of AFDC recipients who were Black	42%	45%
% of Blacks who were recipients of AFDC	7%	21%

7. Unemployment

	1960	1965	1970	1974	1977 (Jan-Apr)
Total in U.S.	5.5%	4.5%	4.9%	5.6%	7.9%
Black and other races — male	10.7	7.4	7.3	9.1	12.8
White male	4.8	3.6	4.0	4.3	6.9
Black and other races — female	9.4	9.2	9.3	10.7	13.5
White female	5.3	5.0	5.4	6.1	7.7
Total Black and other races	10.2	8.1	8.2	9.9	13.1
Total White	4.9	4.1	4.5	5.0	7.2
Ratio Black and other races to whites	2.1	2.0	1.8	2.0	1.8

8. Education — median number of years completed

	1960	1970	1976
Black men	7.7	9.6	10.8
White men	10.7	12.2	12.5
Black women	8.6	10.2	11.4
White women	11.2	12.2	12.4
Total blacks	8.0	9.9	11.1
Total whites	10.9	12.2	12.4

9. Negro Students in Schools with Whites in 17 Southern States

1960	1965	1966	1968	1974
6.4%	10.9%	15.9%	39.6%	84.3%

10. Life expectancy at birth in years

	1960	1965	1970	1975
White male	67.4	67.6	68.0	69.4
White female	74.1	74.7	75.6	77.2
Black and other races — male	61.1	61.1	61.3	63.6
Black and other races — female	66.3	67.4	69.4	72.3

11. Infant mortality rate per 1,000 live births

	1960	1965	1970	1975
Total	26.0	24.7	20.0	16.1
Whites	22.9	21.5	17.8	14.2
Blacks and other races	43.2	40.3	30.9	24.2

12. Elected Black Officials

	Total	U.S. and State Legislators	County and State Officials	Law Enforcement	Education
1964		115			
1970	1,472	182	715	213	362
1972	2,264	224	1,108	263	669
1974	2,991	256	1,602	340	793
1976	3,979	299	2,274	412	994
1977	4,311	316	2,497	447	1,051

*Data gained from *Historical Statistics of the United States, Colonial Times to 1970,* Vols. I and II; *Statistical Abstract of the United States,* 1976 and 1977; and *Money Income and Poverty Status of Families and Persons in the United States: 1977* — Department of Commerce, Bureau of the Census.

Chapter Eight

The Presidency: Politics and Power

"The Buck Stops Here"
           — a paperweight on President Truman's desk.
"We have a cancer, close to the Presidency, that's growing" —
    —John Dean to President Nixon, March 21, 1973.

       Shortly after 2:00 a.m. on June 17, 1972, a former CIA agent, James W. McCord, and four Cuban Bay of Pigs veterans were arrested for breaking into and bugging the Democratic National Committee (DNC) offices in the Watergate Hotel in Washington, D.C. The two leaders of the burglary, G. Gordon Liddy, a former FBI agent and then legal counsel of the Commitee to Re-elect the President (CREEP), and E. Howard Hunt, a former CIA agent involved in the Bay of Pigs invasion and responsible for security at CREEP, watched from a motel room across the street as off-duty policemen arrested the burglars. President Nixon's press secretary quickly dismissed the break-in as a "third-rate" burglary, and most Americans during the 1972 campaign saw the burglary as "just politics". But "Watergate" soon became the word used to describe the most ugly political crimes in American history. Most Americans considered that the Nixon administration subverted the democratic electoral process and grossly abused the powers of the American Presidency.

THE AMERICAN ELECTORATE

      American voting   In a discussion of the American Presidency, one should begin with an examination of the source of sovereign political power in the United States — the voters. In 1920 both of the major political parties had almost the same percentage of party loyalists; 47 percent of the voters said they were Democrats, 43 percent Republicans, and only 9 percent, Independents. The Democrats gained supporters in the New Deal and Kennedy-Johnson years. In the mid-1970's, the Democrats could still claim 42 percent of the electorate. But the Republican loyalists dropped steadily to a low in 1974 of 18 percent, while Independents rose to 40 percent.

Party Identification

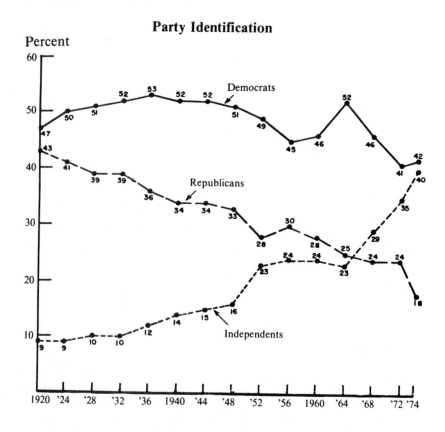

Failure to Vote   In Presidential elections in the post World War II era the vote increased each year from 48,794,000 in 1948 to 81,551,000 in 1976; but the percent of eligible voters actually voting ranged from lows of *51.1* percent in 1948 and *54.4* percent in 1976 to a high of *61.8* percent in 1960. It is a popular opinion that Americans take their politics seriously, but these figures do not compare favorably with those of West European democracies.

A Democratic Majority in Congress   The Democrats won a majority of the seats in the House of Representatives in twenty-eight of the thirty-two years from 1946 through 1978, all except the years 1946-48 and 1952-54, and they won a majority of the popular votes in all but the 1946 election. Since 1964 the Democrats have held approximately a 2-1 margin in the House and almost the same lead in the Senate since 1958.

An Elite Electorate   Elections demonstrated clearly that men are more likely to vote than women, whites more likely than blacks; fifty-year-olds vote at twice the rate of eighteen-year-olds; city people slightly more than country people, Northerners and Westerners more than Southerners; and college graduates and the employed vote in substantially higher percentages than high school dropouts and the unemployed.

The Black Voter   The major change between 1960 and 1975 was the increase in black voting. In 1960 in the eleven states of the Old Confederacy, 61.1 of the voting age whites were registered to vote compared to 29.1 percent of the voting age blacks; in 1967, 67.9 percent of the voting age whites, and 63.1 percent of the voting age blacks were registered. The civil rights movement and the 1965 Voting Rights Act made blacks a political force in the South.

The Decline of Party Loyalty and the Rise of Independent Voting   Despite Democratic strength and Republican decline, the Democrats have won only one overwhelming Presidential election victory since Roosevelt in 1936 — Lyndon B. Johnson's record 61.1 percent of the vote over Barry Goldwater in 1964. In the post-war years the Republicans won three big Presidential victories, Eisenhower in 1952 and 1956, and Nixon's landslide over McGovern, 60.7 percent to 37.5 percent in 1972. Voters have become increasingly independent when they cast their votes for President. American political parties are not disciplined national organizations committed to certain principles. They are loose coalitions of local and state organizations and personal followings held together by the quadrennial spectacles of Presidential elections with their months of primaries, conventions, and all the hoopla of compaigning.

Changes in American Society and the Decline of Political Parties   Increased voter independence coincided with and was strongly influenced by changes in American society. Americans move more often than other people. In 1975, 48.5 percent of Americans lived in a different house from the one they lived in in 1970. Not only do Americans move physically, but many continue to follow the American dream and move up the income ladder. These changes loosen old ties and allegiances, including those to a political party. As

Americans acquire more education — in 1940 the average American had finished 8.6 years of school; in 1975, 12.3 years — they seem to become more independent of party leaders and more ready to make up their own minds.

The old party bosses who traded favors and jobs to unskilled immigrants for votes found that times had changed. The 1,218,480 immigrants of 1914 dropped to 386,000 by 1975. A professional civil service, with job appointments by merit demonstrated on examinations, long ago reduced political patronage. Moreover, the federal government's social welfare programs increasingly replaced the ward boss's influence once exercised through handouts of coal, Christmas bundles, and emergency aid. In 1930 the federal government spent $817,000,000 on social welfare (social insurance, health, housing, education, etc.) or 0.9 percent of the Gross National Product; but in 1976 the federal government spent $198,300,000,000 or 12.3 percent of the GNP on social welfare programs. Union halls have often replaced political clubs as places to gather and gain help, and union membership increased from 3,728,000 in 1934 to 21,643,000 in 1974.

Increased physical and class mobility, the expansion of education, the decline of immigration, the introduction of a professional civil service, the development of a welfare state, and the growth of labor unions cut into "party politics as usual" and encouraged the new independence.

TV, Polls, and the New Politics   In Presidential campaigns the candidates have found other reasons to rely less on regular party organizations. Television, which first covered the national conventions in 1948 and played a major role in the election of 1952, gives candidates direct access to the voters. No longer must a candidate work as carefully through a chain of command of state chairmen, district leaders, ward bosses and precinct captains. He may speak directly to the voters. New polling techniques provide the candidates ready access to voter attitudes and wants. Communication is direct and continuous both ways. Political workers are still needed to register voters, identify supporters and get them to the polls, but increasingly candidates have built personal organizations to do these jobs. Such organizations as "Citizens for Eisenhower," the extraordinary Kennedy "machine," and the Committee to Re-Elect the President (CREEP) have become the norm since 1952.

The new battleground for votes in the years since 1950 has become the sprawling, rapidly growing, politically unorganized suburbs. Candidates fly in by helicopter, "press the flesh" at shopping malls, and get on the local 6:00 TV news. Such techniques have replaced the railroad "whistle stop speech" and partisan exhortation to the regulars in the political clubhouse.

The "New Politics" still demands solid organization, hard work, voter registration, doorbell ringing, and "get out 'our' vote" campaigning. But the old party organizations run by the regulars from the clubhouse have been increasingly replaced by professional campaign managers, TV imagemakers, sophisticated pollsters, computer experts and telephone "banks." The process and the electorate have changed markedly.

The "Vital Center"   In most of the post-World War II years the American electorate has been in the "middle of the road," rejecting the politics of the Left or Right. One historian described these moderate voters as the "vital center." All the Presidents in these years have been "centrists," at least that is the message they have conveyed to the people. Harry S. Truman won the upset victory of 1948 while renouncing splinter groups on each flank of the Democratic Party, the Henry Wallace Progressives on the Left and the Strom Thurmond Dixiecrats on the Right. In 1952 Eisenhower won a victory for "moderate Republicans" in the GOP convention over the conservative favorite, Robert A. Taft. In 1960 both John F. Kennedy and Richard M. Nixon appealed to the middle. In 1964 LBJ seized the center and won a smashing victory over a candidate regarded by many as a right-wing ideologue, Barry Goldwater.

By 1968 American society was torn by the Vietnam War, urban riots, campus turmoil, the youth revolt and racial conflict. The center seemed to collapse. But two old political warhorses, Hubert Humphrey and Richard Nixon, played the game as usual and attempted to win the moderate majority. In 1972 Nixon carried forty-nine states and won the second highest percentage of the popular vote in the twentieth century by portraying Democratic candidate George McGovern as an irresponsible radical. In 1976 Jimmy Carter and Gerry Ford attempted to restore legitimacy to a government subverted by Vietnam and Watergate. They both stood for honesty, efficient government and traditional virtues. A centrist approach to Presidential politics makes sense for that is where the majority of the voters are.

PRESIDENTIAL POLITICS

President Truman   On April 12, 1945, Vice-President Harry S. Truman was called to the White House where Eleanor Roosevelt told him, "Harry, the President is dead." The stunned Truman answered "Is there anything I can do for you?" Mrs. Roosevelt replied, "Is there anything *we* can do for *you*? For you are the one in trouble now." Truman faced many critical decisions in foreign affairs (see Chapters One and Two). At home the new President faced the pressing problems of the demobilization of our armed forces and the conversion of the economy to peacetime production. The list of problems seemed endless, including a rash of strikes, shortages of many raw materials and consumer goods and inflation. In November, 1946, the Republicans took political advantage of popular discontent and won the Congressional elections for the first time since the 1928 election. In foreign affairs the Republican Congress led by Senator Arthur H. Vandenberg continued the bipartisanship begun in 1940 and supported bold administration initiatives such as the Truman Doctrine, Marshall Plan and NATO; but at home the 80th Congress was conservative and even saw socialist dangers in federal aid to school lunch programs. Truman's attempts to continue the Roosevelt New Deal failed.

The Election of 1948   In 1948 the Democrats faced a strong Republican challenger, Thomas E. Dewey, former Governor of New York and the GOP presidential nominee in 1944. The Democratic Party appeared to be falling apart. Some who believed Truman's policy towards the Soviets was too antagonistic and had caused the Cold War rallied to the banner of the Progressive Party under the leadership of former Vice-President Henry A. Wallace who pledged better relations with Stalin's Russia and radical extensions of the New Deal at home. Truman's bold support of civil rights antagonized many Southerners and led to the formation of the Dixiecrat Party under Governor Strom Thurmond of South Carolina. Some members of the Americans for Democratic Action and the CIO unions wanted the Democrats to draft General Eisenhower.

But Truman won the nomination and told the convention "... I will win this election and make those Republicans like it — don't you forget that." Truman blasted the "Do Nothing 80th Congress" and the Wall Street "gluttons of privilege," as he crisscrossed the country on the Presidential train in an old-fashioned "whistle stop" campaign. The Democrats lacked money, and all the polls indicated a certain Dewey victory, but this Missourian did not quit. He gave "sharp speeches fairly criticizing Republican policy and defending New Deal liberalism, [he] mixed [the criticism] with sophistries, bunkum piled higher than haystacks, and demagoguery...." Before his first cross country tour he told his Vice-Presidential running mate, Senator Alvin W. Barkley of Kentucky, "I'll give 'em hell."

Wherever Truman went, the cry went up, "Give 'em hell, Harry." And he did.

Truman had advantages which are easier to see in hindsight. He was the incumbent; the Communists' brutal coup in Czechoslovakia and the Russian Berlin blockade hurt Wallace; only four Deep South states followed Thurmond "into exile"; and the New Dealers finally rallied to Truman. The powerful legions of the AFL and the CIO worked tirelessly for Truman, the vetoer of Taft-Hartley. Farmers voted for Truman and his farm subsidies. Blacks, crucial in big electoral states, supported Truman in response to his strong civil rights position. Jewish voters backed Truman's recognition of Israel. Truman defended Roosevelt's New Deal. A decade before the New Deal programs seemed dangerously radical to many, but now these same programs had large numbers of supporters who benefited from them and feared victorious Republicans would repeal their hard won gains. Last, and possibly most important, were the candidates. Truman was the fighting underdog that Americans love. Once a farmer, a World War I artillery officer, a haberdasher, a Kansas City machine politician, Truman was a

A jubilant Harry Truman, a decided underdog in the presidential election of 1948, enjoys the last laugh the day after the election. *(Photo; UPI)*

plain-speaking, straight-from-the-shoulder sort of man. Dewey appeared cold, egotistical, and over-confident. He announced his Cabinet before the election! The result was Truman's victory with 49.6 percent of the popular vote and 303 electoral votes to Dewey's 45.1 percent of the popular vote and 189 electors. Thurmond won South Carolina, Alabama, Mississippi, and Louisiana; while Wallace won less than 2 percent of the vote. The voters gave the courageous little man from Independence whose desk top paperweight read "The Buck Stops Here," one of the greatest Presidential election upset victories in American history.

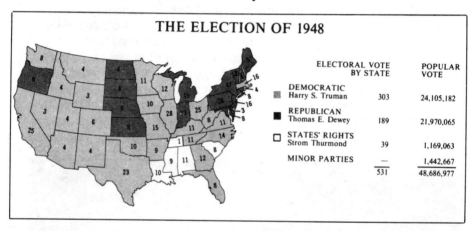

THE ELECTION OF 1948

	ELECTORAL VOTE BY STATE	POPULAR VOTE
DEMOCRATIC Harry S. Truman	303	24,105,182
REPUBLICAN Thomas E. Dewey	189	21,970,065
STATES' RIGHTS Strom Thurmond	39	1,169,063
MINOR PARTIES	—	1,442,667
	531	48,686,977

The Fair Deal   Truman pledged to the Americans a "Fair Deal." It was the New Deal with the addition of federal aid to education, national medical insurance, sweeping civil rights proposals, the Brannan farm plan and a greatly expanded federal housing program. Truman won passage of only the last proposal and the extension of some New Deal measures, for Congressional Republicans joined conservative Southern Democrats to block him.

Corruption, Communism, and Korea   The last years of the Truman administration were sour ones. There was petty corruption with bribes of mink coats and deep freezers, and Republicans charged there was a "mess in Washington." The worst scandal involved the Internal Revenue Service — nine eventually went to jail — and most of the crooks were Truman's old cronies to whom he remained loyal too long. McCarthyism was born when the junior Republican Senator from Wisconsin in a speech to a Republican Women's Club in Wheeling, West Virginia, in February, 1950, made sensational and unsubstantiated charges of Communist infiltration into the State Department. A red scare, exceeding that of 1919-20, diverted the attention of the American government for the next four years. The Truman administration was accused of being "soft on Communism" and guilty of "losing China" in 1949. The Korean War settled into a deadly stalemate in 1951 and became "Truman's War" (see Chapter Two), a seemingly endless and futile bloodletting. The Republicans raised cries of "Corruption, Communism, and Korea."

The Elections of 1952 and 1956 Republican regulars favored the able, conservative, isolationist Ohio Senator, Robert A. Taft; but the managers of a "citizens' movement" for Dwight E. Eisenhower won the "battle of the delegates" at the Republican Convention and nominated the hero of World War II. Eisenhower was a committed internationalist and a moderate on domestic issues. The sixty-one-year-old Eisenhower, above politics, well-connected to the Eastern Establishment, little known to the party professionals, was balanced on the ticket by the thirty-nine-year-old California Senator, Richard M. Nixon, who reassured the party conservatives by his hardnosed partisanship and his anti-communist record. The Democratic Convention drafted Adlai E. Stevenson, Governor of Illinois. Though some detractors called him indecisive, Stevenson combined rare qualities of brilliance, elegance and wit. He pledged to "talk sense to the American people." His finely honed rhetoric, however, did not win the people. The personable, grandfatherly Ike pledged "to go to Korea" and to clean up the "mess in Washington." Other Republicans lashed "Communists" in government. After twenty years in power the Democrats looked a little frayed around the edges. The people yelled "We like Ike." He won handily. Almost 13,000,000 more people voted in 1952 than in 1948, a 27 percent increase. Corruption, Communism and Korea, and especially the magic of the Eisenhower personality brought out the big vote. Ike won 33,936,234 popular votes or 55.1 percent and 442 electors; while Stevenson trailed with 27,314,992 votes and carried only nine southern states. Although the Democrats lost control of Congress by the narrow margin of one in the Senate and ten in the House, the Republican victory was a great tribute to the personal popularity of Eisenhower and did not mark a resurgence of the Republican Party.

Since 1955 the Democrats have controlled both Houses of Congress, and in Eisenhower's last two years from 1959 to 1961 their margin stood at 283 to 153 in the House and 64 to 34 in the Senate. Yet Eisenhower in a rematch with Adlai in 1956 rolled up an even greater victory than in 1952, 35,590,471 to 26,022,752. Eisenhower negotiated an end to the Korean War, kept us out of any new wars, presided over a general prosperity (interrupted by recessions in 1953-54 and 1958) and ran a businessman's administration. He didn't call for bold new starts nor for a repeal of the New-Fair Deal legislation. The 1950's was a period of governmental consolidation, a political pause; and Eisenhower was the man to preside.

The Election of 1960   The Republicans in 1960 nominated Richard Nixon. Unlike Eisenhower, Nixon had been in politics since 1946, serving a Washington apprenticeship, first as a Representative, then as a Senator, and then as Eisenhower's Vice-President. A child of poverty, raised in rootless southern California, his life seemed a series of lonely struggles and crises. Nixon was a strong partisan who as a campaigner played to feelings of popular resentment. Some critics thought him a gut-fighter who hit below the belt and played on the fears of Communists in government as he charged his opponents with being "soft on Communism." Using this technique he won election to the House in 1946 and the Senate in 1950. He made a national reputation as a member of the House Un-American Activities Committee (HUAC) in its investigation of Alger Hiss in 1948. In the Presidential campaign of 1952 he called Stevenson, "Adlai the appeaser... who got a Ph.D. from Dean Acheson's College of Cowardly Communist Containment." Many Democrats would never forget nor forgive such charges. Nixon campaigned for Republican candidates year-in and year-out, and he earned the support of delegates at the Republican National Convention in 1960.

Eisenhower gave Nixon a more prominent role than previous Vice-Presidents. Nixon was sent on numerous diplomatic trips abroad. A party loyalist, he would have to win Democratic and Independent votes to gain the White House, no mean feat. In the campaign, he tried to put the "red-baiting, hatchet-man" image to rest and posed as a "New Nixon." He presented himself as an experienced leader, knowledgeable in foreign affairs, who would continue the peace and prosperity of the Eisenhower years.

The Democratic nominee was the handsome young Massachusetts Senator, forty-three-year-old John F. Kennedy. Kennedy — the grandson of an immigrant Irish Catholic Boston politician, son of a wealthy financier, schooled at Choate and Harvard, World War II hero of P.T. boat 109, husband of Jackie — symbolized the arrival of a new generation and style in American politics. He won in primary battles over a trio of Senators, Lyndon Johnson of Texas, Stuart Symington of Missouri, and Hubert Humphrey of Minnesota, and the still-willing Adlai Stevenson. Kennedy assembled a superbly-organized and well-financed Presidential campaign. By publicly pledging his support to the separation of church and state, Kennedy put to rest the Catholic issue, which haunted many old-line Democratic leaders from Al Smith's ill-fated 1928 race. Kennedy called upon Americans to face the challenges of a "New Frontier." He brought a new generation, that came to maturity in the Depression, World War II and the Cold War, into politics. He had a rare ability to inspire. His youth, call for sacrifice, and charisma contrasted strikingly with the Eisenhower Presidency. Kennedy was also a practical politician, as his choice of the Texas Senator Lyndon Johnson as his Vice-Presidential running mate demonstrated. The Catholic Kennedy from the urban Northeast needed Johnson to hold the South in the Democratic column.

In the campaign Kennedy and Nixon did not differ much on the issues. Both proclaimed support of the Cold War abroad and civil rights at home. They pledged vigorous exercise of presidential power. In fact, Kennedy attacked the Eisenhower administration for not being tough enough against Castro's Cuba. Kennedy inaccurately charged that the Eisenhower administration had allowed a "missile gap" to grow between the United States and the Soviet Union. He called for a major buildup of America's conventional armed forces to fight local, small-scale wars around the globe. He claimed that America was losing the Cold War — "the tide is running out." The Democrat pledged to increase America's rate of economic growth, to expand our space efforts, and supported civil rights, medicare, and federal aid to education. Kennedy saw the federal government as the vehicle to achieve these goals and the Presidency as the initiator of action.

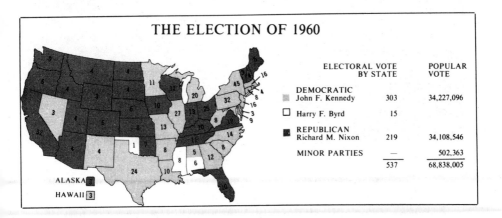

THE ELECTION OF 1960

	ELECTORAL VOTE BY STATE	POPULAR VOTE
DEMOCRATIC John F. Kennedy	303	34,227,096
Harry F. Byrd	15	
REPUBLICAN Richard M. Nixon	219	34,108,546
MINOR PARTIES	—	502,363
	537	68,838,005

ALASKA

HAWAII 3

Four televised debates, viewed by about 70,000,000 Americans, were the high point of the campaign. In the first debate a vigorous Kennedy spoke with confidence to the television viewers; Nixon, thin from a recent illness, his TV makeup running under the hot lights, his five o'clock shadow showing, busied himself debating Kennedy, not talking to the viewers. Kennedy proved at least Nixon's equal, if not his victor, and neutralized Nixon's primary strength, that of more diplomatic experience and mature leadership. The campaign was fiercely contested and extremely close. Of the almost 69,000,000 votes, Kennedy won by only 118,574 — no mandate. Kennedy won a smaller percentage of the votes than his fellow Democrats. He, as all Democratic presidents since 1938, faced a conservative Republican-Southern Democratic Congressional opposition.

Kennedy-Nixon TV Debate, 1960   *(CREDIT: THE NEW YORK TIMES)*

The "New Frontier"   The "One Thousands Days" of John F. Kennedy were marked more by promise than achievement. The Kennedy style captivated many Americans. After the assassination in Dallas on November 22, 1963, there was heartfelt mourning world-wide. In fact, in 1961 and 1962, President Kennedy was stalemated in Congress. In foreign affairs he stumbled badly in the Bay of Pigs fiasco, was thwarted by the Berlin Wall, and slid into increased involvement in Vietnam. But as 1963 opened, JFK had a new confidence resulting from his victory in the Cuban Missile Crisis and the added Democratic support won in the 1962 Congressional elections. He attempted to lead Congress to enact major bills to guarantee civil rights and to cut taxes to stimulate economic growth. He gained Soviet acceptance and Senate ratification of a treaty to ban atomic tests in the atmosphere. The President had his economic advisers draft a major program to combat poverty. Then the bullet struck, a symbol of the irrational violence that dominated the 1960's.

LBJ Lyndon B. Johnson took the oath of office beside the blood-spattered Jacqueline Kennedy on Air Force One as it flew back to Washington from Dallas. Johnson was the complete politician. This big, energetic, earthy, often profane man seemed born to lead. From the hill country of Texas, Johnson was a graduate of South West Texas State Teachers college. A master politician in Congress from 1937 to 1960, he was frustrated in the Vice-Presidency. His old Texas friend and former Vice-President John Nance Garner had once said the Vice-Presidency was "not worth a pitcher of warm spit." Johnson felt out of place and often snubbed by the bright, young, Ivy League "New Frontiersmen." But in 1963 Johnson was probably the best-prepared politician, at least on domestic affairs, to assume the Presidency since Teddy Roosevelt. At home Johnson planned to follow the humanitarianism of the New Deal. Abroad he set himself against appeasement and the "Communist menace."

The "War on Poverty" and the "Great Society" Johnson acted decisively to pull the nation together and kept the Kennedy team in the White House. In 1964, invoking the memory of the martyred President and using all his legislative skills, the new President pushed Kennedy's tax cut and civil rights bills through Congress. These were the first pieces of legislation to break new ground since the closing days of the New Deal in 1938. Johnson held a strong majority of Congressional and popular support. In his first State of the Union address, he called for an "unconditional war on poverty." He soon named his program the "Great Society," and convinced Congress to establish the Office of Economic Opportunity to wage the "war" in August, 1964.

The Election of 1964 In the 1964 election the Republican Party was taken over by right-wing ideologues who nominated their favorite, Senator Barry M. Goldwater of Arizona. Goldwater was an amiable man who had written a book, *The Conscience of a Conservative,* which denounced the welfare state at home and called for victory over Communism abroad. For the first time since 1932 the Republicans dropped their centrist position and "me too" stance and gave the voters a "choice not an echo." Goldwater captured the spirit of his supporters in his acceptance speech with the words, *"Extremism in the defense of liberty is no vice!... moderation in the pursuit of justice is no virtue!"* The Goldwater nomination was a triumph for the South and Southwest and the new wealth of the Sunbelt over the older Republican establishment of the Northeast and Midwest. The Goldwater fundraisers raised and spent over $16,000,000, 60 percent more than any previous Presidential candidate. Some moderate Republicans, such as Governor Nelson Rockefeller of New York, " sat on their hands" in November or voted Democratic.

President Johnson relished the Goldwater challenge. Johnson pictured himself as the successor of the martyred Kennedy and the mastermind behind the legislative majority which enacted major tax, civil rights and anti-poverty laws. Goldwater gave Johnson a chance to do battle with a self-styled conservative who talked of selling TVA, ending Social Security, defoliating trees in Vietnam with "tactical atomic weapons," and who had voted against civil rights and the war on poverty. The Goldwaterites' slogan, "In your heart you know he's right" was twisted by some Democrats to "In your guts you know he's nuts." Johnson campaigned in favor of humanitarian reform at home and against war abroad, especially in Vietnam!

Johnson won the highest percentage of popular votes of any Presidential candidate in American history, 61.1 percent. Goldwater won only his home state of Arizona and five states of the Deep South.

The Johnson landslide carried in an 89th Congress with overwhelming Democratic majorities, 295 to 140 in the House and 68 to 32 in the Senate. It was a Congress eager to enact LBJ's Great Society programs. The new Congress enacted bills such as medicare, federal aid to education, voting rights, air and water pollution controls, model cities, rent supplements, war on poverty measures — legislative action without parallel since 1935.

Confrontation Replaces Consensus   The euphoria of 1964-65 was soon replaced by disillusion in northern racial ghettos with the failure of the war on poverty and the civil rights movement to fulfill rising expectations. Racial riots tore at the fabric of urban America from 1964 to 1968. The endless misery of Vietnam, viewed nightly on the television news, crushed the hopes of more Americans. Confrontation politics in the streets replaced Johnson's efforts to build broad-based popular and legislative majorities.

The Election of 1968   As 1968 began, the country was as divided as at any time since the Civil War. In the Republican Party a "New, New Nixon" made an extraordinary comeback from his defeats in the Presidential race of 1960 and the California gubernatorial election of 1962 to gain the nomination. Nixon appealed to the party regulars in control of the GOP since 1964. He played on public fears. He campaigned for "law and order" and appealed to what he called the "silent majority," who feared racial violence, anti-war protesters, campus turmoil and the lifestyles of the counterculture. He actively sought southern votes the "Southern Strategy." He sought the "white backlash" vote (see p. 241). Nixon raised over $25,402,000 in campaign funds, a 64 percent increase over Goldwater's record fund in 1964 and more than twice the Democrat's monies

The third party candidacy of Alabama segregationist Governor George C. Wallace appealed to the racists, North and South, the lower middle class ethnics who felt ignored, those who demanded victory in Vietnam, and those who had a grudge. He blasted the "pointy-headed intellectuals," "the briefcase totin' bureaucrats," and yelled, "Ah hadn' meant to say this tonight but *yew* know, if one of those hippies lays down in front of mah car when *Ah* become President. . . ." The end was usually drowned out by his audiences' roaring response. He told them to "send Washington a message." He didn't say what the message was. It was one of rage, bitterness, resentment. Civility disappeared in American politics.

Senator Eugene McCarthy of Minnesota seriously challenged President Johnson on the war issue in the New Hampshire primary on March 13. Robert F. Kennedy, President Kennedy's younger brother and the Attorney General under Kennedy, joined the race three days later. The ferocity of the "Tet offensive" launched by the Vietcong and North Vietnamese on January 29, 1968 shocked Americans. President Johnson announced on March 31 that he would not run. In June after an apparently decisive victory in the California primary, Robert F. Kennedy was shot by an assassin in Los Angeles. The Johnson administration candidate at the Democratic Party Convention in Chicago was Vice-President Hubert H. Humphrey, who, for two decades until he became LBJ's man as Vice-President, had been one of the nation's leading spokesmen for the working man and the underprivileged. But Humphrey's foreign policy views were those of the Cold War and he was a "hawk" on Vietnam. Despite anti-war demonstrations in the streets and the impassioned "peace forces" in the hall, the administration rammed through a pro-war plank and the delegates nominated Humphrey. But the streets ran with blood as the police attacked youthful protesters, and the nation watched on TV. The Democratic Party was torn apart. The nomination was worth little, and Humphrey "went home heartbroken, battered, and beaten."

Campaign crowds chanted "Dump the Hump" and drowned out Humphrey's speeches. Wallace's candidacy threatened to deny any candidate an electoral majority and to throw the election into the House of Representatives where Wallace could bargain for his constituency and himself. Nixon took the high road and called for "law and order," while the Republican Vice-Presidential candidate Spiro Agnew became the partisan whose slashing rhetoric led some critics to call him "Nixon's Nixon." Finally Humphrey in late September broke with LBJ's Vietnam policy and called for an unconditional halt to the bombing in Vietnam. His support grew, but not enough. Nixon, with only 43.4 percent of the popular vote, .7 percent more than Humphrey, won the Presidency by a majority of 110 in the electoral college. Republicans had made a comeback since the Goldwater debacle of 1964, and they made additional gains in the South. Humphrey held the old New Deal coalition in the North, but he carried only Texas in the once Solid Democratic South.

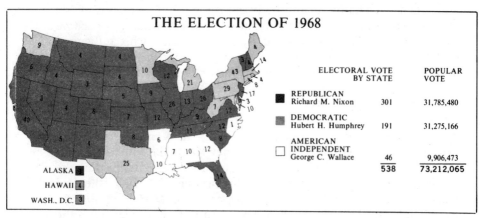

THE ELECTION OF 1968

	ELECTORAL VOTE BY STATE	POPULAR VOTE
REPUBLICAN Richard M. Nixon	301	31,785,480
DEMOCRATIC Hubert H. Humphrey	191	31,275,166
AMERICAN INDEPENDENT George C. Wallace	46	9,906,473
	538	73,212,065

Richard Nixon Nixon said he would bring Americans together. He gradually deescalated the Vietnam War, but he did not get all American troops out until March, 1973. The anti-war protests grew larger with Nixon's invasion of Cambodia in 1970 (see p. 139). Public anger increased with the 1970 shootings at Kent State University and Jackson State College. Nixon called youthful protesters "bums," offered blacks "benign neglect," lashed his Democratic critics as "radicals," and put together an "enemies" list. His achievements such as the "opening to China" and "detente" with the Soviets, were overshadowed by his self-imposed political isolation and criminal actions to protect his power.

The Election of 1972   President Nixon won a smashing victory over the Democratic candidate, Senator George McGovern of South Dakota, however, in 1972. The Republicans renominated Nixon and Agnew in a carefully staged performance in Miami. The Democrats presented a very different story. In May the political violence of the 60's spilled over into the 1972 campaign. George Wallace, who had returned to the Democratic Party, was removed from the race when he was shot and permanently crippled during the Maryland primary. The little-known McGovern won a first ballot nomination. A January, 1972 Gallup Poll showed McGovern had 3 percent of the Democratic support. But twenty-three primaries later he was the leader. In the process strange things happened. Letters appeared which "proved" one candidate was a bigot, another a homosexual and father of an illegitimate child, and that Humphrey had a record of drunken driving and cavorting with prostitutes. These sordid charges were part of the "dirty tricks" campaign orchestrated from the White House, paid for by a secret fund and carried out by Donald Segretti. The use of sabotage, spies, wire taps and bugs, finally culminated in the break-in and bugging of the Democratic National Committee headquarters in the Watergate Hotel by employees of CREEP, former CIA and FBI agents and Cuban refugees, on the night of June 17, 1972.

McGovern, long an opponent of the Vietnam War, attracted many from the groups who had entered politics in large numbers in the previous decade — blacks in 1964, young people in 1968, and women in 1972. The Democratic Party rewrote its party and convention rules to welcome the newcomers. "McGovern's army" was a winner within the party, but most of middle class America was alienated by the demands of blacks, Hispanics and feminists, the youth revolt, the liberation rhetoric, the militant anti-war activists' stance and the newcomers' appearance at the Miami Convention. In the older cities many of the ethnic groups and trade unionists, the backbone of the Democratic Party for decades in the big industrial states, felt forgotten, if not discriminated against, by the McGovern forces. Many of these traditional Democrats "sat out" the 1972 campaign; some even voted Republican.

McGovern made campaign mistakes. He pledged welfare reform with a federal payment of $1,000 per American, but he could not say how he would finance it. He chose Missouri Senator Thomas

F. Eagleton to be his Vice-Presidential running mate. When he learned that Eagleton had been hospitalized for mental illness, McGovern said he backed him "1000 percent," and then he dropped him. The Democratic organization was demoralized and desperate for money. Republicans pictured McGovern as a dangerous extremist determined to redistribute income by a radical overhaul of the tax structure. They charged McGovern was the candidate of "acid, amnesty and abortion." The Democrats brought a suit against CREEP for $1,000,000 for the Watergate burglary, and McGovern denounced the Nixon administration as "the most corrupt in history." Few listened. A Harris Poll in October revealed that 62 percent of the voters dismissed Watergate as "just politics."

Nixon, the picture of a statesman after his trips to China and Russia early in 1972, took the high road as Agnew and the agents of CREEP slugged it out underground. The CREEP organization raised $60,200,000, the previous record being $25,402,000. Nixon's campaign won forty-nine states (losing only Massachusetts and the District of Columbia) while piling up a record 47,167,319 votes to McGovern's 29,168,509. Yet the Democrats continued to control Congress, 239 to 192 in the House and 56 to 42 in the Senate.

"Watergate"   As 1973 wore on, Watergate and a host of "White House horrors" came to light. For eighteen months the government was almost paralyzed and Americans shocked by the constant revelations that flowed from the *Washington Post*, Senator Sam Ervin's Committee, the Special Prosecutor's Office, Judge Sirica's courtroom, and the House Judiciary Committee impeachment proceedings. Most political corruption in the past had involved more ordinary crimes, bribe-taking and kick-backs, such as led to Vice-President Agnew's unprecedented resignation in September, 1973. The "President's men," however, in their grasp for power attempted to subvert America's constitutional procedures and end the rule of law. They came dangerously close to succeeding. The American constitutional and democratic system worked, the guilty were brought to justice, and Nixon resigned on August 9, 1974. Gerald R. Ford, the former Republican leader of the House of Representatives whom Nixon had nominated as Vice-President to succeed Agnew, in accord with the Twenty-fifth Amendment, took the oath of office that day. He was the first man to reach the White House without ever being elected President or Vice-President.

Gerald R. Ford   Ford, a one-time football star at the University of Michigan, had been a Republican regular during his years in the House from 1949 to 1973. Though partisan, he was a friendly and decent man, who in the next two years did much to restore

Americans' trust in their government. In September, 1974, however, in an act of compassion for a man he believed extremely ill and thoroughly discredited, Ford granted Nixon a Presidential pardon for all illegal acts Nixon may have committed while President. Many cried "deal" and feared the complete story of Watergate would never come out. The act of mercy temporarily undermined Ford's primary asset, personal credibility and moral authority.

As President, Ford had to deal with the backlog of unsolved problems of the 1973-74 years, particularly the twin economic crises of the worst inflation since 1946 and the highest unemployment since the 1930's. The energy crisis, environmental problems, the welfare mess, long time tax inequities, and the decay of the cities joined the Middle East and Southeast Asian crises and the challenges of stabilizing new relations with Russia and China to test the new President. These were, and still are, tough problems, and in Ford's brief tenure as President little progress was made to resolve them.

The Election of 1976   In 1976 President Ford used the powers of incumbency to beat back a right-wing challenge from former movie star and California Governor Ronald Reagan. The Democrats had a large field of aspirants eager to contest the wounded Party of Watergate. A dark horse, former Georgia governor, Annapolis graduate, and peanut farmer, Jimmy Carter showed his strength in the first Iowa caucuses and fought through the primaries to a first ballot victory at the convention.

Carter was the first Southerner to be nominated by either party since 1848. An "outsider," untainted by the corruption of Washington, he pledged never to lie to the American people. Pledged to reorganize the mammoth federal bureaucracy, cut the budget, and make the government more efficient and responsive, he promised to reduce the pretentions of the "imperial Presidency."

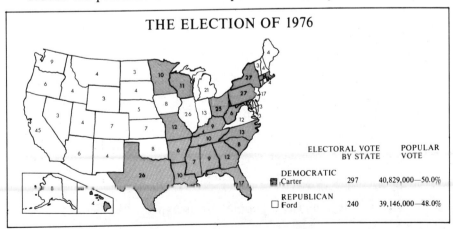

THE ELECTION OF 1976

	ELECTORAL VOTE BY STATE	POPULAR VOTE
DEMOCRATIC Carter	297	40,829,000—50.0%
REPUBLICAN Ford	240	39,146,000—48.0%

Both candidates stressed honesty, trust and character and set themselves apart from all the odors of Watergate. This was difficult for the long-time Washingtonian, Nixon's hand-picked successor and pardoner, President Ford. Even a series of TV debates couldn't enliven this dull campaign. Ford narrowed the gap, but the Georgian won with 50.1 percent of the vote to Ford's 48.0 percent. The Democrats maintained control of Congress, 292 to 143 and 61 to 38.

By mid-term Carter had difficulties with domestic policies. He was unable to gain the government reorganization, or successful energy program or tax reform that he seemed to promise the voters in 1976. Problems of unemployment and particularly inflation continued. No progress was made in solving the welfare mess or in implementing his pledge of national health insurance. Carter, the outsider, had trouble with a Democratic Congress. He stumbled, either from ineptness or the complex and difficult nature of these problems. In foreign affairs he had more success. He spoke boldly for human rights. He succeeded in getting ratification of the Panama Canal Treaties in 1978. In September, 1978, President Carter achieved a major breakthrough in the Middle East when he hosted a thirteen-day conference at Camp David between Egypt's President Anwar Sadat and Israel's Prime Minister Menachem Begin which produced unprecedented "accords" between the old enemies and a formal peace treaty in 1979. In late 1978, President Carter, building on earlier Nixon-Kissinger initiatives, announced the establishment of full diplomatic relations with Communist China. The United States ended formal diplomatic relations with the Nationalist Chinese regime on Formosa and gave formal one-year notice that the United States-Nationalist China military alliance would terminate at year's end. The administration also signed a treaty with the Soviet Union to limit offensive nuclear weapons (SALT II).

PRESIDENTIAL POWER

The President has great powers. Some are granted to him by the Constitution, such as those of Commander-in-Chief, the power to appoint ambassadors, judges and various executive officials, and the duty to execute the laws. By act of Congress he has authority to close all the member banks of the Federal Reserve System in a financial crisis, or to guarantee that all foods and drugs sold in interstate commerce meet certain safety standards. By historical developments he became the leader of his political party and the major spokesman of the "free world." He has become the focal point of the political feelings of the American people. He is expected to help "people make sense of politics. . . he is the top man. . . he ought to know what is going on and set it right."

When Franklin Delano Roosevelt died in April, 1945, the powers of the Presidency were extraordinary. The Congress delegated and the Court upheld great grants of authority to the President to combat the Depression and to lead the nation in World War II.

The Power to Persuade   The essence of Presidential power is not the legal right to command, but it is the power to *persuade*. If he is to succeed, he must sense the many moods of the public. He must realize what is possible. He must be able to persuade members of his administration, the bureaucracy, his party, a majority in Congress, the Washington community, the media, the leaders of corporations, unions, universities and various interest groups, the American people, foreign heads of state, and people in other lands that what he wants to do is right, possible, and reasonable. Harry Truman commented privately of Ike in 1952 concerning the Presidency and the bureaucracy,

> He'll sit here, and he'll say 'Do this! Do that!' *and nothing will happen.* Poor Ike — it won't be a bit like the army. He'll find it very frustrating.

Truman summed up his view of Presidential power,

> I sit here all day trying to persuade people to do the things they ought to have sense enough to do without my persuading them. . . . That's all the powers of the President amount to.

Access to Information   Crucial to any successful exercise of Presidential power is access to information. A President needs to have accurate and complete information if he is to define problems clearly, propose reasonable policies, make wise decisions and see that the desired results are achieved. He must understand the views, wishes and needs of many different groups.

Roosevelt was a master at keeping the lines of information open. He asked questions and listened to all sorts of politicians, interest group spokesmen, reporters, academics, and private citizens. Roosevelt actively sought out the widest range of opinion and information. He would even put administration officials of differing views to work, often unbeknownst to one another, on the same problem. Some called such procedures those of a messy administrator, but clear administrative charts were not important to Roosevelt. He wanted and received the information to make sound decisions.

In the post-World War II era John F. Kennedy most closely imitated Roosevelt's accessibility and fact-gathering techniques. Eisenhower, with an Army staff system and desire for staff prepared one-page summaries of the issue, and Nixon, with his demands for long hours of isolated study, deviated most from the maxim that information is a key to power.

The Use of Executive Orders — Civil Rights   President Truman, stalemated by the 80th Congress, exercised initiative in civil rights by executive order. In 1946 he created the President's Committee on Civil Rights which issued a memorable report, *To Secure These Rights,* in 1947 (see p. 220). It was a blueprint for civil rights action for the next two decades. In 1948 as Commander-in-Chief he ordered the desegregation of the Armed Forces, and as Chief Executive he ordered fair employment in the federal government. President Kennedy also used executive orders to combat discrimination in housing and employment until public opinion, mobilized by the Birmingham crisis of 1963, finally stirred significant Congressional action.

"Loyalty" Programs   The House Un-American Activities Committee (HUAC), established by Congressional conservatives in 1938 to investigate "un-American" activities on the eve of World War II, and, many feared, to harass liberal New Dealers, held sensational hearings in 1946. President Truman acted to head off Congressional witchhunts, to protect himself from charges of "being soft on Communism," and to prevent Communist infiltration of the federal service. Truman, by executive order in 1947 established a domestic loyalty review program in federal employment. The Cold War, the Soviets' rejection of international control of nuclear weapons, a Soviet atomic spy ring uncovered in Ottawa, Canada, and conservatives' fears of "radicalism"made a red scare similar to 1919-20 seem likely. When the Russians vetoed United Nations control of atomic energy, the Congress established the Atomic Energy Commission in 1946 to develop military and civilian uses of the atom. The combination of this doomsday weapon and the fears of the Soviets led to extraordinary executive secrecy measures and loyalty procedures to protect national security and prevent the employment of "security risks." The most famous casualty of the excesses of such procedures took place in 1953 when the Atomic Energy Commission withheld the security clearance of the great physicist, J. Robert Oppenheimer, the "father of the atomic bomb" and dismissed him as an AEC consultant.

Loyalty programs raise serious questions. How does one define "un-American," "subversive," or "disloyal"? Do they involve only actions or also associations and beliefs? Attorney General Tom Clark convinced Truman in July, 1946, to allow the FBI to use bugs and wiretaps, as he said Roosevelt had done since 1940, because of the "increase in subversive activities." Truman did not realize that Roosevelt's actions of World War II had been restricted to aliens and "grave matters involving the defense of the nation," whereas the Justice Department under Clark moved on domestic subversives. In November, 1946, Truman established a temporary Committee on Employee Loyalty. The committee reported in 1947 that there were disloyal people in government and that the procedures for ousting them were "ineffective." Truman wrote in the winter of 1946-47,

> People are very much wrought up about the Communist 'buga-boo' but I am of the opinion that the country is perfectly safe so far as Communism is concerned — we have far too many sane people. Our Government is made for the welfare of the people and I don't believe there will ever come a time when anyone will really want to overturn it.

But by March, 1947, President Truman issued Executive Order 9835 to insure the "maximum protection. . . against the infiltration of disloyal persons" into the United States government. The Civil Service Commission was to investigate the loyalty of every applicant for a federal job, and the FBI would do the same for all present federal employees. The executive order allowed for dismissal if "reasonable grounds exist for belief that the person involved is disloyal to the Government of the United States." The Attorney General compiled a list of eighty-two subversive organizations in which past or present membership could be grounds for dismissal. A person accused of disloyalty was entitled to an administrative hearing before a loyalty board in his department. He could hear the evidence against him, be represented by a lawyer and present sworn evidence in his own behalf. He had the right to appeal to a Loyalty Review Board in the Civil Service Commission.

The Presidential program violated traditional American rules of fair play. Disloyalty was not clearly defined. The accused had no right to confront his accusers and cross-examine them or examine the FBI's incriminating files. A man could lose his job and reputation by an administrative procedure without a day in court. The Attorney General's list seemed to some an "executive bill of attainder," in which organizations, over two hundred by 1953, were "branded in secret" without a chance to defend themselves. Individuals were judged untrustworthy because of their political ideas and associations, motives attributed to them or suspicions of their future conduct.

In 1951, with the coming of the Korean War, Truman went further with Executive Order 10241 and ruled that an employee could be fired if there were "reasonable doubt" as to his loyalties, the government need not prove his disloyalty. Under President Truman, 4,750,000 employees were checked, 26,000 cases went to loyalty board hearings, 7,000 quit the service or withdrew job applications while under investigation, most were given loyalty clearance, and only 560 persons were actually removed or denied employment on loyalty charges.

President Eisenhower in Executive Order 10450 in April, 1953, took another step and ordered that employees be dismissed if their "employment may not be clearly consistent with the interests of national security." The Presidents attempted to blunt the public and Congressional red hysteria, but the loyalty programs demoralized the federal service and produced a bland conformity to safe ideas in the bureaucracy. In the 1950's the Court checked some major excesses in the loyalty program, and the red scare gradually diminished. But in a dangerous world, the public demanded loyalty programs, and they became accepted as grim necessities.

"Executive Privilege"   In 1949 a Department of Justice attorney claimed that Presidents and Cabinet heads, by 150 years of precedent, had the right to confidential papers and information "which require secrecy." He wrote that the judgment as to what a President might withhold from a Congressional investigation was entirely the President's and that his "uncontrolled discretion" had long been upheld by the Court. Such a claim was unsupported by court precedents, but many civil libertarians applauded Eisenhower's use of the doctrine in the face of Congressional demands for loyalty files of government workers.

While such executive action could be used for the laudable end of blocking irresponsible Congressional investigators, it could also be used to stop Congress from fulfilling its constitutional role to inform itself and the public of Presidential folly or wrongdoing. The sword cut two ways. In fact, Presidential withholding of information from Congress had traditionally been very limited, and executive compliance with Congressional requests had been the rule. But in 1954 Eisenhower ordered that all material generated by the internal deliberative processes in the executive branch of government, not just Presidential conversations with aides, were privileged and established a "claim of boundless and unreviewable executive control of information."

From 1955 to 1960 the Eisenhower administration withheld information in response to forty-four Congressional requests, and in 1958 Attorney General William P. Rogers made the Justice Department attorney's memo of nine years earlier a constitutional doctrine — *executive privilege.* Although Kennedy cited executive privilege only once, it was invoked increasingly in the late 1960's and early 1970's, though its constitutionality was never ruled on by the Supreme Court until *U.S. v. Nixon* in 1974. Executive privilege was an example of the growth of Presidential power.

Executive Secrecy   While executive privilege was cited by the Presidency versus the Congress, the post-World War II Presidency also invoked a rule of secrecy relative to the press and public on matters of "national security." Again, this policy was established by executive order, not by act of Congress. It was a product of two World Wars, and, especially, the Cold War. Executive officials institutionalized an elaborate system of secrecy classifications and the "eyes only," "confidential," and "strictly confidential" stamps came into use.

In 1950 President Truman extended the right "to classify information" to any executive department or agency which believed such action "necessary in the interst of national security." In a dangerous world certain ongoing diplomatic negotiations, active military preparations, and intelligence activities had to be secret. But Presidents could use secrecy stamps to bury errors, cover up crimes, manipulate public opinion, and abuse Presidential powers. If Presidents had the public's trust and limited the use of secrecy to a "reasonable level," then such actions seemed acceptable; but if Presidents, as did Johnson and Nixon, developed a "credibility gap," then secrecy seemed intolerable. By the late 1960's many Americans believed that their Presidents in their own self-interest withheld information and misled the American people. In a Gallup Poll in October, 1967, in response to the question, "Do you believe the Johnson Administration is or is not telling the public all they should know about the Vietnam War?" 70 percent of the American people said "is not," and only 21 percent said "is" (9 percent had "no opinion"). That response held steady through the Nixon administration.

The government has a need for secrecy in certain areas; and the people have a right, in fact a need, to know in other areas if self-government is to work. In 1966 Congress after years of giving in to Presidential claims of the need for secrecy — once a member of the Joint Chiefs of Staff wrote another saying that too many undeserving papers were being stamped 'top secret' and then his note itself was stamped 'top secret'!— enacted the Freedom of Information Act. That law declares disclosure is the rule, and the burden of proof for withholding a document is on the government, not on the person who requests it. It further provides for judicial review if the request for information is denied. The act, however, does allow for secrecy in matters deemed necessary by the executive for national defense or foreign policy. Such legislation opened the flow of information to the public and investigative reporters in the 1970's.

Powers as Commander-in-Chief   In foreign affairs the President's constitutional authority as Commander-in-Chief and "chief diplomat" give him the greatest opportunity to exercise power. On June 25, 1950, the Cold War turned hot in Korea (see p. 55). President Truman initiated and then responded to United Nations Security Council resolutions calling for troops under the U.N. flag to combat North Korea's aggression and sent American boys into combat. He did not ask for a Congressional declaration of war, nor even for a Congressional resolution to authorize limited war. He did not cite the U.N. charter as his legal authority to act. On the advice of his Secretary of State, Dean Acheson, Truman claimed the power to send troops into battle in Korea under his constitutional power as Commander-in-Chief. The State Department claimed there were ample precedents, but none were in situations so grave, nor in a war so major, as the Korean conflict. Truman claimed power and set a precedent for later "Presidential wars."

In 1951 Truman sent four divisions of American troops to Europe to fulfill America's commitment to NATO (see p. 21). He claimed the power to deploy such troops as Commander-in-Chief. Congressional Republicans, upset by the events in Korea and the President's firing of General Douglas MacArthur (see p. 60), challenged Truman's authority to send troops to NATO without Congressional authorization. Truman had his way; Congress did not check him.

The Steel Seizure Case   The Supreme Court did check President Truman at home. In 1952 the Court in *Youngstown Sheet and Tube Co. v. Sawyer* ruled 6-3 that President Truman's unprecedented takeover of the American steel industry during the Korean War was unconstitutional. A strike had long threatened. All government mediation efforts and White House intervention failed to prevent the strike which began on April 9, 1952. Truman cited the national emergency and the need for steel production for the Korean War effort and the atomic energy program and issued his order for a federal takeover of the steel industry "under the Constitution and laws of the United States and as Commander-in-Chief." The President reported his action to Congress and invited them to take any legislative action they might deem helpful. Congress did not act. Truman not only acted without statutory authority, but Congress in its debates over the Taft-Hartley Act of 1947 had considered and rejected just such use of Presidential power. The Taft-Hartley Act gave the President an alternative, the right to seek an eighty-day federal court injunction to stop strikes which threaten the national welfare. Truman had vetoed and condemned Taft-Hartley as a "slave-labor act," and Democrats had long denounced "government by injunction" in labor disputes. Truman's basic defense rested on his claim to an "executive prerogative" inherent in his powers as Chief Executive.

Justice Black for the Supreme Court ruled Truman's seizure an unconstitutional usurpation of legislative power in violation of the fundamental constitutional provision for a separation of powers between the legislative and the executive. He rejected summarily any theory of executive prerogative flowing from the Constitution which would empower the President to take over the steel industry. Black denied that the President could so act as Commander-in-Chief. The five other justices for the majority wrote separate concurring opinions, but only one other, Douglas, denied in all circumstances the constitutionality of special executive prerogative. The President complied with the Court's ruling and restored the steel industry to its private ownership.

Eisenhower Global Anti-Communism   President Eisenhower practiced executive restraint at home. He significantly increased Presidential power, however, in foreign affairs. The United States ratification of NATO and the fighting in Korea changed the Cold War from one of finely tuned economic and political containment of Soviet expansion to an increasingly military policy. Americans came to see America's role as a global mission to resist any nation's conquest or subversion by Communism.

To carry out this policy, the United States maintained enormous military forces, and the Eisenhower administration added to our traditional European, Latin American, and Pacific commitments, military pacts and agreements with almost fifty nations (see pp. 52). In both the Formosan Straits in 1955 and in the Middle East in 1957 Eisenhower was able to gain from Congress the authority to use military force if certain "contingencies" arose. Congress gave the President "prior authorization" to use military force in certain geographical areas under certain vaguely defined circumstances. Modern weapons, it was claimed, made swift executive action imperative. In the nineteenth century Congress flatly rejected such requests, but in the 1950's public opinion and Congress favored such requests.

Kennedy and Cuba, the Bay of Pigs and the Missile Crisis   In the spring of 1961 President Kennedy carried out the Eisenhower-initiated and CIA-directed invasion of the Bay of Pigs in Cuba (p. 75). The United States action violated Presidential pledges, hemispheric treaties, the U.N. charter, the American Constitution, and basic morality. And the invasion failed. The most common assessment in the post-mortems was that the United States failed to use sufficient force to depose Castro, not that the President had exceeded his constitutional powers, violated international law or contradicted common morality. A year later in 1962 President Kennedy, in the Cuban missile crisis, "quarantined" Cuba. The quarantine was really a blockade which under international law assumes a declaration of war. To many, Kennedy's "brinkmanship" was a spectacular success, for the Russians removed their missiles from Cuba. But critics contend that Kennedy clearly exceeded his constitutional authority as Commander-in-Chief. Congress not only did not authorize his actions, particularly a blockade, Congress was not even consulted. Kennedy defenders have justified his extraordinary actions in the missile crisis as necessary for our national survival. Possibly the administration's actions in the missile crisis were wise, certainly they were successful; but they set precedents that later Presidents in lesser crises would cite as justification for unilateral Presidential decisions to use military force.

LBJ and the Dominican Republic   In 1965 President Johnson sent 22,000 troops into the Dominican Republic (p. 82). The administration claimed the troops were sent to rescue American citizens in a moment of Dominican revolutionary violence, but in reality they were to prevent another Castro revolution in the Caribbean. Johnson did prevent a new Castro regime, but he violated Presidential promises and treaty commitments of American nonintervention in this hemisphere, and he exceeded constitutional limits on Presidential use of military force. Johnson's "successful" use of military force in the Dominican Republic gave his administration the false belief that if the United States used sufficient military force, it could achieve its political goals in the Third World. This belief was painfully disproved in Vietnam.

VIETNAM AND THE PRESIDENCY

Political struggle and the uses and abuses of Presidential power characterized the Vietnam war. The war destroyed Johnson's broad base of popular support and created bitter divisions in the nation. The "imperial Presidency" rose to full power.

Background   During the Truman and Eisenhower years, the United States extended military and economic aid first to the French and then to the South Vietnamese Diem regimes in their wars with the Communist Nationalist Vietminh and Vietcong. Eisenhower also sent military advisers to train the South Vietnamese army. These actions seemed consistent with the containment policy, and Congress supported them through annual appropriations. President Kennedy increased the military advisers from about 350 in December, 1960, to 16,900 in November, 1963, and expanded economic and military assistance to the Saigon government. He developed an elite corps — the "Green Berets" — to wage political and military struggles against Communist revolutionaries in the Third World. The Kennedy administration used the CIA in South Vietnam to make covert attacks against the Vietcong.

LBJ and the Tonkin Gulf Resolution   After Johnson assumed the Presidency, he said, "I am not going to lose Vietnam." During the Presidential election of 1964, the peace candidate, Johnson, manipulated the Tonkin Gulf incident (see pp. 107-9) to gain Congressional passage of the Tonkin Gulf Resolution. One constitutional expert, Senator Sam Ervin of North Carolina, said the resolution constituted a declaration of war. Senator J. William Fulbright, the floor manager of the resolution, believed it granted the President only limited authority. Fulbright felt betrayed by the White House when the resolution was used as constitutional justification for Presidential decisions to send over 500,000 troops to Vietnam in a war that Americans fought until 1973! Johnson regarded the Congressional resolution as good politics. He believed Truman's failure to gain such Congressional authorization in the Korean War was a political blunder.

LBJ and His Power as Commander-in-Chief   Johnson believed that he had the constitutional authority as Commander-in-Chief to commit troops to battle in Vietnam as part of his power to wage war in defense of the United States. The administration claimed ". . . an attack on a country far from our shores can impinge directly on the nation's security," and the President has the power alone to determine if the situation is so threatening to the United States "that he should act without formally consulting with Congress." This expansive view of Presidential power gave the Chief Executive greatly increased war-making authority.

Secret Wars   Beyond American overt and covert actions in Vietnam, the United States had long engaged in secret wars in other nations in Southeast Asia. The Nixon administration carried out secret bombing raids in Cambodia in 1969-70, and the United States waged a secret war by the CIA against Communist forces in Laos from 1964 to 1970.

Nixon's Rationale for His Exercise of Power in Southeast Asia
President Nixon accepted Congress's repeal of the Tonkin Gulf

Resolution in 1971. Nixon justified his military actions in Southeast Asia under his constitutional authority as Commander-in-Chief. He argued that when he assumed the Presidency, there were over 500,000 American troops in Vietnam and that he had the constitutional power and moral duty to do whatever was necessary to protect those troops. He used that rationale to wage war until the last soldier was withdrawn on March 28, 1973.

President Nixon argued that a *potential* attack on American troops anywhere in the world was sufficient justification for a President to wage war. He used this reasoning to justify the invasion of neutral Cambodia in 1970. Critics argued that that invasion was illegal. They argued: Cambodia represented no threat to the United States; the Communist sanctuaries in Cambodia were less of a threat to American troops in South Vietnam in 1970 than in 1968; this assault was not a case of the lawful pursuit of an invader back across an international border; there was no precedent for an American President to make a massive attack on a neutral country to protect American troops in a third country. Nixon acted alone. He simply told Congress and the nation what he was doing.

A Resurgent Congress   Efforts in Congress to end the war in Southeast Asia by cutting appropriations long proved futile, but they finally gained ground in 1969 and 1970 as Congress denied funds for American ground forces in Laos, Thailand, and after the invasion, in Cambodia. In 1971 Congress forbade the President to send any United States troops into Cambodia. These resolutions forbade funds for ground troops, but said nothing about bombing. After all American troops were withdrawn from South Vietnam, Nixon's constitutional basis for waging war seemed to end. But the United States continued to bomb Cambodia — the Nixon administration argued the continuing Cambodian civil war violated the Paris Peace Accords of 1973 and gave the United States justification to bomb. Congress finally used its power of the purse to stop all bombing in August, 1973. The Paris Accords were never submitted to the Senate as a treaty nor to Congress as a resolution. The American war in Vietnam was Presidentially begun and ended. Congress played little role except for the passage of the ambiguous Tonkin Gulf Resolution. They did raise and supply armed forces, and appropriate monies. Finally, however, Congress moved to pressure the President to stop the war.

A Professional Army   During the closing days of the Vietnam War, Congress ended the draft and created a professional military. This was popular among those faced with conscription, but many feared it gave the President a tool which he could more easily use for "international adventures" without the restraining influence or protest which use of a "citizen army" might raise.

Executive Agreements   The Senate's role in diplomacy, particularly its approval of treaties, was downgraded. The two Roosevelts had often used "executive agreements," which in international usage had the legal standing of treaties, in place of formal treaties. Nowhere in the Constitution is there explicit provision for Presidents to make such agreements, but the Supreme Court in 1937 declared executive agreements constitutional.

In the early 1950's the isolationist Republican Senator, John Bricker of Ohio, in reaction to the Democratic Roosevelt's secret agreements at Yalta, attempted to amend the Constitution to forbid executive agreements. His efforts narrowly failed, but in the wake of Vietnam many feared that executive agreements, often secret, could lead the nation into war. Senator Stuart Symington's investigation into the extent of executive agreements and resulting commitments uncovered, after numerous battles over executive secrecy, American commitments from Spain to Ethiopia to Thailand, a six-year secret war in Laos, and the deployment of over 7,000 nuclear warheads in Europe without Congressional consultation.

Congress Acts to Restrain the Imperial Presidency in the 1970's   The Congress in the 1970's took steps to limit the Presidency in the areas of executive agreements, making war, deploying troops, and CIA "dirty tricks." In 1972 Congress mandated that all executive agreements must be submitted to Congress within sixty days and made public, unless "national security" required secrecy, and then the agreement had to be shared with the Senate and House Foreign Relations Committees. The President could still make executive agreements and under certain circumstances they could be kept secret, but Congress took steps to reassert itself.

In November, 1973, Congress took a major step — after the Vietnam War! — and passed the War Powers Act. The act declared the President may send United States military forces into combat, but the President must immediately inform Congress of his actions, and the Congress must pass a resolution to support the war within sixty days or the President must end American fighting. The President can continue the fighting another thirty days, if need be, to make a safe withdrawal of American forces. Congress can stop American involvement before the sixty days are up by a simple majority vote which the President cannot veto. Congress has also taken a more active role in troop deployment overseas through more careful scrutiny of military appropriations. The Congress established special oversight committees to monitor the activities of the

CIA and the intelligence community after the unprecedented Congressional investigations of 1975 and 1976 into the activities of the American intelligence agencies.

Some complained that Congressional efforts were insufficient and made legal such abuses as Presidential wars and the CIA's "dirty tricks." Presidents Ford and Carter complained that the new laws were so restrictive as to make effective Presidential leadership in foreign affairs difficult. It is clear that there is need for regular consultation and cooperation between the executive and legislative branches if there is to be a foreign policy which serves the national interest and has popular support.

WATERGATE AND THE PRESIDENCY

The June 17, 1972, Watergate burglary was simply the tip of the iceberg of corruption of the Nixon Presidency. Eventually, because of two young *Washington Post* investigative reporters, Robert Woodward and Carl Bernstein; a tough federal judge, John J. Sirica; a tenacious guardian of the Constitution, Senator Sam J. Ervin (D., N.C.); two relentless special prosecutors, Harvard Law professor Archibald Cox and Houston lawyer Leon Jaworski; a little-known Newark Congressman, Peter W. Rodino (D., N.J.); the Presidential "tapes"; the United States Supreme Court — and some good luck — the White House Horrors came to light, President Nixon resigned, his principal aides went to jail, and the Presidential abuse of power was exposed.

Wiretaps and "Enemies"   Wiretaps and bugs were widely used by the Nixon administration to find out who was leaking information to the press and to gain advantages in the political in-fighting in the White House. The Nixon administration, between May 10, 1969 and February 10, 1971, without court authorization, wiretapped and bugged thirteen government officials — ten on the White House staff, five reporters, and even the President's brother, Donald Nixon. The Supreme Court in 1972 ruled such unauthorized electronic surveillance an unconstitutional "search" in violation of the Fourth Amendment. In the years 1969-1971 the White House staff mirrored President Nixon's view that the government was under a "state of siege" from waves of anti-war protesters, campus radicals, and black militants. The Nixon men held that drastic steps were necessary to stop the "enemies" before a mob overthrew the president as they believed Lyndon Johnson was overthrown in 1968.

Nixon and the Court, Congress, the Bureaucracy and the Press
President Nixon attempted to control or manipulate the courts, the

Congress, the Bureaucracy, and the press. He demonstrated his contempt for the Supreme Court by his nominations of Haynsworth and particularly Carswell (p. 211). The President impounded and refused to spend $15 billion that Congress appropriated in one hundred federal programs and thus created an absolute veto over legislation and he refused to "take Care that the Laws be faithfully executed." He refused to cut off federal funds in order to desegregate schools as directed by the 1964 Civil Rights Act. Nixon directed an aide to dismantle the Office of Economic Opportunity before its legal life expired in 1973. The courts eventually rebuked the President on all these actions. Nixon claimed executive privilege in March, 1973, for all past and present White House employees relative to Congress, the FBI and grand juries. His Attorney General said Congress could not command any of the two and one half million members of the executive department to testify if the President said no.

Nixon also worried about opposition in the bureaucracy. He appointed political loyalists at middle levels of the bureaucracy to get "the bad guys — the guys down in the woodwork." After the 1972 election Nixon reduced the influence of the department heads and concentrated increased power in the White House under his principal aides, John Ehrlichman, Henry Kissinger, and H. R. Haldeman, men not confirmed by the Senate nor required to testify before Congress. Under Nixon the White House staff grew rapidly. Presidential assistants rose from an average of twenty in the Johnson administration to forty-eight under Nixon. The Executive Office budget went up 129 percent between 1968 and 1972.

Nixon's hostility towards the press was old and deep. He had Spiro Agnew blast the networks and the "eastern establishment press." In 1971 he requested a court injunction to prevent publication of the "Pentagon Papers" which had been leaked to *The New York Times*. The Pentagon Papers were a history of the Vietnam War prepared by the Defense Department. This attempt at "prior restraint" was ruled unconstitutional by the Supreme Court. The administration tapped reporters' phones and pressured editors to fire newsmen. The FBI ran a complete field investigation on veteran CBS reporter Daniel Schorr to intimidate him; then, when discovered, the White House said Schorr was being screened for a government job! The administration won a decision before the Supreme Court forcing reporters to reveal confidential sources in grand jury investigations. Nixon's allies challenged the FCC licenses to two *Washington Post*-owned TV stations in Florida. The war against the press was systematic and thorough.

"Screw" the Enemies   John Mitchell's Justice Department prosecuted a number of "conspiracy cases" against black militants, radicals, and anti-war activists without success. The White House compiled an "enemies list" of some two hundred people and eighteen organizations. Few of the enemies were radical. They were mostly liberals and included Ted Kennedy, professional football player, Joe Namath, and the Harvard Law School. Nixon planned, after the 1972 election, to use the CIA, the FBI, and the IRS to "screw our enemies."

The Huston Plan and the Plumbers   In 1970 Nixon was upset that the FBI was not "doing the job" of exposing press leaks. The President approved in July, 1970, a young White House aide's plan for wiretaps, bugs, opening mail, campus informants, and "surreptitious" entries — breaking and entering. The so-called Huston Plan involved clearly illegal and unethical activities. It was shelved when FBI chief J. Edgar Hoover protested that such action would bring the FBI bad public relations and "unleash the jackals of the press." The CIA, the FBI, and the Secret Service had long been carrying on such illegal activities in the United States in the name of national security, but Hoover had grown leery under press critizcism.

After Daniel Ellsberg leaked the "Pentagon Papers" to *The New York Times* in June 1971, the White House quickly set up a secret Special Investigations Unit, in Room 16 of the Executive Office Building, and named it the "plumbers" after its job of "fixing" leaks. The plumbers were headed by two young aides from Kissinger's and Ehrlichman's staffs. Nixon's orders were ". . . do whatever has to be done to stop these leaks. . . . I don't want to be told why it can't be done. . . I want it done, whatever the cost." The plumbers hired G. Gordon Liddy and E. Howard Hunt. The plumbers went beyond leaks. They tried to get "dirt" on the leading Democratic challenger, Ted Kennedy; they forged and leaked a cablegram to "prove" President Kennedy ordered the assassination of Diem; they broke into the office of Ellsberg's California psychiatrist to get damaging information to "destroy" Ellsberg; and finally they broke into the Watergate Democratic National Committee headquarters. That break-in had the approval of CREEP chairman and former Attorney General John Mitchell. The "dirty tricks" of the CIA and the Cold War had come home to American politics.

Containing Watergate — or Obstructing Justice   The administration denied any involvement in the burglary, and John Dean, the legal counsel to the President, was put in charge of efforts to "contain" Watergate during the 1972 campaign. G. Gordon Liddy offered, in the best tradition of a spy thriller, to have himself shot on a Washington street corner. The administration did not take his offer. Instead they launched a public relations campaign to down-grade the break-in as a "third-rate burglary" and to push the "most strenuous criminal investigation in history" to bring all the wrong-doers to justice. In fact, the President on June 23, 1972, ordered the CIA to head off the FBI investigation into monies found on the bur-glars which could be traced through a Mexican "laundering" opera-tion back to CREEP. Nixon found willing political appointees in the CIA and the FBI who carried out these orders from June 23 to July 5,1972. John Dean sat in on FBI interrogations, counselled CREEP officials on perjury before the grand jury, had access to all FBI field reports, and obtained daily reports from the Assistant Attorney General on the progress of the investigation. Nixon's private lawyer arranged to pay the seven burglars "hush money." An ex-New York City cop "dropped off" the money in brown paper bags in predesig-nated telephone booths. After a sloppy job of investigation, the fed-eral prosecutors on September 15, 1972, gained a grand jury indictment of only the seven burglars. CREEP, the White House and Nixon seemed safe. That afternoon Nixon congratulated John Dean for containing Watergate. On November 7, 1972, he won his landslide Presidential victory.

Judge Sirica and Woodward and Bernstein   Five Watergate burglars pleaded guilty, and the other two were tried and convicted in January, 1973. But Judge John Sirica announced that he was "not satisfied that all the pertinent facts that might be available. . . have been produced before an American jury." Judge Sirica often ques-tioned the defendants in the trial when he felt the prosecutors were doing a superficial job. Earlier, in the summer of 1972 two young *Washington Post* reporters, Robert Woodward and Carl Bernstein, began a lonely and relentless investigation into Watergate. For the 1972 campaign the Republicans raised $60,200,000, and almost $2,000,000 of this was in "untraceable cash." Woodward and Bern-stein, at the suggestion of a mysterious informant, "Deep Throat," traced $100 bills found on the burglars through a Miami bank to Mexico to CREEP. It turned out that the Nixon campaign was awash in money. Special interests bought favors — such as an ITT contribution to head off an antitrust suit and a mysterious Howard Hughes loan. Seventeen corporations were later convicted of illegal contributions. Numerous corporate individuals gave a total of $1,433,830 to the Nixon campaign, some illegally, such as George Steinbrenner, a shipbuilder and later owner of the New York Yan-kees. Ambassadorships were sold — in 1968 and 1972 a total of $1,800,000 came to Nixon from people later named ambassadors. From August to November, 1972, Woodward and Bernstein wrote about the CREEP-Watergate money connections, the secret funds of Haldeman and CREEP officials, and of the White House ties to Donald Segretti and "dirty tricks" used in the campaign. Few took heed.

McCord Cracks, Dean Talks, Ervin Investigates   In March, 1973 as sentencing day for the Watergate burglars approached, one of them, James W. McCord cracked and told Judge Sirica that there had been political pressure and perjury in the trial and undisclosed criminal involvement by higher-ups. John Dean, on the same day, March 21, 1973, told President Nixon that "we have a cancer — within — close to the Presidency, that's growing." He told Nixon of E. Howard Hunt's demands for executive clemency and more money, that the blackmail might last two years and cost $1,000,000, and that many high officials were guilty of obstruction of justice. Nixon's response was ". . . you better damn well get that [payment to Hunt] done, but fast. . . . Well, for Christ's sake get it. . . ." Nixon told John Mitchell the next day, "I want you all to stonewall it, let them plead the Fifth Amendment, cover up or anything else, if it'll save it — save the [cover up] plan."

The administration put out public relations stories, and erected constitutional defenses. Citing the confidentiality of Presidential deliberations and the separation of powers, the Attorney General announced that the President could invoke executive privilege for all employees of the executive branch, past and present. Previously, on February 7, the Senate unanimously passed a resolution to establish the Select Committee on Presidential Campaign Activities under Senator Sam Ervin. Dean saw the cover-up crumbling, and on April 8 he began talking to the prosecutors and entered into plea bargaining in return for his complete testimony. Others followed.

New Developments, April, 1973   Nixon announced new "developments" in Watergate on April 17 and presented himself as a vigorous investigator. Throughout Watergate Nixon "the criminal" posed as Nixon "the investigator," two irreconcilable roles. The public relation scenarios that the president's men hoped would "play in Peoria" changed so often that the President, as the tapes would later reveal, confused the truth with the numerous cover stories. On April 30, 1973, in a dramatic TV speech, Nixon accepted the resignation of John Dean, regretted the resignation of "two of the finest public servants it has ever been my privilege to know," Haldeman and Ehrlichman, and announced the appointment of a new Attorney General, Elliott Richardson, with the right to name a "special supervising prosecutor," to get to "the bottom of Watergate." He waived executive privilege for White House aides before the Ervin committee.

Dean Versus Nixon — the Tapes   In five dramatic days in June, John Dean told a detailed story of the cover-up, including the role of President Nixon, to the Ervin committee and a spellbound national TV audience. It now seemed a test of Dean's word against Nixon's. But on July 13, 1973, a Presidential aide, in response to Ervin committee investigators, revealed that President Nixon had installed automatic taping equipment in the White House, the Executive Office Building and at Camp David. He had bugged himself! The public was amazed and outraged! On July 23 Senator Ervin and the Special Prosecutor, Archibald Cox, obtained subpoenas for nine key tapes. The President refused to surrender the tapes and invoked executive privilege based on Presidential confidentiality, the constitutional separation of powers and a plea to protect national security. Cox requested Judge Sirica issue a court order. Cox claimed that the President was not above the law and could not withhold evidence in a criminal proceeding. Judge Sirica and the Circuit Court of Appeals ordered Nixon to give over the tapes.

On October 20, 1973, Nixon fired Cox, abolished the special Prosecutor's Office, and Attorney General Richardson resigned in protest, in what became known as the "Saturday Night Massacre." There was a "firestorm,"of public protest. Nixon felt compelled to name a new Special Prosecutor, Leon Jaworski, with added assurances of independence, and Nixon promised to deliver the tapes. It was then revealed that two of the subpoenaed tapes were missing and a third, a conversation between Nixon and Haldeman on June 20, 1972, three days after the burglary, had a mysterious erasure, an "eighteen-and-one-half-minute gap." General Haig, Nixon's new Chief of Staff, attributed the erasures to "some sinister force." Experts later testified that the erasures were done by hand.

Nixon in November told newspaper editors in Disney World, ". . . I am not a crook." Spiro Agnew, who clearly was a crook, resigned as Vice-President in October, and the Congress confirmed the nomination of Representative Gerald R. Ford to be Vice-President in December. As the year 1973 ended, the Nixon administration launched a new public relations campaign, "Operation Candor," to "get out in front" on Watergate while the House Judiciary Committee under Chairman Peter W. Rodino and Counsel John M. Doar began an impeachment inquiry.

The Special Prosecutor and House Impeachment   The Special Prosecutor and the House Judiciary Committee moved ahead relentlessly. More and more it came down to Dean versus Nixon, and the tapes were the "best evidence." On February 29, 1974, a grand jury indicted Mitchell, Ehrlichman, Haldeman, and four others for conspiracy and obstruction of justice. Jaworski, for the grand jury, handed to Judge Sirica a brown briefcase for delivery to the House Judiciary Committee. The grand jury named Richard M. Nixon an "unindicted co-conspirator," though this did not become public knowledge until June. The Special Prosecutor believed a grand jury, under the constitutional separation of powers, could not indict a sitting President.

Nixon continued to stonewall and refused to honor subpoenas from the House of Representatives and the Special Prosecutor. On April 29, 1974, Nixon went on TV to "tell all." He presented 1,254 pages of transcripts of the tapes. The Senate Republican leader, Hugh Scott of Pennsylvania, called them "deplorable, disgusting, shabby, immoral." When the public learned that these tapes were edited to make the President look innocent, there was rage. The House Judiciary Committee rejected the edited tapes and voted that Nixon's refusal to deliver the tapes as subpoenaed blocked the House from carrying out its constitutional duty.

U.S. v. Nixon   Nixon tried to quash Jaworski's subpoenas, but on May 20, 1974, Judge Sirica ordered the President again to hand over the tapes. Nixon refused. Jaworski requested and the Supreme Court agreed to take the case on immediate appeal to resolve the nation's constitutional and political crisis. The arguments were familiar. Jaworski claimed the tapes were needed in the Watergate prosecutions, that they were the best possible evidence, and that no one is above the law. Nixon's lawyers claimed the executive, as a co-equal and separate branch of government, was immune from judicial orders, and was only responsible to the constitutional impeachment proceedings in the House of Representatives (he had already refused to comply with the House's subpoena!)

The Supreme Court, in an 8 to 0 decision written by Chief Justice Warren Burger, ruled on July 24 that the Supreme Court had the constitutional responsibility to "say what the law is," and that the President could not invoke privilege in a domestic criminal proceeding. Chief Justice Burger ruled,

> . . . It is imperative to the function of courts that compulsory process be available for the production of evidence needed either by the prosecution or by the defense. . . . The generalized assertion of privilege must yield to the demonstrated, specific need for evidence in a pending criminal trial.

The Court ordered the President to deliver the subpoenaed tapes to Judge Sirica. Nixon complied.

In the closing days of July, 1974, the House Judiciary Committee voted three articles of impeachment for obstruction of justice, abuse of Presidential power, and refusal to obey a House subpoena. The votes were bipartisan, 27-11, 28-10, and 21-17. On Monday, August 5, 1974, the tapes were made public and the June 23, 1972 Nixon order to the CIA to block the FBI Watergate investigation destroyed Nixon's last defenses. The House Judiciary Committee now stood 38 to 0 for impeachment. Republican leaders told the President that conviction on impeachment charges was certain, for he had no more than fifteen supporting votes in the Senate. On August 9, 1974, the Watergate agony ended with an unprecedented Presidential resignation and Nixon's self-imposed exile to his home in San Clemente, California. The jail doors soon closed behind his colleagues.

Post-Watergate Politics The major post-Watergate public reactions were ambiguous. Many Americans lost confidence and interest in the political process. The percentage of eligible voters voting in the Congressional election of 1974 reached the lowest level, 36.1 percent, since the war year of 1942. In 1978 fewer than 35 percent voted. Those figures compare with the so-called apathetic 1950's, when 41.7 percent and 43 percent voted in the off-year elections of 1954 and 1958. Cynicism about politicians and apathy about politics were the norms. At the same time there was a demand for a "new morality" in politics. Codes of ethics, conflict of interest and financial disclosure laws, and puritanical political styles were demanded — politicians must be "cleaner than a hound's tooth." The major reforms enacted by Congress came in 1974 in a law to limit individual campaign contributions, tighten reporting and disclosure rules and to establish public financing of Presidential campaigns.

The nation was badly wounded by the twin Presidential blows of Vietnam and Watergate. The injury to America's political process was great; the recuperation was painful and drawn out. It slowly continues.

Suggested Additional Reading

Chapter One

Basic to the study of the foreign policies of the United States is the series published by the State Department, *The Foreign Relations of The United States.* Unfortunately, publication of this series, containing declassified government documents lags more than twenty-five years after the event. Another indispensable primary source is the series *Public Papers of the Presidents of the United States,* an annual collection of public statements and executive documents. The Council on Foreign Relations publishes annually two important volumes, *The United States in World Affairs* and *Documents on American Foreign Relations.*

Historians have disagreed sharply in interpreting the Cold War. The early orthodox or official position held that the policy of the United States was nothing more than a defensive move against Soviet expansion. This view is ably presented in John Spanier, *American Foreign Policy Since World War II** (1965); and Herbert Feis, *From Trust To Terror** (1965). William A. Williams' study, *The Tragedy of American Diplomacy** (1962) sparked a school of revisionist writing, often referred to as the New Left. Important revisionist works blaming the economic and strategic interests of the United States as the expansionist force responsible for the Cold War include: Dana L. Fleming, *The Cold War And Its Origins,* 2 vol. (1961); Gabriel Kolko, *The Roots of American Foreign Policy** (1963); Gar Alperovitz, *Atomic Diplomacy: Hiroshima and Potsdam* (1965); and Walter LaFeber, *America, Russia, and The Cold War, 1945-1975** (3rd. ed., 1976). While acknowledging that American policy makers failed to accept the reality that World War II had produced, post-revisionist writers have placed varying blame on both sides. Among these are: Louis Halle, *The Cold War As History** (1967); John L. Gaddis, *The United States and the Origins of The Cold War** (1972); and Daniel Yergin, *Shattered Peace: The Origins of The Cold War and The National Security State* (1977).

Specialized studies of the Truman era include John Gimbel, *The Origins of the Marshall Plan* (1976); Bruce Kuklick, *American Policy and The Division of Germany* (1972); and Barton J. Bernstein, *Politics and Policies of the Truman Administration** (1970). Participants in the shaping of policies in Europe during the Truman administration, who have written personal accounts, include: Harry S. Truman, *Memoirs,* 2 vol. (1955-6); Dean Acheson, *Present At The Creation* (1969); George F. Kennan, *Memoirs, 1925-1950* (1967); James F. Byrnes, *Speaking Frankly* (1947); Lucius D. Clay, *Decision in Germany* (1950); Charles E. Bohlen, *The Transformation of American Foreign Policy* (1969); and Arthur H. Vandenberg, Jr., ed., *The Private Papers of Senator Vandenberg* (1952). For a counterview consult Robert A. Taft, *A Foreign Policy For America* (1951).

Policies of the Eisenhower administration are treated somewhat critically in Herbert S. Parmet, *Eisenhower and The American Crusades* (1972); Norman Graebner, *The New Isolationism** (1956); and Townsend Hoopes, *The Devil and John Foster Dulles* (1973). More favorable interpretations of Republican policies appear in James Burnham, *Containment or Liberation* (1953); William H. Chamberlain, *Beyond Containment* (1953); and Thomas K. Finletter, *Foreign Policy: The Next Phase* (1955). Eisenhower has written

*available in paperback

289

his own account in *Mandate For Change* (1963) and *Waging Peace* (1965). The standard account of the U-2 incident is Thomas Ross and David Wise, *The U-2 Affair** (1962).

Close advisers of Kennedy have written accounts that must be used carefully (see references in Chapter 8). In addition are Roger Hilsman, *To Move A Nation* (1967), and Robert S. McNamara, *The Essence of Security* (1968). More critical are Richard J. Walton, *Cold War and Counter-Revolution: The Foreign Policy of John F. Kennedy** (1972); and Donald C. Lord, *John F. Kennedy, The Politics of Confrontation and Conciliation* (1977).

Chapter Two

In 1946 two correspondents of *Time*, Theodore H. White and Annalee Jacoby, wrote *Thunder Out of China*, a surprisingly frank treatment of both Chiang-Kai-shek and Patrick Hurley's mission. For the next two decades journalists, public officials, and historians debated in print the reasons for the Communist triumph in China. Among the studies critical of American policy toward China's Civil War are: Tang Tsou, *America's Failure in China, 1941-1950** (1963); and Herbert Feis, *The China Tangle** (1953). In 1949 the State Department published *United States Relations With China, 1944-1949*, a white paper defending American policies. Among the important works by participants in making and carrying out policy in China are: O. Edmund Clubb, *The Witness and I* (1974); and Karl Lott Rankin, *China Assignment* (1964). The role of the "China Lobby" in influencing policy is investigated in Ross Koen, *The China Lobby In American Politics* (1974); and S.D. Bachrack, *The Committee of One Million: "China Lobby" Politics, 1953-1971* (1976). One should also consult Russell Buhite, *Patrick J. Hurley and American Foreign Policy* (1973); and Warren Cohen, *America's Response To China* (1971). General Wedemeyer has written his account of events in China in *Wedemeyer Reports* (1958).

The factors influencing Truman's decision to aid South Korea have been analyzed in T.R. Fehrenbach, *This Kind of War* (1963); and Glenn Paige, *The Korean Decision* (1968). Important works critical of America's role in Korea include: I.F. Stone, *The Hidden History of The Korean War* (1952); and Joyce and Gabriel Kolko, *Limits of Power** (1972). General MacArthur has written his views in *Reminiscences* (1964), while his chief aide, General Courtney Whitney has made a strong defense in *MacArthur: His Rendezvous With Destiny* (1956). Allen Whiting, *China Crosses The Yalu* (1960); and David Rees, *Korea: The Limited War* (1964) offer different views. More critical voices appear in John W. Spanier, *The Truman-MacArthur Controversy** (1959); and William Manchester, *American Caesar: Douglas MacArthur, 1880-1964* (1978).

One should also consult the primary sources listed in chapter one.

Chapter Three

There are few good surveys of the United States in the Third World. Useful studies include: Robert A. Packman, *Liberal America and The Third World** (1973); and James W. Howe, *The United States And The Developing World: Agenda For Action*, an annual beginning in 1973. Two accounts critical of American policy are: Richard J. Barnet, *Intervention and Revolution, The United States In The Third World** (1968); and Melvin Gurtov, *The United States Against The Third World** (1974).

An extensive literature treats the relations of the United States with Latin America. Samuel Baily, *The United States And The Development of South America, 1945-1975* (1977) and David Green, *The Containment of Latin America* (1971) offer differing views. For the role of the CIA in Guatemala consult David Wise and Thomas Ross, *The Invisible Government** (1964). Problems with Castro's Cuba are analyzed by Haynes Johnson, *The Bay of Pigs* (1964); Elie Abel, *The Missile Crisis* (1966); Graham Allison, *Essense of Decision* (1971); and Herbert Dinerstein, *The Making of A Missile Crisis: October 1962** (1976). Robert F. Kennedy had described the actions of ExCom in *Thirteen Days** (1969). Intervention in the Dominican Republic is discussed by U.S. Ambassador John Bartlow Martin, *Overtaken By Events* (1966); Theodore Draper, *The Dominican Revolt: A Case Study In American Policy* (1968); and Jerome Slater, *Intervention and Negotiation: The United States and Dominican Revolution* (1970). For the Alliance for Progress see Jerome Levinson and Juan De Onis, *The Alliance That Lost Its Way* (1971).

The various crises in the Middle East are detailed in Walter Laquer, *Confrontation: The Middle East and World Politics* (1974). Robert W. Stookey, *America and The Arab States* (1975); and J.C. Hurewitz, *Soviet-American Rivalry in The Middle East* (1969). More specialized studies include Hugh Thomas, *The Suez Affair** (1966); and Edward R.F. Sheehan, *The Arabs, Israelis, and Kissinger* (1976). Kissinger's role is also the subject of John Stoessinger, *Henry Kissinger: The Anguish of Power* (1976).

Among the useful studies of American policies in Africa are: Stephen Weissman, *American Foreign Policy In The Congo, 1960-1964* (1974); Anthony Lake, *The "Tar Baby" Option: American Policy Toward Southern Rhodesia* (1976); and Barbara Rogers, *White Wealth and Black Poverty: American Investments In Southern Africa* (1976).

One should also consult works noted that cover the Truman, Eisenhower, and Kennedy administrations. An important interpretations of foreign policy in the Johnson administration is Philip Geyelin, *Lyndon Johnson and The World* (1966). Johnson has written his own account in *The Vantage Point* (1971). Nixon has offered his explanation in *RN: The Memoirs of Richard Nixon* (1976).

Chapter Four

The intense battle of words over the Vietnam War fought by journalists and historians, as well as by military and political leaders, poses many pitfalls for the unwary reader. Even such collections of documents as *The Pentagon Papers* in both the Senator Mike Gravel four volume edition (1971) and in *The New York Times* single volume edition (1971) must be used carefully as partial records only. The Defense Department has published a more complete record in *U.S. – Vietnam Relations, 1945-1967.* Another useful primary source is United States Senate Committee On Foreign Relations, *The United States and Vietnam, 1944-1947* (1972).

The best study of the early phases of the war remains Bernard Fall, *The*

Two Vietnams: A Political and Military Analysis* (1963). George Kahin and John W. Lewis, *The United States In Vietnam** (1967) offers useful insights. For a survey see Peter Poole, *The United States and Indochina From FDR To Nixon* (1973).

For accounts critical of the Vietnam policies of the United States consult Theordore Draper, *Abuse of Power** (1967); Townsend Hoopes, *The Limits of Intervention** (1969); J.C. Goulden, *Truth Is The First Casualty: The Gulf of Tonkin Affair* (1969); David Halberstam, *The Best and The Brightest* (1972); Daniel Ellsberg, *Papers On The War* (1972); and Frances Fitzgerald, *Fire In The Lake** (1972). Senator Fulbright has written two criticisms of U.S. policies, *The Arrogance of Power** (1966) and *The Crippled Giant* (1972). For a defense of American action in Vietnam see Guenter Lewy, *American In Vietnam* (1978). The My Lai incident is covered in Seymour Harsh, *My Lai 4* (1970). Two commanding generals of U.S. forces in Vietnam have written their accounts: Maxwell Taylor, *Responsibility and Response* (1967); William C. Westmoreland, *Report On The War In Vietnam* (1969) and *A Soldier Reports* (1976).

For policy in Laos consult Bernard Fall, *Anatomy of A Crisis: The Laotian Crisis of 1960-1961* (1969). The Nixon Doctrine is discussed by Virginia Brodine and Mark Selden, *Open Secret: The Kissinger-Nixon Doctrine In Asia* (1972).

One should also consult references listed in previous chapters on each administration.

Chapter Five

In spite of a welter of commentary on specific areas of the economy and material culture of the United States since 1945, there is no serious, comprehensive economic history of the post-war era. The best starting place is the surveys of economic theory, full of historical description and information: Paul Samuelson, *Economics* (10th ed., 1976) is unparalleled. Campbell McConnell, *Economics* (7th ed., 1978) is excellent, and in places, more readable than Samuelson. For key documents and statistical data read *The Economic Reports of the President* (1947 on) and the annual statistical abstracts published by the Department of Commerce. The Department of Commerce also has compiled *Historical Statistics of the United States: Colonial Times to 1970* (1975). The best introduction to the economic assumptions of post-war Americans is David Potter, *People of Plenty** (1954). When contrasted to recent, grimmer assessments of the economic climate, such as The Club of Rome, *The Limits to Growth* (1971) or Robert Heilbroner, *An Inquiry into the Human Prospect* (1974), Potter's book is invaluable in understanding the confusion over the material future in the last several years.

A standard introduction to American economic history is Harry Schieber, Harold Vatter, and Harold Faulkner, *American Economic History* (1976) which covers the post-war economy in some detail. Eric Goldman, *The Crucial Decade** (1956) is a spirited account of economic conditions in the decade after 1945. The best treatment of the government's policies and the economic development of the 1950's is Harold Vatter, *The United States Economy in the 1950's** (1963).

To understand the Keynesian orthodoxy that developed after 1945, read Robert Lekachman, *Age of Keynes** (1975). Gabriel Kolko, *Wealth and Power** (1964) is a penetrating, quite critical, look at the status of capitalism a generation after the inception of the New Deal. Key to dealing with post-war consumption and corporate power are John Kenneth Galbraith's *The Affluent Society** (1958) and *The New Industrial State** (rev. ed. 1972). Milton Friedman makes an eloquent case against welfare capitalism and regulated enterprise in *Capitalism and Freedom** (1963).

Two social commentaries of the 1950's attracted special attention, David Riesman, Nathan Glazer and Reuel Denney, *The Lonely Crowd** (1953) and William H. Whyte, Jr., *The Organization Man** (1957).

Many books were written after 1960 exploring the paradoxes and failures of the American economy and society. Some of the best were: Michael Harrington, *The Other America** (1962); Charles Silberman, *Crisis in the Classroom** (1971); Rachel Carson, *The Silent Spring* (1962). On the counter culture, the best sympathetic treatment is Theodore Roszak's perceptive *Making of a Counter Culture** (1969). Charles Reich, *The Greening of America* (1970) is an interesting document of the times and a polemic in behalf of youth. It has not aged well as social analysis. A more sober, pessimistic treatment of the convulsions of the 1960's is found in Joan Didion, *Slouching toward Bethlehem** (1968), a collection of essays. Two recent, important looks at the social temperament in the late 1970's are Richard Sennett, *The Fall of Public Man* (1977) and Christopher Lasch, *The Culture of Narcissism* (1979).

Chapter Six

A strong introduction to constitutional history is Alfred H. Kelly and Winfred A. Harbison, *The American Constitution, Its Origins and Development* (5th edition, 1976). Edward S. Corwin's *The Constitution and What It Means Today** (1974) is a standard. The best case book has long been Alpheus T. Mason and William M. Beaney, *Supreme Court in a Free Society**, (1968). A study of the role of the Court in our constitutional system is David F. Forte, *Supreme Court in American Politics: Judicial Activism vs. Judicial Restraint** (1972). A reading of Alan F. Westin's documentary study of the Truman Steel Seizure Case in 1952, *The Anatomy of a Constitutional Law Case** (1967), is an excellent way to learn how the American judicial system works.

The Warren Court, 1953 to 1969, dominated the judicial history of the post World War II years. The leading legal scholars' assessments are Alexander Bickel's *Least Dangerous Branch, The Supreme Court at the Bar of Politics** (1962), *The Supreme Court and the Idea of Progress** (1978); Archibald Cox's, *The Warren Court** (1968), Philip B. Kurkland's *Politics, The Constitution,* and *The Warren Court** (1970) and Clifford M. Lytle, *Warren Court and Its Critics* (1968).

Important issues faced by the Court are studied in Alan F. Westin's *Privacy and Freedom* (1967), Milton R. Konvitz's, *Expanding Liberties; Freedom's Gains in Post War America** (1966), Alan Barth's, *The Price of Liberty,* (1972), Albert P. Blaustein and Robert L. Zangrando's, *Civil Rights and the American Negro** (1970), Robert G. Dixon, Jr.'s, *Democratic Representation: Reappointment in Law and Politics* (1968), Norman Dorsen's, editor, *The Rights of Americans** (1972), and Fred P. Graham's, *The Due Process Revolution: The Warren Court's Impact on Criminal Law** (1971). Two brilliantly written case studies are Anthony Lewis' *Gideon's Trumpet** (1964) on the right of counsel and Richard Kluger's *Simple Justice** (1977), the definitive work on the legal struggle of black Americans to bring desegregation, culminating in *Brown v. Board of Education of Topeka*. The President's Commission on Law Enforcement and the Administration of Justice Report, *The Challenge of Crime in a Free Society** (1967) is central to the law and order issue.

The papers of Justices Warren, Douglas, Brennan, Frankfurter and Harlan are available. Indispensable to study of the Supreme Court are the decisions themselves in *United States Reports*. The articles published in law school *Law Reviews* are the most thoughtful commentaries. Also, *The New York Times* reporting of the Supreme Court in the Post-World War II era is excellent.

Chapter Seven

The study of race relations in the years after World War II should begin with Gunnar Myrdal, *An American Dilemma** (2 Vols., 1944). Path-breaking black scholarship is the sociologist E. Franklin Frazier's works on *Black Bourgeoizie** (1965), *Negro Family in the United States** (1966), *E. Franklin Frazier on Race Relations** (1968), historian John Hope Franklin's *From Slavery to Freedom** (1974), sociologists St. Clair Drake and Horace Cayton, *Black Metropolis** (2 Vols. 1945), and the social psychologist, Kenneth Clark's *Dark Ghetto** (1965). Gordon Allport's *The Nature of Prejudice** (1958) and Thomas Pettigrew's, *A Profile of the Negro American**   (1964), broke new ground. A major contribution at the height of the civil   rights movement was *Daedalus, The Negro American** (1966), edited by Talcott Parsons and Kenneth B. Clark.

Journalists have written popular and thoughtful works chronicling the years of the civil rights movement's triumphs: Anthony Lewis, *Portrait of a Decade** (1964), Benjamin Muse, *The Negro Revolution: From Non-Violence to Black Power** (1970), Nat Hentoff, *The New Equality** (1964), and Louis Lomax, *The Negro Revolution** (1962). The first major synthesis on American race relations since Myrdal was Charles E. Silberman's *Crisis in Black and White** (1964).

E.U. Essien-Udom's *Black Nationalism: A Search for An Identity in America** (1962) is a clear statement. Harold Cruse's *The Crisis of the Negro Intellectual** (1967) is a provocative work. Two psychiatrists, William H. Grier and Price M. Cobbs in *Black Rage** (1968), helped explain the depths of black anger and anguish. Robert Conot's *Rivers of Blood, Years of Darkness** (1967) is the best account of the Watts riot.

To Secure These Rights* (1947) — Report of the President's Committee on Civil Rights; United State Commission on Civil Rights (1957 on) — annual and special reports; and the *Report of the National Advisory Commission on Civil Disorders** (1968) are invaluable government studies.

The regular reports of the Bureaus of the Census and Labor Statistics help the serious student cut through the stereotypes and misinformation.

The role and actions of civil rights organizations in these years are analyzed in a case study by August Meier and Elliot Rudwick *CORE: A Study
in the Civil Rights Movement, 1942-1969**, (1975). The best biography of
the years' leading black figure is David L. Lewis, *King, A Biography** (2nd
ed., 1978). James W. Silver's *Mississippi: The Closed Society* (1964) is trenchant on racial problems in the author's home state. Two journal articles
stand out. August Meier wrote a brilliant essay, "On the Role of Martin
Luther King," *New Politics*, Winter, 1965, and Richard M. Scammon and
Ben J. Wattenberg, "Black Progress and Liberal Rhetoric," *Commentary*,
April, 1973, provoked much thought and controversy.

The most powerful and influential writings are autobiographical state-
ments by participants in the racial cauldron of these years: Martin Luther
King, Jr., *Stride Toward Freedom, The Montgomery Story** (1958), *Why We
Can't Wait** (1964), *Where Do We Go From Here: Chaos or Community**
(1967), *The Autobiography of Malcolm X** (1965), James Baldwin, *The
Fire Next Time** (1962), John Howard Griffin, *Black Like Me** (1960),
Claude Brown, *Manchild in the Promised Land** (1965), Stokely Carmichael
and Charles V. Hamilton, *Black Power: The Politics of Liberation in America**
(1967), Frantz Fanon, *The Wretched of the Earth** (1963), and Eldridge
Cleaver, *Soul on Ice** (1968).

Chapter Eight

Any study of the Presidency would profit from an examination of *The
Federalist Papers** (numbers 67 to 77). Political scientists Clinton Rossiter's
The American Presidency* (rev. ed., 1960), Edward S. Corwin, *The President,
Office and Powers, 1787-1957** (4th rev. ed.,1957), and Richard E. Neustadt's
Presidential Power* (rev. ed., 1976) are particularly useful on the sources and
uses of presidential power. James D. Barber combines political science and
psycho-biography to write a most thoughtful study of presidents since the
first Roosevelt in *Presidential Character** (rev. ed., 1977). Arthur M. Schlesinger, Jr.'s historical account is a trenchant, through partisan study of the
Imperial Presidency* (1973).

The fourth volume of the *History of American Presidential Elections,
1789-1968*, ed. by Arthur M. Schlesinger, Jr. and Fred L. Israel (1971) and
Theodore H. White's four books on the *Making of the President, 1960**,
1964*, *1968, 1972* examine elections. Joe McGinnes worked in the Nixon
1968 campaign and then wrote a scary but hilarious little book, *The Selling
of the President, 1968** (1969).

The electorate is studied in the 1940's and 1950's by pollster-journalist
Samuel Lubell, *The Future of American Politics** (1950) and *The Revolt
of the Moderates* (1956); a generation later by two pollsters, Richard M.
Scammon and Ben J. Wattenberg, *The Real Majority** (1970), and by Norman
H. Nie, Sidney Verba, and John R. Petrocik, *The Changing American Voter**
(1978).

Truman's *Memoirs* (2 Vols., 1955-6) are the best by a twentieth century
president. Cabell Phillips, *The Truman Presidency* (1966) is a journalist's account. Barton J. Bernstein and Allen J. Matusow made a fine collection of

documents in *The Truman Administration* (1966). Robert J. Donovan's has launched the best biography, really a history of the Truman years, with *Conflict and Crisis: The Presidency of Harry S. Truman, 1945-1948* (1977).

The Eisenhower presidency is viewed with a critical eye by historian Peter Lyon, *Eisenhower, Portrait of the Hero* (1974), and Emmet J. Hughes, a speechwriter for Ike, in *Ordeal of Power: Eisenhower Years* (1963). Arthur N. Larson's, *Eisenhower, The President Nobody Knows* (1968) is a more favorable treatment by an administration official, Charles C. Alexander's *Holding the Line: The Eisenhower Era, 1952-1961** (1975), is a thorough work.

The Kennedy years are brilliantly and favorably told in Arthur M. Schlesinger's *A Thousand Days: John F. Kennedy* (1965) and critically examined in British journalist Henry Fairlie's *The Kennedy Promise** (1973). The massive and controversial *Report of the Warren Commission* (1964) is the starting point for study of the assassination.

Historian turned White House aide, Eric F. Goldman, wrote a critical work on President Johnson, *The Tragedy of Lyndon Johnson** (1969) and Doris Kearns, wrote a fine piece of psycho-biography in *Lyndon Johnson and the American Dream** (1976). *New York Times* reporter, Tom Wicker's little book, *JFK and LBJ** (1968), tells much about both men and presidential decision-making. Johnson's Press Secretary, George E. Reedy's, *The Twilight of the Presidency** (1971), is insightful and critical of Johnson and of the modern Presidency. Jim F. Heath's *Decade of Disillusionment: The Kennedy-Johnson Years** (1975) is a fine survey. Barry Goldwater's, *Conscience of a Conservative** (1961), was the bible of the right-wing ideologues.

The best work on Richard Nixon, and much of post-World War II politics, remains Gary Wills, *Nixon Agonistes: The Crisis of the Self-made Man** (1970). Richard Nixon's *Six Crises** (1962) is most revealing. The Watergate literature is exhaustive, but the best overall study is Anthony Lukac's *Nightmare: The Underside of the Nixon Years* (1976). Jonathan Schell's *The Time of Illusion** (1976) is a most thoughtful interpretation of "Watergate". *The Washington Post's* Robert Woodward and Carl Bernstein's two books, *All the President's Men** (1974), and the *Final Days** (1976) are extraordinary examples of investigative reporting and lively writing. James Doyle, the Press Secretary for Cox and Jaworski, tells the story brilliantly from the Special Prosecutor's office in *Not Above the Law* (1977). John Dean, the man who accused the President and made it stick, tells all in *Blind Ambition** (1977). Judge John J. Sirica describes the Watergate story as he saw it from the bench in *To Set the Record Straight* (1979). The report of the House Judiciary Committee, *Impeachment of Richard M. Nixon, President of the United States** (1974) is most important. Harvard Law professor, Raoul Berger's two studies, *Impeachment* (1973) and *Executive Privilege* (1974), were timely and scholarly.

William Lee Miller's *Yankee from Georgia: The Emergence of Jimmy Carter,* (1978), is the best book yet on Carter.

Index